3/02

949.7
Benson, Leslie.
Yugoslavia : a concise
history
Houndsmills, Basingstoke,
Hampshire ; New York :
Palgrave, 2001.

02   03

GAYLORD MG

Yugoslavia: A Concise History

Yugoslavia:
A Concise History

Leslie Benson

palgrave

First published 2001 by
PALGRAVE
Houndmills, Basingstoke, Hampshire RG21 6XS and
175 Fifth Avenue, New York, N. Y. 10010
Companies and representatives throughout the world

PALGRAVE is the new global academic imprint of
St. Martin's Press LLC Scholarly and Reference Division and
Palgrave Publishers Ltd (formerly Macmillan Press Ltd).

ISBN 0–333–79241–6

This book is printed on paper suitable for recycling and made from fully managed and sustained forest sources.

A catalogue record for this book is available from the British Library.

Library of Congress Cataloging-in-Publication Data
Benson, Leslie.
　　Yugoslavia: a concise history / Leslie Benson.
　　　　p. cm.
　　Includes bibliographical references and index.
　　ISBN 0–333–79241–6 (cloth)
　　　　1. Yugoslavia—History. I. Title.

DR1246 .B464 2001
949.7—dc21

2001133052

10　9　8　7　6　5　4　3　2　1
10　09　08　07　06　05　04　03　02　01

Printed and bound in Great Britain by
Antony Rowe Ltd, Chippenham, Wiltshire

For James and David,
and in memory of
Marija ('Mis'), Ivan and Bora Milojević,
their grandparents and uncle

Contents

Acknowledgements

Many thanks to my friends and colleagues at University College, Northampton, who relieved me of teaching for a term so that I was able to get this book properly started. John McDonald very kindly offered to read the final draft for me, and I am indebted to him for his comments. I am also glad to have this chance, however belated, of thanking Stane Saksida and Veljko Rus in Ljubljana, Dragoljub Kavran in Belgrade, Dimitar Mirčev in Skopje and Mustafa Imamović in Sarajevo, for their kindness and hospitality during my travels around (the former) Yugoslavia. My years there now seem to belong to another existence altogether, but memories of (former) family and old friends still tug, and the book's dedication is intended to embrace them all. These personal debts of gratitude are a cheering reminder of other Balkan realities.

I am extremely grateful to the Librarians at the School of Slavonic and East European Studies, University of London, for permission to use their outstanding collection.

Maps are an important part of the book. Maps 1–7 are based on maps in *Jugoslavia*, volume II, published by the Naval Intelligence Division, 1944. These maps are out of copyright, but I should like to express my appreciation of the cartographic skills of Miss K.S.A. Froggatt, Miss M. Garside, Mrs Marion Plant and Mrs Gwen Raverat. They have been redrawn by Peter Cory. The original titles of the maps have been retained.

Map 8 is based on the map in F. Singleton, *A Short History of the Yugoslav Peoples*, Cambridge: Cambridge University Press, 1985 (Fig. 4), reproduced by kind permission.

Maps 9, 10 and 11 are based on maps in John B. Allcock, Marko Milivojević and John J. Horton (eds), *Conflict in the Former Yugoslavia: An Encyclopedia*, published by ABC-CLIO: Denver, CO; Santa Barbara, CA; Oxford, 1998 (map 1, p. xxii; map 3, p. xxv; map 9, p. xxxi), reproduced by kind permission.

Linda Nicol of Cambridge University Press was most helpful in response to my several enquiries, and gave permission to reproduce Map 8. Dr Robert Neville of ABC-CLIO and Mrs J.M. Braithwaite of the University of Bradford very generously allowed me to reproduce Maps 9, 10 and 11.

My IT skills were frequently not up to the demands of modern publishing methods, but David Benson plugged the worst gaps, with patience and aplomb. Many thanks to Luciana O'Flaherty at Palgrave Publishers, and to Ray Addicott of Chase Publishing Services, for their help in getting the book in shape for publication. My wife Anne Marie was at the heart of everything.

Notes on Serbo-Croatian Language

Croatian and Serbian are nowadays the national languages of two sovereign states, but linguistically they are one, created by political design during the nineteenth century (see Chapter 1). The South Slavs spoke three major dialects of a common tongue: štokavian, čakavian and kajkavian, terms derived from the variant interrogative pronoun (što?, ča? and kaj?) meaning 'what'? The Vienna Agreement of 1850 between Serb and Croat scholars adopted the štokavian dialect as the foundation of a common Serbo-Croatian language with two separate but equal varieties, which became the standard language of Serbia, Croatia, Bosnia-Hercegovina and Montenegro. This speech community is bounded to the north-west by Slovenia, where the kajkavian dialect forms the basis of the modern standard language, and to the south-east by Macedonia, where the national language of the Slav inhabitants is close kin to standard Bulgarian. The čakavian dialect now survives only as an attenuated vernacular in the remoter island regions of Dalmatia.

Apart from the aesthetically and politically very sensitive question of the two different alphabets, the differences between the Serbian and Croatian varieties are linguistically quite minor. The main one is the way in which they signal the varying quantity (long or short) of the letter e. Thus, for example, the 'ekavian' (eastern/Serbian) and 'ijekavian' (western/Croatian) variants of the word 'river' are 'reka' and 'rijeka'. The 'ekavian' form is normally written in Cyrillic script, but can be transliterated exactly using the modified Latin alphabet adopted in Croatian orthography.

Serbo-Croatian is completely regular in pronunciation, and there are no silent letters. Eight Serbo-Croatian consonants do not feature in English, and four consonants appear identical but are pronounced differently. They are:

č	*ch* in 'church'
ć	*t* in 'mixture'
dž	*j* in 'jam'
dj	*d* in 'duke'
š	*sh* in 'shoe'
ž	*s* in 'treasure'

lj	*ll* in 'million'
nj	*n* in 'new'
c	*ts* in 'Tsar'
h	*ch* in Scots-English 'loch'
j	*y* in 'yet'
r	*r* in Scots-English 'person', always sounded

Of the remaining consonants it need only be pointed out that *g* is always hard (as in 'gag'), and so is *s* (as in 'sack'). The English letters w, x and y are absent. The vowels in Serbo-Croatian are sounded as follows:

a	*a* in 'father'
e	e in 'pet'
i	*i* in 'machine'
o	*o* in 'hot'
u	*u* in 'rule'

Maps

Glossary

Ausgleich   'Compromise', of 1867 between Vienna and Budapest that created the Dual Monarchy within the Austro-Hungarian Empire.

AVNOJ   (Antifašističko Veće Narodnog Oslobodjenja Jugoslavije) 'Antifascist Council for the National Liberation of Yugoslavia.

Ban   Vice-regal governor, especially associated with Croatia.

Banovina   Vice-regal province.

Bosniak   Self-appellation of the Bosnian Muslims.

četa   A guerrilla band, hence četnik.

četnik   A member of the band – see also hajduk.

Chetniks   (Četnici) Serbian nationalist fighters during World War II.

hajduk   Bandit and leader of resistance to Otttoman rule in Serbia during the nineteenth century.

Muslim–Croat Federation   A joint entity within Bosnia-Hercegovina, created by the Dayton Agreements (1995). The Serb entity is Republika Srpska.

Nagodba   'Agreement' between the Hungarians and Croats in 1868 on a measure of autonomy for Croatia.

NDH   (Nezavisna Država Hrvatska) Independent State of Croatia, puppet regime under Ante Pavelić established by the Axis occupiers in April 1941.

Obznana   'Proclamation' outlawing the Communist Party in 1921.

Old Serbia   The name for Macedonia and Kosovo in the first Yugoslavia.

Old Kingdom   Serbia within the frontiers established in 1878.

Partizans   (Partizani) Communist-led resistance fighters during World War II.

prečani Serbs   Literally those Serbs living 'on the other side' of the River Drina from the Old Kingdom, under Austro-Hungarian and Ottoman rule.

Republika Srpska   The Serb entity within the Republic of Bosnia-Hercegovina established by the Dayton Agreements – normally appears in its Serbian form so as to avoid confusion with the Republic of Serbia.

Ustashas   (Ustaše) 'Insurgents', fascist followers of Ante Pavelić in the Independent State of Croatia

vilayet   Ottoman administrative district.

VMRO/IMRO   Internal Macedonian Revolutionary Organization.
zadruga   Communal form of land ownership based on extended families.

Chronology of Events

1 December 1918	Kingdom of Serbs, Croats and Slovenes proclaimed
28 June 1921	Constituent Assembly adopts Vidovdan Constitution
20 June 1928	Shootings in the Assembly lead to the death of Radić
6 January 1929	King Aleksandar suspends Vidovdan Constitution. Kingdom of Yugoslavia comes into being on 3 October
November 1932	'Zagreb Theses' signal strengthening opposition to dictatorship
9 October 1934	King Aleksandar assassinated in Marseille. Prince Pavle becomes Regent
May–June 1935	Elections fail to give the government party a convincing mandate. Stojadinović appointed premier
August 1937	Josip Broz Tito becomes General Secretary of the Communist Party of Yugoslavia (CPY)
October 1937	Bloc of National Agreement forms a united opposition
March 1938	Austria incorporated into the Third Reich
September 1938	Munich agreement between Chamberlain and Hitler
December 1938	Stojadinović's poor showing in elections leads to his resignation
15 March 1939	Germany invades Czechoslovakia
3 September 1939	Britain and France declare war on Germany
October 1940	Italy invades Albania
6 April 1941	Luftwaffe bombs Belgrade. Yugoslavia surrenders 17 April
10 April 1941	Independent State of Croatia (Nezavisna Država Hrvatska – NDH) founded
8 September 1943	Italy surrenders

29 November 1943	The Anti-fascist Council for the Peoples' Liberation of Yugoslavia (AVNOJ) proclaims itself a future government of Yugoslavia
31 January 1946	Constitution establishing the Federative Peoples' Republic of Yugoslavia (FNRJ)
28 April 1947	Five Year Plan adopted
28 June 1948	Fifth Congress of the CPY learns of Yugoslavia's expulsion from Cominform
November 1952	Sixth Congress renames the Party as the League of Communists of Yugoslavia (LCY), and announces a programme of reform
January 1953	New Constitution. Djilas expelled from Party
October 1956	Hungarian revolution crushed by Red Army
April 1958	LCY Seventh Congress
April 1963	New Constitution. The state is renamed the Socialist Federal Republic of Yugoslavia
December 1964	LCY Eighth Congress endorses market reforms
August 1965	Market reforms implemented
July 1966	Brioni Plenum dismisses Ranković
March 1969	LCY Ninth Congress
1 December 1971	Purges of republican leaderships begin, and extend to all levels of the political bureaucracy
January 1974	New Constitution confirms the powers of the republics won during the reform years
May 1974	LCY Tenth Congress
June 1978	LCY Eleventh Congress
May 1980	Death of Tito. Collective Presidency installed
March 1981	Riots break out in Kosovo
June 1982	LCY Twelfth Congress
August 1983	Death of Ranković
April–May 1986	Kučan and Milošević elected to lead their republican League of Communist organizations
July 1986	LCY Thirteenth Congress
October 1986	Memorandum of the Serbian Academy of Sciences and Arts is leaked to a Belgrade evening newspaper, attacking the 'genocide' of the Serbs in Kosovo
Autumn 1987	Yugoslavia rocked by 'Agrokomerc' fraud
September 1987	Milošević ousts 'liberal' opposition within the Serbian party organization

Spring 1988	Tensions between the Yugoslav People's Army and the Slovenes erupt in protests with the arrest of the 'Ljubljana Four'
October 1988	Autonomous federal status of Vojvodina abolished by a new Serbian republican constitution
March 1989	Autonomous federal status of Kosovo surrendered by the provincial assembly in Priština, amid a strong show of armed force. Serious riots, shootings and thousands of arrests
28 June 1989	Milošević addresses a million Serbs at the 600th anniversary of Kosovo Field, and warns of 'armed struggles' to come
December 1989	Hyperinflation hits the Yugoslav economy
January 22 1990	LCY Fourteenth Congress abandoned after the Slovenian delegates walk out
February 1990	Serbian Democratic Party founded, representing the Serbs in Croatia and Bosnia-Hercegovina
April 1990	Multi-party elections in Croatia and Slovenia
July 1990	Milošević announces that the Serbian League of Communists will from now on be known as the Socialist Party of Serbia
November–December 1990	Multi-party elections in Bosnia, Montenegro and Serbia
9 March 1991	Huge anti-government demonstrations in Belgrade
25 June 1991	Army moves into Slovenia to restore federal authority but is forced to withdraw after only ten days
8 October 1991	Slovenia and Croatia declare independence. War in Croatia
December 1991–April 1992	Croatia, Slovenia and Bosnia-Hercegovina are all recognized as independent states by the EU and the United States
27 April 1992	Communist Yugoslavia ceases to exist. Federal Republic of Yugoslavia proclaimed, comprising Serbia and Montenegro
April 1992	Full-scale war breaks out in Bosnia-Hercegovina. Sarajevo comes under years of siege

2 January 1993	Vance–Owen Peace Plan, rejected by Bosnian Serbs
November 1993	Mostar falls to Croatian forces
April 1994	Contact Group formed, superseding Vance–Owen
Summer 1995	Combined Croat–Bosniak offensives roll Serbs back
July 1995	Massacre of Bosnian Muslims at Srebrenica
14 December 1995	Dayton Agreements end war in Bosnia-Hercegovina
April–May 1996	Mass demonstrations against government in Serbia
3 November 1996	Opposition coalition 'Zajedno' contests elections. Milošević refuses to concede losses, triggering mass protests which last for months
Spring 1997	Increasing activity by the Kosovo Liberation Army
March 1998	Šešelj joins government. Serbian reprisals in Kosovo escalate the conflict
February 1999	West brings Serbs and Kosovars to Rambouillet, to engineer a peace agreement. Negotiations break down
24 March 1999	NATO launches airstrikes against targets in Kosovo and Serbia, in a campaign of 78 days of continuous bombing
10 June 1999	Serbia begins withdrawing its forces from Kosovo

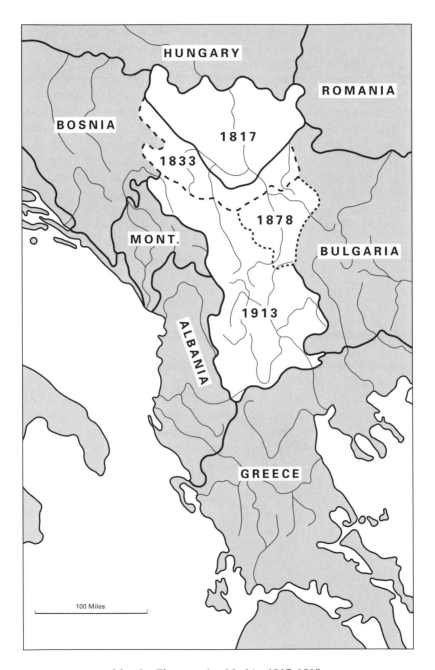

Map 1   The growth of Serbia, 1817–1913

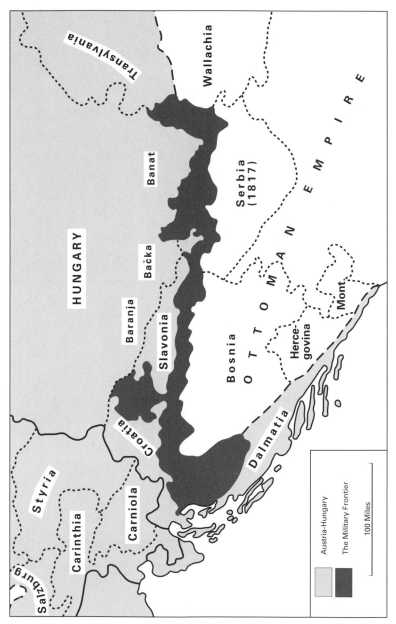

Map 2   The military frontier of Austria and Hungary

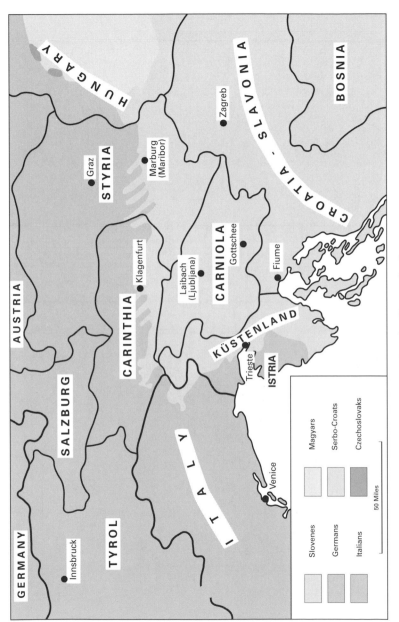

Map 3   The Slovene lands

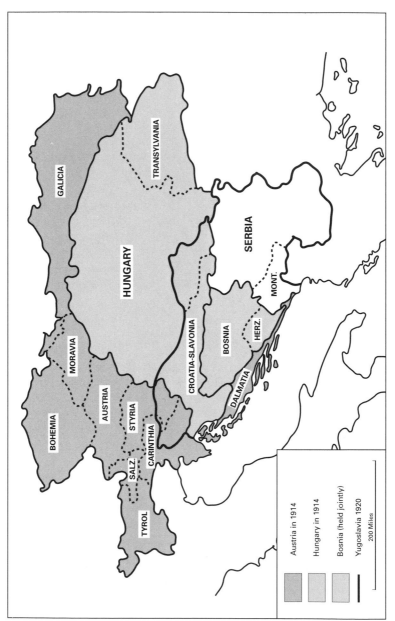

Map 4 Yugoslavia in relation to Austria-Hungary

Austria in 1914

Hungary in 1914

Bosnia (held jointly)

Yugoslavia 1920

200 Miles

GALICIA

TRANSYLVANIA

HUNGARY

SERBIA

MONT.

BOHEMIA

MORAVIA

AUSTRIA

STYRIA

CARINTHIA

SALZ.

TYROL

CROATIA-SLAVONIA

BOSNIA

HERZ.

DALMATIA

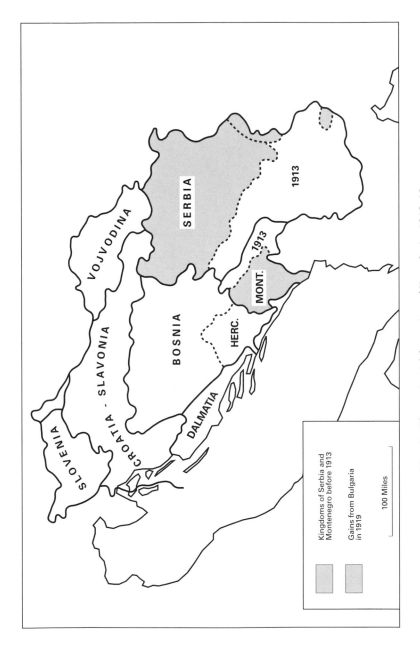

Map 5   The territorial formation of Yugoslavia, 1913–19

SLOVENIA

CROATIA - SLAVONIA

VOJVODINA

SERBIA

BOSNIA

HERC.

DALMATIA

MONT.

1913

1913

Kingdoms of Serbia and
Montenegro before 1913

Gains from Bulgaria
in 1919

100 Miles

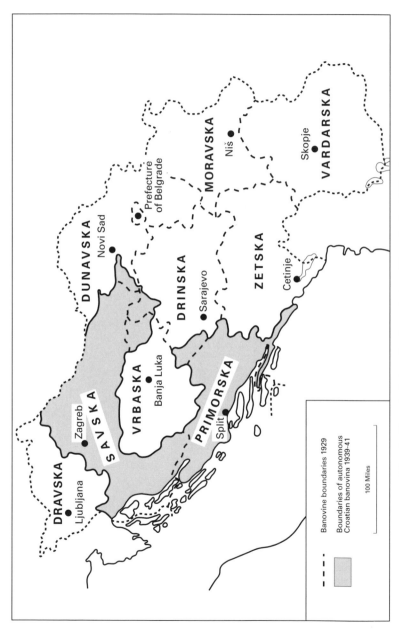

Map 6   The administrative boundaries of Yugoslavia, 1929–41

DRAVSKA
Ljubljana

SAVSKA
Zagreb

VRBASKA
Banja Luka

PRIMORSKA
Split

DUNAVSKA
Novi Sad

Prefecture
of Belgrade

MORAVSKA
Niš

DRINSKA
Sarajevo

ZETSKA
Cetinje

VARDARSKA
Skopje

Banovine boundaries 1929

Boundaries of autonomous
Croatian banovina 1939–41

100 Miles

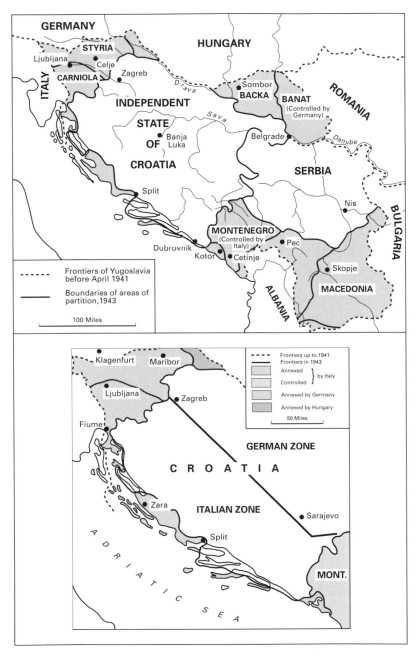

Map 7 The dismemberment of Yugoslavia, 1941

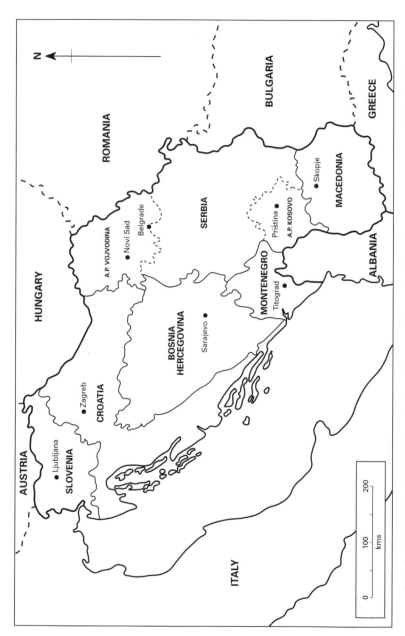

Map 8 Yugoslavia 1945–91: boundaries of the republics and of the autonomous provinces within Serbia

* Declared by Serbia and Montenegro in April 1992, the Federal Repubic of
Yugoslavia is not recognized internationally as being sole successor of the former
Yugoslav Federation.

Map 9   The former Yugoslavia and its successor republics
in their regional context

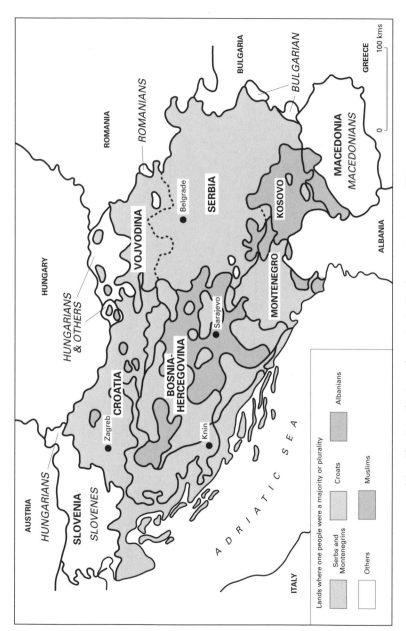

Map 10   Distribution of peoples in the former Yugoslavia, 1991

Lands where one people were a majority or plurality

Serbs and Montenegrins

Croats

Muslims

Albanians

Others

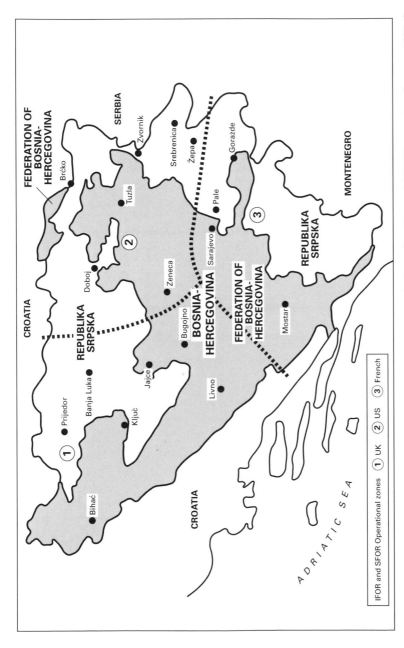

Map 11   Dayton Peace Agreement territorial dispensation, inter-entity boundary line and I/SFOR operational zones, 1995–8

1
Prologue: The Road to Kumanovo

It took the destruction of two great empires to make room for the formation of the Kingdom of the Serbs, Croats and Slovenes in 1918, a new state created out of the marcher lands straddling the Ottoman and Habsburg dominions. The histories of the Slav tribes settled south of the Danube[1] have diverged since earliest times, when the power of Byzantium won the Serbs for the Orthodox rite, while the Croats and Slovenes adhered to Rome. The Ottoman victory at Kosovo Field in 1389 completed the separation, dealing a mortal blow to the crumbling Serbian empire carved out by Stefan Nemanja and his successors over two centuries. Serbia and Bosnia-Hercegovina came under Ottoman sway for half a millennium, leaving the Croatian and Slovene lands under Habsburg rule.

By the end of the Napoleonic wars both empires were in disarray, laggards in the race to modernization. Turkey was the pivotal state in the European balance of power throughout the nineteenth century, and it was in the Ottoman possessions that revolutionary national movements had their early successes. In Serbia, a peasant rising led by Kara Djordje ('Black George') Petrović, in 1804, was suppressed after a decade of guerrilla warfare, only to be followed by another rebellion under Miloš Obrenović, in 1815. Within two years, the Serbs of the Šumadija, the forest fastness south of Belgrade, had driven out all foreigners, and in November 1817 an assembly (skupština) of the people acclaimed Miloš as hereditary Prince of Serbia – he sent the stuffed head of Black George to Istanbul as a propitiating gift. Miloš succeeded in securing the formation of an autonomous principality in 1830, sponsored by Russia; then, after fomenting trouble in adjacent Turkish

1

districts to the south, he moved in to restore order, adding them to his domains in 1833.

For most of the nineteenth century, Serbia remained a backward satrapy of empire. As late as 1894, the Civil Code continued to recognize the zadruga as a legal entity, a form of communal ownership of property vested in the extended family or clan, reflecting the embedded social power of localism and tradition.[2] Serbia was untroubled by the forces of capital and labour which elsewhere favoured the development of liberal democracy. In mid-century, there were 43 varieties of foreign coinages in circulation, and by 1884 Serbia was the only country in the Balkans still without a single kilometre of railway track. Miloš and his successors fought doggedly against constitutionalism. The Prince was the district headman writ large, and it was not until 1858 that the first national Skupština was elected on a franchise restricted to direct taxpayers, thus excluding most of the peasantry. Two dynasties locked in blood feud (Karadjordjević and Obrenović) alternated in power in a cycle of assassination and exile, constantly embroiled in domestic and international intrigues in which the consular representatives of the great powers regularly took a hand.[3]

The fledgling state was puny, and Turkish garrisons continued to occupy key strongholds until 1867, including Belgrade, which, despite its commanding position on the confluence of the River Danube and the River Sava, was slow to develop its later pre-eminence as a capital city – in 1840 it numbered just 6000 people, and by 1863 still had fewer than 15 000 inhabitants. For years Kragujevac, in the heart of the Šumadija, was the preferred seat of Serbia's rulers. Ottoman conquest had eliminated the native aristocracy, and Prince Miloš withheld grants of land in order to prevent the creation of large estates. The result was a remarkably homogeneous society of peasant smallholders, unscathed by industrialization, and immune to social and intellectual novelty. Even the revival of Serbian linguistic and historical studies inspired by Vuk Karadžić (1787–1864) was not a native plant – Vuk himself lived in Vienna. Indigenous Serbian culture was oral, contained in the folk epics recited by traditional bards, and rooted in the authority of the Orthodox Church, the only institution that connected Serbs with their remote past as a free people.[4]

The achievement of Vuk Karadžić was to consecrate the language and poetry of the 'common people' (his term) as an expression of nationhood. Vuk was a towering figure in the South Slav renaissance, whose work attracted the admiring attention of Jakob Grimm, Ranke and Goethe, but his sympathies were all with the Serbs, with no trace of pan-Slavism. He codified and rationalized the Serbian language, taking as the norm the štokavian dialect spoken in eastern Hercegovina, where it was least corrupted by foreign influences. All who spoke it were Serbs, according to Vuk, irrespective of religious or ethnic affiliation. In an essay entitled 'Serbs all, and everywhere', he argued that the Serbs were the most ancient inhabitants of the Balkan lands, a true aboriginal people; even the Muslims in Bosnia (he called them 'Turks') were in fact Serbs. Vuk's vision of Serbdom as united by immemorial ties of blood and language exerted a powerful hold on the collective consciousness of succeeding generations, and more than any statesman or general he symbolizes Serbian national identity to this day.

Serbian nationalism was stamped during the nineteenth century by the harsh struggle to carve out an independent state amid the long, slow dissolution of Ottoman power in Europe. In content it was militaristic and Orthodox, bound together by a mythopoeic history celebrating the fullness of empire under Stefan Dušan (1331–55), who was crowned at Skopje, and established the Patriarchate of Peć (in Kosovo), the religious centre of Serbian life under Ottoman rule. Orthodox piety was enshrined in the cult of St Sava, the monastic name taken by Stefan Nemanja's younger son, who became the first archbishop of a Serbian auto-cephalous church in 1219. In the nature of the case, the contours of medieval Serbia could never be determined, but the call to recover 'the cradle of the nation' carried a powerful emotional appeal to a peasant people accustomed by the liturgy to reverence their ancient rulers as martyrs in the fight for freedom against the Turk.

A nationalism constructed around the epochal defeat at Kosovo Field bred a culture suffused by the themes of purification, and of revenge for the dishonour inflicted by Ottoman conquest. Among the many legends engraved in folk-memory was the exodus of Serbs from their native Kosovo in 1690, led by their Patriarch northwards to escape Turkish reprisals, following an invasion by Austrian forces.[5] Serbia's national aims encompassed the recovery of Kosovo and other ancient lands, and the unification of all Serbs within a single state. In 1844, Serbian statesman Ilija Garašanin published his 'Outlines' ('Načertanije') of a future Great Serbia comprising Kosovo and northern Albania, Bosnia-Hercegovina, Montenegro, Macedonia and the Vojvodina. The 'Outlines' epitomize the expansionism inscribed in the character of Serbian nationalism. Serbia survived only in the political space created by the rivalries between the great powers. Squeezed between warring empires, the Serbs had to seek security through an increase of population and territories, and an outlet to the sea.

Serbia's only ally in the Balkans was Montenegro. Serbia was divided from Montenegro by the Sandžak of Novi Pazar, a land-corridor linking Bosnia with Macedonia, and so on to the port of Salonika (Thessaloniki), which the Serbs called Solun. Possession of the Sandžak delivered control of the great wedge-shaped salient of Bosnia, with its large population of Serbs. A barren tract of mountain (Montenegrins call it 'the land behind God's back'), Montenegro was never entirely subjugated by Turkey. When not engaged in their own clan feuds, Montenegrins warred against the authority of Istanbul with legendary ferocity, ruled by a dynasty of prince-bishops who maintained personal links to the Tsar of Russia stretching back to the time of Peter the Great. Parallel histories and common interests against Ottoman power made union between Montenegro and Serbia a natural object of policy. But although Serbs and Montenegrins shared an Orthodox culture and spoke in the language of Vuk, Montenegro has always preserved its own strong tradition of independent statehood.

In contrast to the situation in Serbia and Bosnia, the Ottoman hold on Croatia-Slavonia was always more tenuous. The Croats appear as an organized, independent community in the tenth century, but their fortunes later became entwined with Hungary, whose king was offered the crown of Croatia in 1102, beginning a connection that lasted for 800 years; and following the Hungarian defeat by the Ottomans at Mohacs (1526) Hungary was itself united with the crown of Austria. Mohacs brought most of Hungary and the Croatian lands under Ottoman control, until they were finally returned to Habsburg possession by the Treaty of Karlowitz (Sremski Karlovci), in 1699. To stem the Ottoman advance, Austria established a Military Frontier in 1578, Vojna Krajina in its Serbo-Croatian rendering, ruled directly from Vienna, a line of defence that incorporated half of Croatia-Slavonia. The depopulation of the war-devastated Frontier zones led to a search for new settlers, who received land in special tenure in return for military service. Most of the newcomers were Orthodox refugees moving northwards in front of the Ottoman armies, creating Serb settlements along the entire line of the Krajina.

Within the relatively loose structure of early Habsburg rule, the Croats were allowed to administer their internal affairs through a Diet (Sabor) in Zagreb, under its own Ban (governor), appointed by the Emperor. In the late eighteenth century, however, the centralizing reforms of Joseph II united the Croats and Hungarians in opposition, and in 1790 the Sabor surrendered most of its traditional autonomy to Hungary, in the hope of receiving protection against Vienna. In the event, Magyar nationalism came to pose the greater menace to Croatian independence. As the ancien regime faltered under the onslaught of revolutionary France, the Hungarians began to agitate for greater independence from Austria, whilst pursuing an aggressive policy of magyarization within their own sphere of influence.

Hungarian assimilationist policy kicked modern Croatian nationalism into life. In its origins, the idea of the Croatian nation referred to an aristocratic estate, to which (as the saying went) the Croat noble would sooner admit his horse than a peasant.[6] The social gulf between lord and peasant bred disdain among the educated classes for the use of the vernacular tongue. Well into the nineteenth century, Latin was the language of administration and learning in Croatia, while German was spoken in polite society. Ljudevit Gaj (1809–72) did for the Croats what Vuk Karadžić accomplished for the Serbs: he created a modern, codified language, likewise based on štokavian speech, with a reformed orthography using the Latin alphabet. The choice of štokavian, in preference to the kajkavian speech of Zagreb, which was more akin to Slovene, had an explicitly political purpose. Gaj (himself a kajkavian speaker) argued that the Catholics of Bosnia, Dalmatia and the Vojvodina who spoke štokavian were not Serbs but Serbo-Croats, Croats who had adopted the language of their Serb neighbours. A common language, he hoped and believed, would reunite the South Slav peoples.

Gaj was the moving spirit in the Illyrian movement, a name celebrating the fleeting life of the Slav Illyrian Provinces (1809–13) created around the north-eastern Adriatic by Napoleon. In 1835, Gaj was licensed by the Emperor to publish newspapers for Croat readers as a counterpoise to Magyar nationalism. By 1841 he was leader of the newly founded Illyrian Party, generally taken as marking the beginnings of modern Croatian nationalism, though for most of the nineteenth century it remained confined to a narrow circle of intellectuals and publicists. Although Gaj always asserted his loyalty to the Habsburg Empire, others within his immediate following were openly speaking of 'cultural Illyrianism' combined with 'political Croatianism' as their programme. Gaj himself opened up channels of communication with Serbia and Russia, seeking support for his movement, and he soon fell out of favour in Vienna.

The Magyars denied the very idea of a Croatian nation. In 1843, the Hungarian Diet made Hungarian the language of public administration, replacing Latin, and decreed that within six years it would also become the official language of Croatia. In 1848, they took advantage of the general European crisis to remove their Diet from Pressburg to Budapest, to which the Croats responded by joining with the Serbs in Slavonia to fight against Hungary on the side of the Emperor. The Hungarians were defeated, in 1849, but neither Croats nor Serbs had any reward for their loyalty to the Emperor, though the Croats did get control of the Adriatic port of Fiume (Rijeka). Having allied themselves with an absolutist state against Hungarian demands for more representative government, the Habsburg South Slavs got no concessions out of system that was becoming less stable and consequently more repressive. The reaction marked the end of the Illyrian movement, and of Gaj's political career.

This was the only occasion during the nineteenth century that Serbs and Croats found themselves confronting a common enemy in armed resistance. The Serbs generally were indifferent to the claims of Slav brotherhood. Vuk Karadžić was dismissive of the pretensions of Illyrianism, and many Serbs saw in Gaj's linguistic reforms an attack upon their language, including the Orthodox clergy, who at first resisted Vuk's tampering with the sacred language. Gaj ensured that Serbs and Croats would speak in variants of a common tongue, but the Serbs could not bring themselves to admit the equality of the two dialects. What was at stake was an entire state of mind. Illyrianism called for mutual toleration, respect for cultural and religious differences, and the call fell on deaf ears in Serbia, an authoritarian peasant society beset by the problems of state-building.

Prince Mihajlo Obrenović (1860–8) was as little concerned with constitutionalism and the rule of law as his father, but he was an energetic modernizer. With Garašanin as his chief minister, Mihajlo began building up a modern bureaucracy and a professional army of some 90 000 men, initiating a new phase in Serbia's struggle for independence. Secret bilateral agreements with the Romanians, the Bulgars and the Greeks were concluded, and, shortly before he was shot dead while taking a walk, Mihajlo secured the withdrawal of the last Turkish garrisons. Ottoman power was ebbing, and it was not long before rebellion broke out in Bosnia-Hercegovina.

The divide between Christianity and Islam, in one sense so fundamental to the structure of Bosnian society, was not related in any simple way to social and political cleavages. A Muslim elite monopolized wealth and power, ruling over a servile Christian populace composed predominantly of Orthodox sharecropping peasants (the Austrian census of 1879 counted about half a million Orthodox believers: 448 000 Muslims, and just over 200 000 Catholics). But most Muslims were small-holding peasants, not big landowners, and shared the hardships of their Christian neighbours in lean years. They were also Slavs. Bosnia was the homeland of their ancestors, who had converted to Islam, and their cherished Bosnian language, with its rich literary tradition, was the tongue of their Christian neighbours.

The most striking source of conflict in early nineteenth-century Bosnia was the power struggle between the indigenous Muslim elite and their Ottoman overlords. In earlier times, Istanbul governed the province through appointed Bosnian Muslim notables who held the title of kapetan, but by the mid-eighteenth century, powerful families had ousted central authority, and made the office of kapetan hereditary. As the rebellion in Serbia gathered strength, the Sultan tried to strengthen his authority in Bosnia by ameliorating the political and social conditions of the Christian peasantry. The Ottoman reform movement ('Tanzimat') threatened the privileges and immunities of the Bosnian Muslim rulers, and ambitious kapetans saw here their chance for an autonomous Bosnia. A Turkish army finally broke them (1851), opening up the way to political reforms, but the authorities could do nothing to halt the relative economic decline of the Ottoman Empire during the nineteenth century, which caused the powerful Muslim landowners to multiply the burden of labour and taxes on the peasantry.[7]

Failures of the harvest bred sporadic peasant rebellions throughout the South Slav lands. One of them, which began at Nevesinje in 1875, spread throughout the province, and beyond, to Bulgaria. The authorities reacted with devastation and killings on a war-like scale. Serbia and Montenegro seized their moment the following year to declare war on Turkey (supported by the Bulgars); and then Russia stepped in to champion its Slav clients, defeating the Turks in January 1878. Later that year, the Congress of Berlin created a new order in the Balkans. Montenegro and Serbia became sovereign kingdoms in 1882, and Serbia made some territorial gains to the south-east.

Five centuries after Kosovo Field, Serbia was finally emancipated from Ottoman rule, but it was not a moment of great triumph. The Congress of Berlin was decisive in limiting the influence of Russia on Balkan affairs. The new power in the region was Austria-Hungary, which was allowed to occupy Bosnia-Hercegovina, and to garrison the Sandžak of Novi Pazar. Bulgaria was now the prime beneficiary of Russian patronage, the outer defence of the Orthodox Christians. The Three Emperors' League (1881) brought together Austria-Hungary, Germany and Russia in an agreement which defined their separate spheres of influence. Within days of that agreement Prince Milan Obrenović was induced by Austria-Hungary to sign a secret convention effectively abrogating his right to an independent foreign policy, together with a trade treaty which turned

Serbia into an agricultural appendage of the Habsburg Empire. The new state remained still without a seaport, dependent on Austria-Hungary for four-fifths of both exports and imports, and the prečani Serbs (literally, 'those on the other side', in Austria-Hungary) were as far away as ever from the day of unification with the homeland.

Prince Milan became King Milan, but Serbia exchanged a weak imperial master for a strong one, and the effect on domestic politics was profound. The Progressives, who formed Milan's government in 1881, were not consulted about his dealings with Vienna, and they were appalled by the concessions he had made. They exploited his isolation (word could not be allowed to get out for fear of public outcry) to pass a number of laws liberalizing political activity and extending the franchise.

The main beneficiary of these changes was the People's Radical Party, formally constituted in 1881. The party had its origins in a circle of Serbian students studying for higher technical degrees at the Federal Polytechnic Institute in Zurich in the years around 1870. They stood in great contrast to the preceding generation of intellectuals, the core of the state political class, whose destination was Paris, and whose profession was the Law. The Radicals were not westward-looking liberals. They drew their inspiration from the Russian narodniks, not least because of the influence on the Zurich group of Svetozar Marković, a revolutionary socialist whose short life (he died in 1875 aged 27) was crammed with political activity. He founded Serbia's first socialist newspaper, but soon came to abandon Marxism – he found the absence of a proletariat theoretically embarrassing. His real political legacy was a populist enthusiasm for the communal life of the peasantry as the moral basis of a new political order.[8]

Some traces of Marković's ideal of a peasant commonwealth survived in the Radicals' inaugural Programme of 1881, published in their newspaper *Samouprava* (Self-government), but already a splinter group was busy organizing an authentic peasant socialist party, aggrieved that his ideas had been abandoned. The true character of the People's Radical Party was in its driving commitment to the unification of all Serbs, and the creation of a strong Serbian national state was the life's work of their leader, Nikola Pašić, who eventually presided over the formation of the first Yugoslavia. Pašić received his advanced training as an engineer in Zurich, where he began an active political cooperation with Marković; he also became friendly with (and disagreed with) Bakunin. In 1875, Pašić deserted engineering for politics (he was a government Surveyor First Class), to which he brought the same methodical, organizing bent, and it was mainly to him that the Radical party owed its centralized, disciplined structure, based on a network of agents in the villages working to mobilize the peasantry as a political force.

The elections of September 1883 were the first involving anything like modern electioneering and the Radicals won them by a two-to-one majority. Milan's answer was to adjourn the Assembly as soon as it was opened, and to reassert his personal control by refusing to invite the Radicals to form the government. In October, rebellion broke out among the peasants of Pašić's Timok region of eastern Serbia (he came from Zaječar), who refused to surrender their rifles to the central authorities. The Radical leaders were implicated in the revolt, which was easily put down, and Pašić (together with 93 others) was sentenced to death, which he escaped by fleeing into exile in Bulgaria.

Despite this setback for the Radicals, the impetus to reform was unstoppable. Milan was faced with a hefty bill for the Serbo-Turkish conflicts of 1875–8, together with new burdens such as maintaining diplomatic missions abroad, and building railways to comply with the treaty obligations imposed on Serbia by Austria-Hungary. Between 1880 and 1886 state expenditure and state revenues doubled by dint of imposing new taxes in place of the uniform poll tax which had stood for half a century, and a National Bank was established (1884) to coordinate finances and regulate the currency. Military service was introduced to augment the standing army, and proper training for officers to lead it. Compulsory elementary schooling, together with founding of the Serbian Academy of Sciences in 1887, initiated that most typical institution of modernity, a national system of public education.

Milan's public standing was badly damaged by Serbia's defeat at the hands of Bulgaria in 1885, in a disastrous war over territory, and by the scandal of his decision to divorce his queen. The military rout shocked the Serbs: Russian aid had turned Bulgaria into a regional military power to be reckoned with. Insecure now in the patronage of Austria-Hungary, which had no use for a weak ruler in Serbia, Milan conceded the liberal Constitution of 1889 (December 1888 os) based upon the joint sovereignty of monarch and elected Assembly. He then abdicated in favour of his son, Aleksandar, who was a minor. Pašić, amnestied by the Regency, returned to take part in the elections in September, which gave the Radicals a massive majority, but the struggle was by no means over. Milan manipulated the Regency, and both he and his son were determined enemies of the Radicals. It took 14 more years of bruising confrontations before the issue was decided against the Obrenović dynasty.

Meanwhile Serbia, forced to turn southwards for expansion, became caught up in a struggle for power in Macedonia. To contemporaries, 'Macedonia' was a geographical expression, comprising the three Ottoman administrative districts (vilayets) of Bitola, Kosovo and Salonika, inhabited mainly by Albanians, Greeks and Macedo-Slavs, but also home to an amazingly variegated ethnic mosaic, including a flourishing Jewish community in Salonika. Most of the Slavs looked to Bulgaria as their homeland, and Bulgarian influence in the region was bolstered by the Bulgarian Orthodox exarchate created in 1870, which encompassed Macedonia. Never averse to dividing their Christian subjects, the Ottoman authorities allowed Serbs, Romanians and Greeks to set up schools in Macedonia, which became the focus of intense cultural competition – the Society of St Sava, founded in Belgrade in 1886, was specifically set up to promote Serbian nationalism in Macedonia, through teaching and propaganda.

Teaching and terrorism went hand-in-hand. Numerous secret societies sprang up, all of them with the aim of ejecting the Turks, but divided against each other. Of the more disciplined and politically self-conscious groups, some aspired to union with Bulgaria, while others, including most importantly the Internal Macedonian Revolutionary Organization (IMRO – VMRO in its Macedonian acronym), wanted autonomy for Macedonia. Both tendencies were opposed by the Serbs and Greeks, though Serbia for tactical reasons supported the bloody and abortive Ilinden (St Elijah's Day) Rising of 2 August 1903, led by IMRO, as a force working against Bulgarian supremacy. Despite (or perhaps because of) the attempt by the great powers to bring order to Macedonia by displacing Ottoman authority, the region sank irretrievably into blood-letting and rapine.[9]

The mainly Albanophone inhabitants of the Kosovo vilayet created at the Treaty of Berlin were inevitably caught up in the revolutionary national movements around them. The Albanians were also predominantly Muslim (Muslims made up about 70 per cent of the population), but it was around language, not religion, that Albanian nationalism crystallized. The League of Prizren, formed in June 1878 to campaign for the incorporation of all Albanian lands within a single vilayet, demanded Albanian-speaking officials and Albanian-language schools. The call for an independent Albanian state was not yet to be heard, or at least not at all clearly, but obvious signs that the League was successfully performing all the functions of an alternative government in Kosovo brought an Ottoman army to Skopje in March 1881, which snuffed the movement out. As in Bosnia, Ottoman civil administration was unequal to the task of reform, and Kosovo relapsed into poverty and misrule.[10]

These were also years of intense domestic conflicts within Serbia. In 1894 Aleksandar suspended the 1889 Constitution, and repressive laws flung Pašić and the Radicals back on the defensive. In 1899 Pašić was again under threat of execution, and in 1901 he was compelled to concede constitutional ground to the Regency, causing a split within his party: a group of younger men, disgusted by what they saw as Pašić's pusillanimous temporizing, formed the Independent Radicals. The day was saved for Pašić when, in May 1903, King Aleksandar and Queen Draga were murdered by a group of army officers, led by Colonel Dragutin Dimitrijević, nicknamed 'Apis' for his bull-like mien. Constitutional government now began to strike deeper roots in Serbia with the accession to the throne of Petar Karadjordjević (1903–14). King Petar was western-educated (he translated J.S. Mill's *On Liberty*), and perhaps too old at 59 to entertain schemes for personal aggrandizement in a country he entered for the first time as monarch – though under the nom de guerre of 'Petar Mrkonjić' he had fought as a guerrilla in Bosnia in 1876, where he came into contact with Pašić. Together they revived and further liberalized the 1889 Constitution, and set about creating a state with real, not fictional, sovereignty.

It is strange that a constitutionalist party should owe its victory to a brutal regicide by serving officers, and the reason for it was the power of dynastic politics in pre-1914 Europe. Royal houses were appalled by the murders. The military needed the Radicals to carry on the business of government, and to represent the Serbs to the world as a civilized nation, but their relationship was a strained one. It took three years of intense pressure from western governments before the last of the conspirators was removed from public life, and the army never was brought firmly under civilian control. What kept the alliance alive was that the Radicals were efficient modernizers, and shared with the generals a vision of a Great Serbia which would bring all the Orthodox faithful within one state, including outposts such as southern Hungary, eastern Croatia (Srem) and southern Dalmatia.

In the chancelleries of Vienna and Budapest, they sniffed trouble. A satellite Serbia was a useful instrument for conducting by proxy the business of undermining Ottoman power along the route to Salonika, and the fall of the Obrenović dynasty threatened the drive to the east. In 1906, the Serbian government flexed its muscles in the 'Pig War', a tariff dispute over the export of livestock to the Habsburg territories, which formed the mainstay of Serbia's trade. This was part of a general programme of innovation and reform led by Pašić, based of necessity on new international links, notably with France, which provided crucial loans, including one to re-equip the army. Still a weak state, Serbia was beginning to behave like a strong one, and the secret of this confidence was the bond between state and people forged by the Radicals.

The achievement of the Radicals, unique among the South Slav parties in the nineteenth century, was to adapt the grass-roots institutions of peasant communities in the cause of nation-building. The early peasant risings were 'national' only in the sense that they were explosions of ethnic fury directed against Turkish janissaries, Greek bishops and Levantine town traders, led by guerrillas bred in the tradition of the Balkan hajduk, more brigand than patriot.[11] Nationalist ideologues were given to celebrating the peasantry as the embodiment of the primordial 'people', but they spoke neither to peasants nor for them. The peasant rebellions endemic throughout the South Slav lands appeared to the thin stratum of educated urban dwellers as a menace to social order, and a barrier to progress.

The Radicals were often accused by their opponents of pandering to lawlessness, and their brand of peasant populism stamped itself on Serbian politics. Corruption, violence, and the absence of any conception of loyal opposition, all were products of the methods the Radicals learned in the cockfight with the monarchy. But they did break with the liberal prejudice that excluded most of the population from the political community on grounds of civic backwardness and uncouthness. Local assemblies, local administration, a developing legal system, an expanding network of schools, military service, provided an everyday framework for a burgeoning of nationalist consciousness based on an identification of the state with the Serbian people. Ethnic solidarity was heightened by the extensive in-migration of displaced Serbs from the disturbed Ottoman Empire: the territories won by Serbia, Montenegro and Bulgaria at the Treaty of Berlin were the scene of large-scale expulsions and exchanges of population.

Austro-Hungarian economic imperialism helped on the process of modernization by breaking down the structure of traditional peasant society. Modern nationalism, the sense of allegiance to a political community bound together by common institutions, presupposes the decline of a peasant way of life grounded in the extended family network, the local economy and customary folkways. A long period of peace, and expanding trade with the Habsburg lands, however unequal, brought increased levels of monetisation and credit. By the turn of the century, the zadrugas were in decay, and there was a spurt in the number of townspeople (Belgrade mushroomed, with about 90 000 inhabitants by the turn of the century), whose levels of literacy were high as a consequence of intensive educational programmes promoted by the government as a means of fostering national consciousness.

Within Austria-Hungary, the effect of capitalist penetration was even more strongly felt. The drive to turn Croatia and Bosnia-Hercegovina into productive units of the Empire gave a major boost to trade and commerce during the period 1890–1914, and there were even distant echoes of western political culture. During the 1890s, embryonic Social Democratic parties appeared in Slovenia, Croatia-Slavonia and the Vojvodina, offshoots of the recently formed parties in Austria and Hungary, but working-class parties remained stunted in the shadow of Croatian nationalism.

The Treaty of Berlin crowned a decade of bitter disappointment among Croats, who coveted Dalmatia and those parts of Bosnia-Hercegovina where Croats were settled. Austria's calamitous defeat by Prussia forced the Emperor to agree to the establishment of the Dual Monarchy by a Compromise (Ausgleich) signed in 1867, and Croatian nationalists hoped for similar status within the Empire. In fact, the effect of the deal between Vienna and Budapest was to return Croatia to Hungarian tutelage. The Hungarians in their turn concluded an Agreement (Nagodba) with the Croats in 1868, in which Croatia was recognized as a national entity, with Serbo-Croatian as the official language, and the Sabor in Zagreb acquired control over internal matters such as justice and education. However, economic and foreign policies were decided in Budapest, and the Ban of Croatia was appointed by the Hungarian premier. Hungary also took back control of Fiume (Rijeka), cutting off Croatia's access to the Adriatic, though by way of easy recompense Budapest supported the Croats in the negotiations that ended with the disbanding of the Military Frontier, in 1881.

Returning the Frontier to Croatian civil administration pleased nationalist sentiment, but it also increased the proportion of Serbs in the population ruled from Budapest to something like one in five, a situation exploited by the Hungarian authorities to fuel the 'Serb problem' which came to dog future generations. In 1883, Count Károly Khuen-Héderváry was appointed Ban of Croatia, beginning two decades of personal rule based on a Sabor packed with the Croatian nobility and senior clergy, who sat there by virtue of their rank, together with deputies elected by 45 000 voters out of a total population of 2.5 million. Serbs organized in numerically small electoral districts sent representatives to Zagreb, where they assiduously supported the government. The

Serbs were deliberately strengthened in their sense of ethnic separatism by encouraging the founding of denominational schools and allowing equality of status for their Cyrillic script. The more restless Croatian districts, prone to return deputies hostile to the creeping magyarization of Khuen-Héderváry, were dismantled.

Growing hostility towards the Serbs living in Croatia found a voice in Ante Starčević, the leader of the Croatian Party of Right (that is to say, the historical and constitutional right to independent statehood). He was a socially marginalized intellectual who might have become a teacher of philosophy but for want of patronage. In his early years a disciple of Illyrianism, Starčević ended as an ideologue of Croatdom, which he identified quite simply with all the South Slavs. He claimed the Serbian Nemanjid dynasty as an illustrious Croatian house, and argued that those he disparagingly termed 'Slavoserbs' were Orthodox Croats. More even than Vuk Karadžić in the case of the Serbs, Starčević found Croats all, and everywhere. His motto was simple: 'Neither Vienna nor Budapest', and he wanted an independent Great Croatia.

The problem was how to get it. Austria-Hungary was unlikely to succumb to armed revolt, as Turkey had done when faced by a series of national movements aided and abetted by predatory great powers. Croatia had no powerful patron, such as the Serbs had found in Russia, and no allies among neighbouring states. Nor did Croatian nationalism ever seriously threaten to take an insurrectionary turn. Starčević's muscular rhetoric appealed to the urban intelligentsia and the lesser bourgeoisie, faced by a huge influx of ethnic Germans and Magyars during Khuen-Héderváry's reign, but despite the severe economic distress which forced half a million Croats into emigration between 1880 and 1914, there was no means of channelling peasant discontents into organized political action. Peasant rebellions, in which Serbs and Croats sometimes joined forces, were directed towards limited ends, and whether the official who taxed them was Hungarian or Croat was of little consequence.[12]

Starčević was by no means a dominant figure in the development of Croatian nationalist doctrine during the nineteenth century, which was more accurately typified by Bishop Josip Strossmayer, with his vision of a Catholic empire in which the Croats would take their rightful place alongside the Austrians and Hungarians. Unlike Starčević, Strossmayer was a pillar of the establishment: he occupied the plum see of Djakovo, and was much favoured at the Viennese court. (He also had the distinction of casting one of only three votes against Papal Infallibility in 1870.) Strossmayer's long life (1815–1905) spanned most of the century, during which he helped found the South Slav Academy of Arts and Sciences (1867) and the Croatian National University (1874) at Zagreb. He intended in this way to foster a commitment to education that would overcome the differences between the Catholic and Orthodox Slavs. In this reading of the future, an enlarged Croatia would assume cultural leadership of a South Slav state within a federalized Habsburg empire, which presupposed a set of political arrangements to sustain a Great Croatia.

In 1894, Starčević and Strossmayer sank a lifetime of acrimonious disagreement in favour of a Programme of united opposition to the 'Magyarite' party through which Khuen-Héderváry ruled virtually unopposed. Strossmayer had long since abandoned hope that the Serbs might be reclaimed for a Catholic South Slav union. In a letter penned ten years earlier, he referred to the Serbs as 'our bloody enemies', guilty of stabbing the Croats in the back in their struggle against Hungarian repression. But the Programme clearly identified the Magyars as its main target, demanding full equality between the Kingdom of Croatia and the Kingdom of Hungary in matters of common concern, though the call for a 'juridical, constitutional and free state' uniting all Croats (and perhaps the Slovenes as well), was carefully qualified by a clause which read 'within the framework of the Habsburg Monarchy'.

Confronted by the brute fact of Austro-Hungarian power, the dominant tenor of Croatian nationalism was understandably cautious. Loyalty to the person of the Emperor, within a reconstituted empire, was its hallmark. For the Croats, all depended on exploiting the divisions between Budapest and Vienna to create a South Slav entity within the Habsburg dominions, a Croatia enlarged by the addition of Dalmatia and Bosnia-Hercegovina, together with the Slovene lands. The Dual Monarchy would become three, all of equal status. The difficulty with this so-called 'trialist' solution was that, even if the Habsburgs could agree to compromise with their Slav subjects – and some of them favoured such a stance, including the Archduke assassinated at Sarajevo – they would first have to wrest control of Croatia from Hungary.

The Slovene lands remained insulated from nationalist currents in Croatia. Among the Slovenes, national consciousness developed under the sheltering wing of the Catholic Church, giving Slovenian nationalism a clericalist and conservative stamp embodied in the dominant Slovene People's Party (SPP) (first organized in 1890 as the Catholic Political Society) led by Monsignor Anton Korošec. The success of the Slovene People's Party in holding off the challenge of its secular rivals for leadership in political affairs was due to the tenacity of the

Catholic hierarchy in securing appointments for Slovene priests (rather than Austrians), and to the party's links with the rural cooperative movement, which turned the Slovene peasants, once known for their poverty and backwardness, into the most prosperous and literate among the South Slavs.[13] From this localized base, parochial in the exact meaning of the word, the SPP devoted it main efforts to securing an extension of the tiny franchise (about 6 per cent of the population were entitled to vote in a system which favoured Austrians anyway), in order to increase the representation of Slovenes in the provincial Diets, and in the Vienna Reichsrat.

The Ausgleich of 1867 placed the Slovenes under the control, not of Hungary, but of Austria, which shielded the Slovenian lands both from the rising power of Italy and from the aggressive language policy of Budapest that so offended the Croats. The Slovenes were scattered throughout six Austrian provinces, and in only two of them did they form a majority of the population, but they did (in 1882) succeed in winning an electoral majority in the provincial Diet of Carniola, and in Ljubljana itself. This limited political advance, coupled with some well-timed cultural concessions, mollified Slovene opinion, and Slovenian nationalism remained at heart a social movement aimed at greater acceptance of the use of the Slovene language in education and admin-istration. It is not clear that the principle of nationality – the idea that nations ought to occupy a defined territorial space with their own state – was something that the Slovenes seriously applied to themselves. Even a 'trialist' reconstruction of the empire was not unambiguously appealing to Slovene opinion, for fear that the South Slav entity would be dominated by the Croats.

In the years 1903–7, conflicts between Vienna and Budapest led to a brief political thaw in Croatia during which a plethora of parties sprang into existence. Two of them were to play a major part in the life of the first Yugoslavia. The Croatian People's Peasant Party (CPPP) was founded in 1904 by Stjepan Radić (together with his brother Ante). Radić set out to mobilize the peasants, just as the Radicals had done in Serbia, and his political vision sprang from a common root. Russian populist beliefs lay at the heart of his claim that the soul of the Croat nation was carried through the centuries by the enduring virtues of the suffering peasantry. This peasant romanticism was wrapped in pan-Slavic sentiments inspired mainly by the need to whip up support against Hungarian domination. The brief programme of the CPPP (1905) stated that 'Slavdom is valued in the world chiefly with Russia and because of Russia', and claimed all the Slavs as brothers, from Bulgaria to Poland. In fact, however, the Radić brothers distrusted expansionist Serbia. Although they eschewed the virulent anti-Serb rhetoric of Josip Frank and his Pure Party of Right, formed in 1894 after a split with Starčević, they argued that the Serbs in Croatia were not really Serbs, but 'people from the Srem' (Sriemci), and that Catholic and Orthodox believers were being misled by malicious priests of both faiths, and by Jews, into false antagonisms.

Svetozar Pribičević, who emerged in 1903 as the leader of the Serbian Independents, representing the Serbs in Croatia, took his party in the direction of cooperation with the Croat deputies in the Zagreb Sabor. This Serb–Croat Coalition in 1905 issued the 'Resolution of Fiume', demanding political reforms and the union of Dalmatia with Croatia. By 1906 the Coalition was strong enough to win a majority of seats in the Sabor. The Resolution can easily be misinterpreted as expressing a prototypical 'Yugoslavism'. It was in fact a variant of the 'trialist' position, in which the Croatian Serbs would have their autonomous place in the scheme of things. No definite programme emerged in the politics of Croatia for union with Serbia because there was no rational basis for such a policy. Serbia was a distinctly improbable candidate to take on Austria-Hungary, and would in any case seize the first opportunity to incorporate Bosnia-Hercegovina. The rulers of Serbia, for their part, had no time for the tepid doctrines of South Slav brotherhood, except as a useful adjunct to foreign policy. If the Croats achieved their nationalist objectives within the framework of a remodelled Habsburg empire, then the Serbs would be the losers.

It was in the battle for hearts and minds in Bosnia-Hercegovina that Croatian and Serbian nationalism first confronted each other on the ground. Benjamin von Kállay, whose period of office as joint Finance Minister (1882–1903) coincided with Khuen-Héderváry's rule in Croatia, pursued a very different kind of policy with respect to ethnic and religious cleavages. His aim was to create a specifically Bosnian ('Bosniak') national consciousness, and he found himself obliged, rather comically, to suppress his own book, a history of the Serbs written while serving as a diplomat in Belgrade, which acknowledged their distinct national identity. Kállay's strategy was to rule with the cooperation of the existing Muslim elites, but his modernizing imperialist projects did too much to offend them, and too little to appease the Orthodox peasants, whose economic conditions deteriorated. Energetic and successful in promoting industrial development (Bosnia far outstripped independent Serbia), Kállay was quite unable to resolve the land question.[14]

The Ottoman retreat left Bosnia's Muslims behind, strangers in their own land; they reacted first by armed resistance, and then by mass emigration to Turkey. Those who remained were compelled to organize themselves on two fronts, to defend rights previously taken for granted. The Muslim clergy were firmly subordinated to the civil authority, including control over the vakuf, the charitable property that underwrote religious life and education, to forestall the development of any ultramontane movement built on links with Islamic leaders in Turkey. The other major source of friction was agrarian reforms. The authorities introduced measures designed to rationalize the whole system of land tenure, cutting clear across Islamic shariat law in order to curtail the arbitrary power of landowners, which a lax and venal Ottoman bureaucracy had allowed to displace central authority, and to encourage the efficient use of land.

Cut off from the aid and comfort of their Orthodox kin in Serbia and Montenegro, the isolation of the Bosnian Serbs bred in them the intense, xenophobic nationalism of exiles. The domination of the Muslim elite was ended, but the occupying power conceded only the right to take part in elections to consultative assemblies based on religious confession, which had no legislative authority. What is more, the structure of land ownership remained largely undisturbed by Austro-Hungarian rule. The Serb tied peasantry was too impoverished to take advantage of the decree, belatedly passed by the Ottoman administration and still in force, which allowed sharecroppers to buy their land: they wanted it for free, and they were encouraged by nationalist propagandists to look to an enlarged Serbia as the giver. Growing trade also created a new class of town-dwellers among the Serbs, who added their weight to demands for union with Serbia.

The appearance of contending Serb, Croat and Muslim political parties in the years 1906–8 confirmed Kállay's failure to quarantine the province, and in order to strengthen its grip Austria-Hungary took advantage of an opportune moment in international affairs to annex Bosnia-Hercegovina, in October 1908. Russia was paralysed by military defeat and internal dissension. In Macedonia, the 'Young Turks', among them energetic, modernizing army officers like Mustafa Kemal – the future Atatürk, were organizing opposition to the Sultan (he was deposed in April 1909) in an attempt to halt the decline of Ottoman power by imposing modernizing reforms. Serbs everywhere were outraged by the annexation: Bosnia was Serbian land, wrongfully seized by Turkish power and ruled over by renegade Slavs. In Belgrade, the press screamed for war, and there were sympathetic riots in Zagreb – even in Ljubljana. In Austria-Hungary, anti-Serb feeling was whipped into fury and the idea of a pre-emptive war began to occupy the minds of the Habsburg generals.

There was, however, no rapprochement between Serb and Croat leaders. On the contrary, Serbian war fever intensified the vision of a Great Serbia. Radić rebuked the Serbs for incitement to war (he was a pacifist, in a political rather than a personal sense), and fell out with Pribičević over the strategy of the Serb–Croat coalition. The faction within the military led by Colonel Apis and his fellow regicides was outraged when the government was forced to state publicly that the annexation of Bosnia-Hercegovina was not a violation of Serbian interests. Rebelling against the restraints that Pašić tried to impose, they formed the 'Unification or Death' organization (1911), better known as the 'Black Hand', a secret blood-brotherhood dedicated to revolutionary violence in the cause of a Great Serbia. The activities of the 'Black Hand' were in fact semi-public knowledge: it even had an official wing called 'National Defence' which published the newspaper *Piedmont*.

The chaotic situation in Macedonia and Kosovo, and the restlessness of the Serb population in Bosnia, offered boundless possibilities for covert operations conducted by military intelligence agencies using armed Serb irregulars. The tradition of the hajduk bands (čete), from which the name 'chetnik' derives, took on a new lease of life. Chetniks were an ideal instrument for fighting 'dirty', subterranean wars. The annexation of Bosnia also swelled the ranks of 'Progressive Youth'. The movement (it was too diffuse to be called a party) attracted mainly students with a romantic attachment to the ideal of freedom for the South Slavs, but no clear political programme. One such group, 'Young Bosnia', supplied the assassins at Sarajevo, youths fired up by notions of revolutionary self-sacrifice in the cause of Bosnian independence and trained for the operation by 'Black Hand' officers inside Serbia.[15]

The threat of being disarmed and subjected to a revitalized Ottoman control sparked off rebellion among the Albanians in 1909–12, intensifying riot and disorder in Macedonia and Kosovo. Hoping to forestall the creation of an Albanian state, Montenegro declared war on Turkey on 12 October 1912, followed by Serbia, Bulgaria and Greece. The Serbs had an instant military triumph on 23–24 October when they crushed an Ottoman army in a massed battle at Kumanovo in northern Macedonia, and then moved on to take Kosovo. The Serbian army now put into effect a policy of terror designed to alter the ethnic composition of Kosovo in order to strengthen Serbia's claims to the province. When the great powers met in December 1912 to decide the fate of the region, about 20 000 Kosovar Albanians had already been massacred, and there followed a campaign of torture, maiming, and forced conversions that caused perhaps five times as many to flee Kosovo for Bosnia.[16]

By May 1913, Ottoman power in Europe had ceased to exist. Then, in a lightning summer campaign, Serbia and Greece, supported by Montenegro and Romania, defeated Bulgaria in a quarrel over the booty. The Treaty of Bucharest, in August, partitioned Macedonia between Serbia and Greece, leaving Bulgaria only the Pirin district, and the Sandžak of Novi Pazar was divided between Montenegro and Serbia, giving the two kingdoms a common frontier. Serbian nationalist fervour boiled over. Old Serbia had been recovered for the nation, the battle of Kosovo was avenged, the Turk routed.

The celebrations were short-lived. Within a year, on a tour provocatively scheduled for the anniversary of Kosovo Field, 28 June 1914, the Archduke Franz Ferdinand was shot dead in Sarajevo by Gavrilo Princip, a Bosnian Serb. Austria-Hungary declared war on Serbia a month later (28 July), triggering the general European conflict which was to obliterate the second imperial obstacle to South Slav unification.

2
War and Unification

The Great War destroyed Serbian power, inflicting losses shocking even in an age of mass slaughter: 40 per cent of the armed forces and a quarter of the total population (about 4 million in 1913, including the newly conquered territories) perished. The conduct of the army was exemplary. Twice during 1914 the Austrians were driven out of Serbia, but during the winter of 1915 the combined armies of Austria, Germany and Bulgaria overran the country, and the most heroic feats of war were performed on the retreat. The Serbian forces trekked through the winter snows of Kosovo and Albania to reach Corfu, where Serbia's government-in-exile was set up, headed by Pašić and Prince Aleksandar, appointed Regent by King Petar at the outbreak of war.

The Serbs learned yet again that Serbian interests and Serbian lives counted for little in Paris, London or even St Petersburg, despite the promise made in September 1914 by the British Foreign Minister, Sir Edward Grey, of limitless assistance. Serbian war aims envisaged the unification of the Serbs, Croats and Slovenes within a single state, but Serbia was too weak to claim a seat at the diplomatic table with the great powers when the secret Treaty of London was signed in April 1915, which gave Serbia Bosnia-Hercegovina, and a portion of southern Dalmatia where there was a concentration of Orthodox faithful. The fate of the Croats and Slovenes was left undecided, since there was no proposal to break up Austria-Hungary, but Italy was offered gains on the eastern Adriatic as an inducement to enter the war on the Allied side.

From the point of view of the Entente powers it made good strategic sense. Serbia was out of the reckoning militarily, both from battle losses and from an epidemic of typhus fever which decimated the population early in 1915. All men between the ages of 18 and 55 were being called up, including many of those previously declared unfit for service. Under pressure from the Allies, the Serbian government agreed (5 September) to cede Macedonia to Bulgaria, as a gesture of appeasement. It was a fatal, futile blunder, and the Serbs knew it. Allied support wavered at a moment when Serbia was still not completely occupied – the government at this time was located in Niš. The combined German and Austrian armies took advantage of the lull to concentrate their forces in a new offensive, and on 12 October Bulgaria joined in, without the formality of a declaration of war. The Serbs were now defending 1000 kilometres of front with 400 000 men, massively outnumbered in troops and artillery, and the outcome was never in doubt. The retreat began in order to save the remnants of the army, the homeland was abandoned. Again Allied help, in the shape of the Italian navy, was strangely slow in coming to transfer the ravaged and exhausted Serbian army to Corfu.[1]

The general terms of the Treaty of London soon became known to a member of the Yugoslav Committee, Frano Supilo, as a consequence of an indiscretion, possibly a deliberate one, by the Russian Foreign Minister during conversations in St Petersburg. In May 1915, the Committee, formed by a group of exiles in Rome during the preceding autumn, shifted its headquarters to London and began an intensive campaign of lobbying to persuade the British government that a Yugoslav solution was the answer. The Yugoslav Committee comprised some score or so members, chiefly drawn from the ranks of the Slovene and Croat intelligentsia, who claimed to speak for the Habsburg Slavs. They proved remarkably adept at politicking – between them, the Committee managed to secure the ear of many prominent Entente statesmen. Outside the western corridors of power, the influence of the Yugoslav Committee was also heavily buttressed by the support of the large emigré populations abroad, especially in the United States.[2]

Inside Austria-Hungary, the introduction of martial law in 1914 put paid to any semblance of oppositional politics. The Croatian People's Peasant Party supported the war, hoping to win concessions by a demonstration of loyalty, and the Serb–Croat coalition continued to attend the Diet in Budapest, dutifully sending representatives to the coronation of the new Emperor in 1916. Whether the Habsburg Slavs fought willingly is a question no easier to answer than for any other people sucked into the juggernaut of a state mobilized for war on an unprecedented scale. They were conscripted in large numbers, and they fought (including Serbs) without mass desertions – except among the Bosnian Serbs, who were savagely victimized from the very onset of the war.[3]

Relations between Pašić and the Yugoslav Committee were always uneasy, despite the fact that the Committee was urged into life and financed by the Serbian government. The Committee was a valuable ally for the Serbs in representing to the world the wishes of the South Slavs for unification, but they had quite different ideas about what form union should take. All Pašić's political instincts led him to think in terms of a Great Serbia, around which the other nationalities would coalesce as associates. The Yugoslav Committee rejected any notion of Serbian hegemony – it was to be unification on the basis of equality, or nothing. Collaboration persisted because each needed the other. Only Serbia, as an 'associated power' of the Entente, existed as a recognized state around which a South Slav union could be constructed. Furthermore, although it early on became transparent that Turkey's empire was to be dismembered, there was no sign that the same fate was intended for Austria-Hungary. Suspicion that the Habsburgs would once again be the beneficiary of great-power machinations was the basis of common action between the Serbs and the Committee.

Events in early 1917 brought matters to a head. The abdication of the Russian Tsar in February robbed Serbia of its most powerful support among the Allies. This was a truly bitter blow for Pašić, who had never quite abandoned the vision of his youth: that the Orthodox Serbs, together with their Russian 'elder sister', would create a form of state and society transcending the false and egocentric values riding in the baggage-train of western capitalism. It also had the effect of splitting the Radicals, with one wing favouring a more liberal and democratic approach to the post-war order, which went down well in western diplomatic and political circles, particularly after the United States entered the war. The Yugoslav Committee, for its part, was faced with a serious challenge to its claim to speak on behalf the Habsburg Slavs. At the end of May, the South Slav deputies in the Vienna Reichsrat (headed by Korošec, the leader of the Slovene People's Party) announced that they would seek the formation of a union of Croats, Slovenes and Serbs within the Empire. The old 'trialist' idea was back on the agenda.

There was an urgent need for compromise. On 20 July 1917, Pašić and Ante Trumbić, the Croat President of the Yugoslav Committee, signed the Corfu Declaration in favour of an independent constitutional monarchy of Serbs, Croats and Slovenes, under the Serbian Karadjordjević dynasty. Point 9 of this document stressed that anything less than the complete liberation of the South Slavs living under Habsburg rule, and their union with Serbia and Montenegro, was unacceptable. Beyond this, the Declaration expressed only a number of general principles of equality between the three peoples, such as freedom of religion, and the use of both alphabets. The drawing up of a constitution was to be left to a Constituent Assembly when peace came, with the proviso that it could be adopted only by a numerically qualified majority. The precise intention of this rider was not explained in the Declaration, which was also vague about whether the state should be centralist or federalist in character: the first point seemed to endorse a unitary model, while the last (of 14) spoke of autonomous units required by natural, social or economic conditions. At the time none of this mattered. The course of the war was still uncertain, and the Declaration was in no way binding on the Allies. The main thing was that Serbia and the Yugoslav Committee had agreed a form of words for the founding of an independent South Slav state. Exactly what they might mean remained to be decided by the outcome of events beyond their control.

The Declaration of Corfu was a diplomatic coup for Pašić. He never budged from his refusal to give formal recognition to the Yugoslav Committee, yet he induced it to sign up to a union with Serbia, under a Serbian dynasty, without first specifying terms. His problem was to make the agreement stick with the Allied powers. In February 1918, a mutiny among the Slavs in the Austro-Hungarian fleet exposed the weakening of imperial authority; and when Bulgaria surrendered in late September, the position of Serbia was immeasurably strengthened. Serbian armies had fought their way back from Salonika into their homeland, alongside the French, and were pushing on towards Belgrade. But the rapid deterioration of Austria-Hungary's military position also had another, contrary effect. The Yugoslav Committee now demanded recognition of the Habsburg South Slavs as an allied people, equal in status and rights to Serbia. Trumbić put forward this claim in a Memorandum to the British government, dated 7 October 1918, complaining that Pašić, in the French press, had stated that the Allies should now authorize the Serbs to liberate their South Slav brethren, and to establish a new state under the aegis of Serbia. Pašić's response was characteristically devious. If Serbia was making unification difficult, then the answer was simple: let the Croats and Slovenes remain 'over there', where they were in a majority.

'Over there', there was no time for such arguments. Bands of armed deserters were terrorizing the countryside, and Italian troops were occupying areas promised by the terms of the Treaty of London, threatening Ljubljana and Karlovac. On 29 October the Croatian Sabor proclaimed a National Council of the Serbs, Croats and Slovenes as the sovereign ruler of the Habsburg Slavs, with Korošec as President, and expressed, without specifying conditions, a desire for union with Serbia.

Korošec then dispatched Trumbić to represent the National Council at Versailles, where the Allies met in early November to decide on the armistice terms for Austria. President Wilson's declaration in favour of independence for the Yugoslavs had already settled the main issue of Allied policy, but faced with two (or perhaps three) groups claiming to speak in the name of the Yugoslav peoples, the French told Pašić and Trumbić to settle their differences, and to agree the composition of a joint government. At the ensuing meeting in Geneva (6–9 November), Pašić found himself confronted by three representatives each from the National Council and the Yugoslav Committee, and three from the Serbian opposition parties. Outvoted nine to one, he formally accepted a Note establishing the dual authority of the Serbian government and the National Council in matters of common concern, whilst retaining sovereignty within their own territories.

Pašić immediately sabotaged this deal by causing his own government to resign in protest with the agreement unratified, and buying off the Serbian opposition with a promise of power sharing.[4] Serbia's military and political clout was strengthening from day to day. On 1 November 1918, Serbian and French troops re-took Belgrade; within days, they had reached Zagreb and overrun southern Hungary. Encouraged by the military situation, Montenegro (which had been occupied by the Austrians), the Vojvodina and 42 out of the 52 districts of Bosnia-Hercegovina, rejected the authority of the National Council in favour of union with Serbia. The complexion of the National Council itself was now transformed by the entry of Svetozar Pribičević and his followers. Faced by the complete breakdown of order in the Habsburg lands, the National Council was persuaded to repudiate the Geneva agreement, and voted unconditionally to join Serbia. Immediately, Stjepan Radić, the leader of the Croatian People's Peasant Party, announced that the Croatian people wanted an agreement with the Serbian people, but only within the framework of a state untarnished by militarism and centralism. Undeterred, Prince Aleksandar proclaimed in Belgrade the formation of the Kingdom of the Serbs, Croats and Slovenes, on 1 December 1918.

Lloyd George, no less, paid tribute to Pašić's guile and tenacity in establishing the new state in advance of the Peace Conference which met in January 1919, before the complex negotiations on international borders were even begun. The Regent proved less appreciative. Despite Pašić's expressed willingness to serve as the first Minister-President, Aleksandar dispatched him to Geneva. Perhaps Pašić's identification with the cause of a Great Serbia offended Aleksandar's sincere and high-minded attachment to the idea that he must become the focus of loyalty of all three founder-peoples; certainly he wanted to get rid of the old man (Pašić was born in 1845) who had wielded so much influence over the Karadjordjević fortunes.

The first government of the Provisional National Administration was headed instead by Stojan Protić, Pašić's Radical rival, with the other portfolios being distributed equally between Serbs and non-Serbs. A Provisional Assembly of 296 deputies was formed by allocating seats in proportion to the strength of the various pre-war parties in their respective assemblies, on a territorial basis. The third element in government was the Regent himself. The Serbian constitution of 1903, with its strong monarchical powers, remained in force for the time being, and the Assembly was an unelected body, untested and unanchored in any firm structure of party allegiances.

Aleksandar used his authority to the limits – some said well beyond – in the struggle to impose order on the new state. He was an aloof autocrat, with a morbid fear of assassination – he always went armed, even in private. A serving officer in the Balkan Wars (he commanded an army corps at Kumanovo), Aleksandar formed a faction within the army, the 'White Hand', to counteract the activities of the 'Black Hand', whose leader since 1911 had been Colonel Dragutin Dimitrijević – 'Apis'. In 1917, Apis was shot on charges, almost certainly false and definitely unproved, of treason and intent to murder Aleksandar.[5] The difference between the two groups of officers was essentially one of circumstances, and boiled down to the question of personal loyalty to the Regent, whose 'Yugoslavism' offended the extreme nationalist faction within the military. The support of the Allies was essential for the founding of the new state, and the military top brass could not appear to be pulling the strings of government in the new multi-ethnic Yugoslavia, but their influence was everywhere. The army was the sole reliable instrument of control and administration, and from day one the first Yugoslavia was dogged by extreme problems of internal and external insecurity.

This new addition to the map of Europe comprised the kingdom of Serbia in its 1913 frontiers, united with the previously independent kingdom of Montenegro; to which were added Croatia-Slavonia, Bosnia-Hercegovina, Dalmatia and the Slovene lands of Carniola, together with part of Styria. However, its final shape emerged only piecemeal, as the various treaties ending hostilities (seven in all) were concluded. Only in the case of Romania and Greece were territorial claims settled relatively quickly. Italian pressure on the north-west Adriatic littoral, beginning with the occupation of Rijeka (Fiume) by D'Annunzio in August 1919, culminated in the Treaty of Rapallo (November 1920), which gave Italy the whole of Istria plus a bit more, sealing the fate of Rijeka, which was formally annexed in 1924.

In the south, Rome was busily extending its sphere of influence into Albania, which in 1921 became an Italian protectorate under the authority of the League of Nations, and the Kosovar Albanians were in open revolt against the re-imposition of Serbian rule. The fear therefore was of a pincer movement of Italian power, and of irredentist movements in Kosovo – the borders with Albania were not finally settled until 1926. The Internal Macedonian Revolutionary Organization launched a series of incursions from Bulgaria into 'South Serbia' (that is, Macedonia), which did not abate until 1923, when relations with Sofia began to improve.

Revolutionary ferment in Germany, the founding of the Third International in Moscow, and the proclamation of Bela Kun's Hungarian Soviet Republic (both in March 1919) were the background to the formation of the Communist Party of Yugoslavia at the 'Unity Congress' of April 1919, bringing together the revolutionary wings of the pre-war Social Democratic parties. Congress adopted the Erfurt Programme as the basis of its own statutes, and voted to join the Third International. Among the soldiers and prisoners of war returning from Russia (Tito was one of them) were many converts to the ideas and methods of the October Revolution. In July, Communists led the way in organizing a two-day general strike, and throughout Croatia and Slavonia a peasant jacquerie was in progress, with armed bands taking possession of the large estates owned by foreigners.

The first and most threatening internal challenge to the legitimacy of the new state came within days of the liberation of Zagreb. While Serbian and French forces were still moving westwards against Italy, Radić demanded the formation of an independent republic of Croatia. The message was rammed home when, in February 1919, his party was re-christened the Croatian *Republican* Peasant Party, and Radić sent a Memorandum to President Wilson, asking the Allies to alter in favour of Croatia the settlement that Pašić had engineered in the face of so many obstacles. Radić spurned the paltry two seats offered in the Provisional Assembly, based on the pre-war representation of his party in the Zagreb Sabor. The Croatian peasants now had the vote for the first time in their history, thanks to a Serbian constitution, and Radić saw the chance to create a mass following. Croatian casualties were high in the service of Austria-Hungary, which was unstinting with Slav lives, and the dissolution of Habsburg power fed old ambitions of Croatian statehood.

The Croats' rejection of union provoked a reaction that was understandable, but quite disastrous. Pribičević, now Minister of the Interior, imprisoned Radić (oddly enough, they were boyhood friends), releasing him only on the day before the elections to the Constituent Assembly, in November 1920. Radić instantly became hero and martyr to the rebellious Croatian peasantry, suffering from a decline in agricultural production of about one-fifth during the three years following unification. Serbia's own economy was in ruins, and there was no sympathy to spare for the misfortunes of Croats – Pribičević more than once advocated sending in the army to subdue peasant unrest. Serb resentment was fuelled by the emergence of Zagreb as the commercial hub of the new state, in which food exports ranked as a major item. The chances of war left the northward rail links intact, and both Austria and Hungary sucked in cereals and livestock from their former imperial hinterland, while many regions of the new state were threatened by hunger. Croatian middlemen easily evaded the clumsy efforts of the authorities to control trade with Serbia's recent enemies. This did nothing the ease the situation of the peasantry, and drove up prices in Zagreb, but to many Serbs it seemed that the Croats, whose leaders had supported Austria-Hungary throughout the war, were now unjustly profiting by the peace.[6]

In Bosnia-Hercegovina, anarchy and murder ruled. Austria-Hungary treated the Serbs on its territory as enemy aliens during the war, using concentration camps and deportations to inflict reprisals on a civilian population saddled with a collective guilt for Serbia's part in the fighting. There was a mass displacement of Serbs from their homes, interspersed with murderous attacks on Serb villages carried out by the Schützkorps, an Austrian militia that recruited both Croats and Muslims into its ranks. The policy of inciting ethnic hatred succeeded only too well. The Bosnian Serbs in turn took revenge upon their Muslim neighbours, mounting a campaign of terror in which racial bigotry and land-grabbing were enmeshed. In eastern Hercegovina alone, 3000 Muslims were murdered in the early post-war years; and as late as 1924, the massacre of 600 Muslims occurred in two villages in the district of Bijelo Polje.[7]

The Yugoslav Muslim Organization (YMO) easily established itself as the voice of a frightened people. The party responded in the only way it could, by affirming the Muslims' loyalty to the Karadjordjević dynasty in return for constitutional guarantees that their property and culture would be respected. The paramount aim of the leadership for the next 20 years was to prevent the partition of Bosnia-Hercegovina between Serbs and Croats, the most likely outcome of a federalist form of government. Their strategy was to stake a claim to minority rights in a state whose very title denied the Muslims the status of a 'people'. The YMO decisively shed the religious conservatism of the pre-war Bosnian Muslim parties. Its leaders were drawn from the urban middle classes, and they were adamant that the choice of a 'Muslim' identity was to distinguish their followers from both Croats and Serbs. Religious confession was not the basis of their distinct ethnic identity, but rather a unique history and culture.

Despite its name, the Yugoslav Muslim Organization did not embrace the southern Muslims (mainly Albanians) of Kosovo and Macedonia. The Islamic Association for the Defence of Justice (Džemijet), founded at Skopje in December 1919, had similar aims, but the leaders, mostly large landowners, could not speak for most Albanians, since Kosovo was in a state of armed revolt. The Kosovars could not be incorporated into the political structure of the new state because they were from the first treated as an alien population to be crushed. The Serbs resumed the policy of retribution first begun in 1912–13. Denied religious freedom and the use of their own language, Albanian rebels ('kachaks') took to armed resistance. Kosovo was in a state of undeclared war, in which thousands were killed. Chetnik armed bands and colonists (they were often the same thing) were the means by which Belgrade tried to pacify the province, but it seems to have been primarily international pressure and the lack of support from Albania that finally sapped the kachak movement.[8]

Isolated on the north-western flank of the Kingdom, the Slovenes needed the continued protection of the Serbian army. Union with the Orthodox Serbs was not particularly welcome – so many Slovenes in Styria voted in the 1920 referendum to remain with Austria that a second referendum in the areas where they were less numerous was abandoned – but it was the best option available. The Slovene People's Party pursued its traditional aim of maintaining autonomy in administration, education and culture, easy enough now that the Slovenes were recognized as a founder-people of the new state. This limited ambition was as much a matter of necessity as of choice. Korošec would have liked a greater independence for Slovenia, but his party had no natural allies. Radić was outspokenly anti-clerical and republican, and the Slovenes were very aware that an independent Croatia would expose them to Italian expansionism.

Drained of blood and treasure, Serbia was struggling to make good its war claims against hostile diplomacy by the Italians. The Serbs had endured the almost unendurable: massive demographic losses, which included half the men of military age, an economy plundered by the Austrian army of occupation, the population of their capital city reduced to the size of a market township – it stood at about 15 000 in 1915. Swollen by conquest in the years of fighting since the Balkan Wars, Serbia now incorporated Hungarians and Germans in the Srem and Vojvodina, Macedo-Slavs and Albanians to the south, none of them disposed to welcome rule from Belgrade. In Montenegro, conflicts between the pro-Serbian 'Whites' and the independent nationalist 'Greens' surfaced again. By no means all Montenegrins were reconciled to the merger of the two kingdoms under a Serbian dynasty.

The Serbs closed ranks. The studiedly balanced character of Protić's first cabinet soon gave way to the predominance of Serb Radicals and Democrats. Of the parties represented in the Provisional Peoples' Assembly, only the People's Radical Party had any experience of government, and any continuity of organization, and the Radicals remained what they had always been, the party of the Serb ascendancy. Whilst acknowledging the confraternity of South Slav peoples within the new state, they saw the Serbs very much as 'elder brothers' to the Croats and Slovenes. But the Radicals controlled less than a quarter of the votes in the Assembly. Their chief rival was the Democratic Club, one of two new parties (the other was the Yugoslav Muslim Organization) formed in February 1919 in Sarajevo, in the scramble for the mandates of Bosnia-Hercegovina. The Democrats made up the largest single grouping (115 deputies) in the Assembly, but they existed only as a loose coalition grouped around a core membership of 82 deputies, itself a coalition constructed out of an alliance between the Independent Radical Party, formed in Serbia in 1901 after the split with Pašić, and the Serbian Independent Party in Croatia, the Serb half of the Serb–Croat coalition of 1905.

The Democratic Club was rightly named: it was essentially a parliamentary caucus, with no grass-roots organization of its own. The aim of the founders was to construct an all-Yugoslav forum capable of bridging the divisions between the Serbs and the other nationalities. They never succeeded. What initially drew the Democrats together was opposition to Pašić, and a sense that a new party might be shaped as a vehicle for their own ambitions. Politicians of every conceivable stripe flocked to join the Democratic Club, which attracted support from dissident Radicals (including four who called themselves republicans), from Slovene and Serbian Liberals – even from the Croatian Party of Right. This ill-assorted alliance could agree on nothing, and in fact the Democratic Club had no programme for the first year of its existence, but as the need to prepare for elections to the Constituent Assembly pressed, the Democrats had to take up a position on the constitutional form of the new state.

They chose centralism and the man chiefly responsible for this was Svetozar Pribičević, the leader of the Serbs in Croatia. He joined the Democrats with the active backing of the Regent: both of them wished to see Pašić's influence diminished, and to prevent the Democratic Club from being taken over by elements favouring a federalist or (still worse) republican form of state, who would make common cause with Radić. Pribičević induced the Democrats to campaign for a unitary monarchical state, and effectively reunited them with the Radicals. True, he took his stand on the need to create a common 'Yugoslav' identity (and hence was opposed to any special status for the Serbs), but argued that this could be achieved only within the framework of centralism. This was the electioneering platform adopted in February 1920, with the slogan 'One king, one state, one people'. The decision meant the dissolution of the Democrats as a broad coalition. Support among Croats and Slovenes fell away, leaving Serbian anti-centralists isolated.

The Democrats can best be characterized as the modernizing wing of the People's Radical Party, from which they never clearly separated, in terms of either personnel or policies. Pribičević was Minister of the Interior in two cabinets, and outdid the Radicals in his zealous devotion to the defence of the state. At the same time, he was also a reformer, and in this he typified the other face of the Democratic Club, which set them apart from the 'Old Radicals' around Pašić. The Democrats wanted the modernization of the state, together with the introduction of social reforms, such as the eight-hour day, which would defuse working-class protest, so creating the basis for cooperation with moderate parties. Above all, they urged a speedy resolution of the land question, as a way of restoring civil order and beginning the urgent task of post-war reconstruction. The liberal wing of the Democratic Club grouped around Davidović disliked Pribičević's strong-arm methods, but their differences were for the moment sunk in the face of the urgent need to give the country a constitution at a time of national emergency.

The six cabinets formed during the lifetime of the Provisional National Administration (20 December 1918–1 January 1921) were too weak to achieve anything beyond concluding peace treaties and establishing a customs' union. This was largely due to the unruliness of the Democrat deputies, who at one point suspended all parliamentary business for an entire month by absenting themselves, leaving the Assembly inquorate. All domestic legislation, including a budget, failed to pass. But one crucial reform did command the support of the Democrats, in the shape of the royal Interim Decree of 15 February 1919, which abolished the indentured sharecropping tenure of land. The land was now declared to belong to those who tilled it, though the questions of indemnity and confirmation of good title were left to be settled at a future date by an elected Assembly.

To the Yugoslav Muslim Organization, the eagerness of the Democrats for land reform smacked of haste and illegality. If endorsed by the Assembly, the Decree would confirm beyond reparation the dispossessions inflicted on an impoverished Muslim population. Rather unexpectedly, the YMO found an ally in the Radicals, who exploited the divisions among their opponents by agreeing to await the work of a commission to decide on the redistribution of land, and promised to offer compensation to the big landowners whose estates had been seized. The Radicals also guaranteed freedom of religion, and claimed no exclusive status for the Orthodox Church, a move that went some way towards reassuring Bosnia's Muslims that their culture would be respected.

Eighteen months into the life of the new state, the government was no nearer to stabilizing its authority. The Communist Party of Yugoslavia (CPY) emerged as a major political force to trouble the weak executive. In the spring and summer of 1920, local elections produced a string of victories for the Communists, who captured power in two dozen municipalities, including Belgrade, Zagreb and Skopje. The reaction of the authorities was to suspend local government in the capital and elsewhere, and to arrest a number individual councillors, among them the Secretary of the CPY. In September, a blundering decision to inventory livestock for military purposes was interpreted by the Croatian peasantry as the beginning of requisitioning, provoking some of the worst disturbances yet seen, which had to be put down by army units. In Kosovo and Bosnia inter-ethnic violence continued to rage.

In the midst of all this turbulence, elections were finally held to choose a Constituent Assembly, on 28 November 1920. The People's Radical Party and the Democratic Party took respectively 91 and 92 of the 419 seats in the Assembly, while the Agrarian Alliance (the successor to the Serbian Agrarians, a peasant populist party with a strong following in Bosnia) gained 39 seats. These three parties commanded the allegiance of the great majority of Serbs. In Croatia, the Croatian Republican Peasant Party easily led the field, with 50 seats, decimating the Croatian Party of Right, which polled less than 3 per cent of the vote, and won only two seats. In Slovenia, the Slovene People's Party enjoyed similar success, with 27 mandates. The Yugoslav Muslim Organization took 24 seats, all of them in Bosnia. The other major contestant proved to be the Communist Party of Yugoslavia, which won 58 seats, making it the third largest party in the Assembly. Nine other parties were represented, with a total of 77 mandates between them, but none returning more than 13 deputies.

The Radicals had their main power-base in the Old Kingdom (that is, Serbia within its 1882 frontiers), but even there they had to face strong competition from the Democrats, who in the elections to the Constituent Assembly polled 18 per cent of the vote (32 seats) compared with the Radicals' 20 per cent (41 seats). The Communist Party and the Agrarian Alliance each won 14 seats in the stronghold of Serbdom, and both the Radicals and Democrats had to look elsewhere for the balance of their support. The Radicals performed strongly in the Vojvodina, which gave them 30 per cent of its vote (21 seats), and were runners-up in Bosnia-Hercegovina, although they polled only 13 per cent of the vote (11 seats). The Democrats fared best in the Vojvodina, Kosovo/Sandžak, and Macedonia, where they topped the poll; and in Croatia, where they ran second, winning 19 seats. The essential point to notice is that the Radicals held 50 of their 91 seats outside the Old Kingdom, and the Democrats 60 out of 92. The Serbs were widely scattered, and this demographic fact was decisive for arguments about the constitution of the new state.

The electoral success of the Communist Party exceeded the worst fears in government circles. The appeal of the CPY spread well beyond the numerically tiny working class. Communist candidates garnered a heavy crop of votes among the national minorities within Serbia, who were not allowed to form parties of their own, a gesture of resistance to Serbian cultural and political domination. Communists actually topped the poll in Macedonia, and in Montenegro, which together provided 19 (15 and 4, respectively) of the total of 58 CPY deputies. Radić and the Communists between them controlled a quarter of the votes in the Constituent Assembly, but it made no practical difference. At a huge rally in Zagreb on 8 December, Radić announced that his party's deputies would not take their seats. There was, in any case, no possibility of a tactical alliance. The Communists wanted a unitary state, and derided Croatian nationalism as a reactionary bourgeois distraction from the task of creating a Yugoslav Soviet Republic of Workers and Peasants.

The disarray of the opposition made the next step all the easier. Faced by strikes and civil unrest, the government issued a Proclamation (Obznana) outlawing Communist political activity pending the passing of the new constitution, though the CPY deputies retained their mandates. The Assembly then promptly elected Pašić as Minister-President of the government that took office on 1 January 1921. The old hand was back at the helm.

Whatever their differences, Serbs, Croats and Slovenes were agreed that that although ethnic Albanians, Macedonians, Germans and Hungarians might be citizens of the Kingdom of the Serbs, Croats and Slovenes, they could not by definition be counted as constituent 'peoples'. The National Minorities Act of 1919, passed at the insistence of the Allies, made provision for the protection of the rights of minorities incorporated in the new state by the Peace settlement, but the government refused to extend its provisions to those areas conquered during the Balkan Wars. Bizarre as it may seem, the thesis was seriously advanced that the Albanians were in fact really Serbs ('Arnauts'), just as Vuk Karadžić had argued in the case of the Bosnian Muslims.[9] Extending this logic, there could be no reason to treat the Macedonian Slavs as anything but Serbs. Both these ethnic groups were left to Serbia to police, and neither figured in the constitutional drafts put forward by the main political parties.

The title of the Kingdom itself enshrined the constitutional principle that Serbs, Croats and Slovenes were the sole bearers of state-right, by virtue of their descent from common ancestors, separated by the accidents of history into three 'branches' or 'tribes' (plemena). In the light of this mythologized past, unification could be presented as reunification, a 'recovery' of the 'historic' lands inhabited by a primordial South Slav people. The triumph of unification persuaded some deputies to the Constituent Assembly that 'Kingdom of Yugoslavia' should be the official title of the new state, but 'Yugoslavism' was already tainted by association with Pribičević, whose heavy-handed authoritarianism made him so many enemies (including among his government colleagues) that Pašić was obliged to remove him from the Ministry of the Interior (to Education!). In any case, the Serbs were unwilling to allow their identity to become submerged in a union they had done so much to bring about. The consensus was that 'Kingdom of the Serbs, Croats and Slovenes' answered best to present realities, and to the need to construct a parliamentary system that reflected the co-ownership of the state. But were the Serbs, Croats and Slovenes one people, or three? If the latter, what rights did they have to self-rule? The ideological fiction of a triune people predictably threw up diametrically opposed interpretations.

The government produced a draft constitution, following intensive consultations between Pašić and Pribičević, which opted for a centralized state with a strong monarchy and a single-chamber parliament, modelled on the Serbian constitution of 1903. Their draft proposed the creation of 35 administrative districts (later reduced to 33), a balkanizing tactic intended to maximize the electoral power of the Serb vote. Each of them would be headed by a Prefect appointed by the Ministry of the Interior in Belgrade, and answerable directly to the Peoples' Assembly and the King, on whose behalf the Prefect would countersign legislation.

The Croatian Republican Peasant Party put forward proposals for what amounted to a confederal form of government, though they left the central authority so weak as to be quite incompatible with any modern notion of confederalism. Serbs, Croats and Slovenes were recognized as three separate 'historic' nations, each entitled to its own homeland, and exercising effective sovereignty within the new state, with each having an independent legislature, and the right to veto any changes in the constitution. There was no mention of executive organs in common; their finances were to be separate; and Croatian 'defence forces' were to be used only with the assent of the Croats. The talk of 'homelands' introduced a quite new element into the equation, because 'Croatia' existed only as a nationalist project, not as a territorial entity. No internal borders could be drawn separating Serbs and Croats over large tracts of territory, and an independent Croatia would sever the state in two.

The Croatian draft also identified three 'semi-historic, semi-tribal' homelands, Macedonia, Montenegro and Bosnia-Hercegovina, whose populations would be allowed to decide by plebiscite to which 'proper national state' (prava narodna država) they wished belong, and under what conditions. It is impossible to see how such a proposal could ever have been implemented, but the principles underlying it are clear enough. Peoples marked out by history for the privilege of state-right would incorporate the 'semi-historic' homelands within their borders. No mention at all was made of the question of non-Slav minorities, or of the special case of the Slav Muslims in Bosnia. Stripped to its essentials, this was a proposal to divide the state between the three authentic peoples named in its founding charter.[10]

The draft of the Slovene People's Party allocated more residual powers to central government, but with strong provincial assemblies, six in number, to protect local democracy. The six units were to be constructed on the basis of religious confession. Three of them would have a Catholic majority (Slovenia, Croatia-Slavonia, and Bosnia-Hercegovina conjoined with Dalmatia); the other three (Serbia-with-Macedonia, Montenegro, and the Vojvodina) an Orthodox majority. The result would have been an ethnically compact Slovenia, conveniently buffered by two extensive 'Catholic' provinces. It would be hard to devise a scheme combining incitement to Serb–Croat hostilities with indifference to the rights of minorities, in such an explosive mix. The Serbs would never assent to a Catholic (Croat) Bosnia-Hercegovina-Dalmatia, and although Catholics probably (just) outnumbered the Orthodox population, the arithmetic left the Bosnian Muslims out of the reckoning completely. The proposed boundaries also left unresolved the competing claims of Serbs and Croats in the Vojvodina and Srem, to say nothing of the Magyars living there. Ethnic Albanians and the Macedonian Slavs were left to the Serbs to police.

The Communist Party deputies contributed nothing to the debate on the new constitution, being wholly preoccupied with demands for a republic of peasants and workers, and with denouncing the Obznana regime. Two weeks ahead of the final vote, they walked out of the Constituent Assembly in protest at the government's repression of working-class unrest. The absentee Croats had in the meantime persuaded the Slovene People's Party to follow their example, and stay away. The upshot was that, when the Constituent Assembly came to vote on the government's draft constitution, 161 opposition deputies were missing from the chamber, a figure not far short of the strength (183) of the Radical and Democrats combined.

Even so, Pašić was hard pressed to secure an absolute majority, and it was the tactics of the Bosnian Muslim deputies which were decisive. Isolated within the Assembly, the Yugoslav Muslim Organization, in an agreement cobbled together the previous night, agreed to vote with Pašić in return for compensation to the dispossessed Muslim landowners, and the recognition of specific cultural rights, spurring on the eight deputies representing the Džemijet to do a similar deal. This, combined with the ten votes bought with concessions to a minor Slovene peasant party, just tipped the scales. The constitution was ratified by only a very narrow majority (53 per cent) of the deputies to the Assembly, in plain disregard (the opposition argued) of the Corfu Declaration. The Regent swore his oath to it on St Vitus' Day (Vidovdan), 28 June 1921 – the anniversary of Kosovo Field, deliberately chosen to mark the event.

The following day, amid the celebrations in Belgrade, a Communist attempt was made on the life of the Regent; and a month later the Minister of the Interior was assassinated by a Bosnian Communist. The government immediately outlawed the Communist Party, depriving its deputies of their mandates in the Assembly, and passed the Law for the Defence of the State, which consolidated and extended the Obznana regime. This piece of legislation read like the ravings of a frustrated village constable – Article 6 listed vagrancy, drunkenness and prostitu-tion within an open-ended category of 'anti-state' activities. Despite its initial references to Communist and anarchist propaganda, the Law did not provide specific penalties for specified offences, nor did it have the character of an emergency measure with a time limit. The authorities were empowered to send in the military to quell civil disorder, the cost to be borne by the offending community; strikes were made illegal; public employees were forbidden to engage in politics; and so on, and so on, in a seemingly endless list. Even some of the Radical and Democrat deputies present protested, and the Law was passed by the vote of barely one-third of the total number of deputies.

The Kingdom of the Serbs, Croats and Slovenes could hardly have got off to a worse start. Of the three founder-peoples, two were recalcitrant joiners. Now a rump 'Serbian' Assembly had passed a law giving apparently limitless power to the executive. The scene was set for two decades of political paralysis, which ended (when it was too late to make any difference) with the partitioning of the state and the outbreak of Hitler's war in the Balkans.

3
The Brief Life of Constitutional Government

Pašić's thumbprint was clearly visible on the Vidovdan Constitution, which was closely modelled on the Serbian constitution of 1903. Although the Constituent Assembly from time to time canvassed the merits of the French and American systems of government, and of an 'English-style Parliament', the constitution created a form of representative democracy which resembled none of them. The title of the new state, 'The Constitutional, Parliamentary and Hereditary Kingdom of the Serbs, Croats and Slovenes', seemed to hint at the 'Westminster' model of government, but Pašić had no such thing in mind. His was an intensely patriarchal vision of a political order rooted in the ties of blood and kinship between rulers and ruled, in which the key terms were not 'state and citizen', but 'people and king'. The Crown was to occupy a constitutional position above the strife and turmoil of party squabbles, and bring about consensus rule. Article 55 described the King as an 'inviolable person', but the cabinet stood 'immediately under the King' (Article 90), who appointed and dismissed ministers, and wielded a real power of veto over legislation. In effect, the constitution established the dual sovereignty of the Peoples' Assembly and the Crown, yet the King could not be called to account for his political acts.[1]

All males over 21 were entitled to vote (women were excluded, with a promise to consider their position in future legislation) in elections for a single-chamber Peoples' Assembly. The nine months of negotiations allowed by the constitution predictably produced no agreement on internal administrative boundaries, so the government created 33 districts deliberately drawn athwart the historic territories forming the state, with the district Prefect being appointed by the King. Serbs dominated in the prefectures – only in Slovenia was the pattern broken. Wherever possible, districts were drawn so as to create Serb majorities, or failing that to prevent any other nationality from becoming one. The constitution also put a limit of 800 000 inhabitants on any one district, and forbade the merging of adjacent districts. Disaffection among the non-Serb nationalities was aggravated by the amended Electoral Law of June 1922, which created electoral constituencies on the basis of pre-war census figures, so that Serbia's huge population losses during the Great War were ignored. The effect was to enfranchise the Serbian war dead at the expense of the other nationalities. The electoral process itself was opaque, and generated distrust. Deputies were returned according to a complicated system of proportional representation, with a threshold below which no party could claim a seat in the Assembly, the remaining mandates being assigned proportionally to those parties achieving the threshold.

Vesting authority in a Serbian dynasty was asking for trouble when combined with the Serb domination of the Peoples' Assembly, leading to repeated charges of collusion between the government and King Aleksandar. The King's wide discretionary powers in the conduct of foreign affairs were a particular source of tension. The Court played host to thousands of White Russian soldiers commanded by General Wrangel, who used Belgrade as a base to plan his strategy against the Bolshevik government in Moscow, provoking an outcry by opposition deputies in the Peoples' Assembly, in March 1922, against 'hidden government'. In the same month, Pašić moved a motion for an enormous increase in the Civil List, much of it payable in gold francs, further evidence to the opposition that the government was the tool of royal intrigue. Pašić's reply as he closed the debate revealed his political credo in a nutshell: '[The King] who cares for the whole people, and we who have striven and died that Serbia should give freedom to Croatia and Slovenia, have always and will always take care to maintain our triune people, and show them that they are happier and more contented living in our free state than when they lived under Austria-Hungary.'[2]

As opposition swelled, Radić demanded that a united Croatian Bloc be included in the government delegation to a conference at Geneva to discuss world peace, to represent Croatian interests. Pašić ignored the request, which pointedly referred to the new state only as 'the present internationally recognised borders of the Serbs, Croats and Slovenes'. The leaders of the Croatian Bloc therefore delivered a Memorandum of their own to Geneva, describing themselves as 'the constitutional representation of Croatia and of the entire Croatian people'. An addendum to the programme of the Croatian Republican Peasant Party sketched out the map of an independent Croatia, which would cooperate with Serbia on the basis of a confederation. The incident showed that Radić was quite prepared to usurp the authority of the government in the conduct of foreign affairs. In Belgrade, murmurings were heard that the time had come to 'amputate' Croatia and let the Serbs get on with their own affairs.

Radić is something of an enigma. His character and policies (if that is not too definite a word) placed him quite outside the gritty world of everyday politics. One principle remained constant: he always rejected political violence. Beyond this, his programme is hard to decipher. Given to airy talk about Croatian sovereignty, the leader of a republican party in a monarchical state, Radić always denied he was a separatist. He sometimes spoke of Croatia as part of a confederation of peasant republics which would include southern Bulgaria, Albania and Serbia, themselves united in a Balkan peasant federation, whilst simultaneously insisting on the ineradicable cultural differences between the 'western' Croats and the 'eastern' Serbs, often in sneering terms. Croatia was not, in Radić's view, a part of the Balkans, nor was Bosnia-Hercegovina, which the Croats had (he claimed) 'de-balkanized'. Whatever construction is put on this medley of ideas, what emerges beyond doubt is that Radić claimed independent status within the new state for the Croats, and that he included Bosnia-Hercegovina within the Croatian sphere of influence. Nothing could be better calculated to antagonize the Serbs, and make them bury their differences.

As Serb–Croat relations continued to deteriorate, the Democratic Party began to break up. Pribičević sided with Pašić in rejecting any attempt to reform the administrative structure of the state, while a group of deputies around Ljuba Davidović, the leader of the Independent Radicals, were inclined towards concessions which would create a political 'centre' to bargain over issues of constitutional reform. The Davidović wing became the core of a liberal opposition movement, providing a focus of leadership for the growing numbers and social influence of the urban middle classes. At two major public meetings, the Congress of Intellectuals (Sarajevo) and the Congress of Public Employees (Zagreb), held in the summer and autumn of 1922, they called for the redrawing of internal boundaries to create divisions 'larger and more fitted for life, composed according to the needs of their peoples, in conformity with the will of the people', as the statement issued by the Zagreb meeting put it.

But which people(s) did they mean, and what, precisely, was to be done? The Zagreb delegates affirmed their commitment to the indivisibility of the state, and Davidović deliberately stopped short of an open demand for a revision of the Vidovdan Constitution, in order not to provoke a split with Pribičević. The lack of political will to construct an alternative programme was exposed when, in November, Belgrade was abuzz with the news that representatives of the Croats had arrived in Belgrade to open up talks on possible cooperation between Davidović and Radić. The talks never took place because the Democrats were in a coalition government with the Radicals, and the dissidents were unwilling to break cover.

Much good it did them. Pašić resigned in order to form an all-Radical administration, and called elections for March 1923. At the elections, the Radicals strengthened their grip on the Serb vote by taking 108 mandates, mostly at the expense of the Democrats, who won only 51 seats. But still the Radicals only commanded about a third of the votes in the Peoples' Assembly. The Croatian Republican Peasant Party (CRPP) did much better, increasing its representation from 50 to 70 seats, while the Slovene People's Party and the Yugoslav Muslim Organization held their ground. Pašić's tactical gamble backfired. He weakened the Democrats, but not enough, and now faced a larger, more confident opposition. Yet still Radić refused to bring his party into the Peoples' Assembly, even when representatives of the Radical caucus went to Zagreb to try and do a deal with him, in return for concessions on local government. Pašić retorted by forming a second all-Radical administration, and exploited Radić's tantrums to discredit the CRPP. By July, Radić was abroad, fleeing from an arrest warrant issued for publicly insulting the Queen in an inflammatory Bastille Day speech.

In the spring of 1924 the CRPP deputies at last broke with the policy of abstention: the cooling between the Democrats and Radicals suggested there was now advantage to be gained by taking their seats in the Peoples' Assembly. Pašić responded by having most of their mandates nullified, on the grounds of Radić's reiterated refusal to acknowledge the legitimacy of the state. At this point, the Democratic Club formally divided, when Pribičević formed the Independent Democrats. However, Pribičević took with him only 14 deputies, which was of little use to Pašić. On 27 July, therefore, the King was obliged to ask Davidović to form a government, composed of the leaders of the Opposition Bloc (the Democrats, the Slovene People's Party and the Yugoslav Muslim Organization); and on 15 September it was agreed that four members of the CRPP would join the cabinet. For the first time, the politics of compromise seemed a real possibility.

Within three months, Davidović was out of office. Radić's maverick antics again proved a fatal handicap in the attempt to build a united opposition. During the summer, his wanderings around the European capitals brought him to Moscow, where (with the prior agreement of the CRPP leadership) he took his party into the Communist Peasant International on 1 July. Back in Zagreb, Radić described the decision as a major success with a great power not implicated in the Versailles settlement, and justified it as an inevitable response to the stupid politicians in Belgrade (his own words). The Radicals jumped at the opportunity to accuse Radić of treasonable commerce with godless Bolshevism. Using their influence at Court, Pašić and Pribičević campaigned to bring down the government 'in the name of those sacrificed in the war'. As Radić continued to attack the 'militarists and shysters' in Belgrade, the war minister, General Hadžić, declared he could not serve in a government associated with the CRPP, and contrived to bring it down. Davidović privately made it clear that the King had forced his resignation, and he complained about the subversion of civilian government by the generals, who consistently exaggerated the degree of unrest in the country in their reports to Aleksandar.[3]

It was typical of Radić that, in order to further Croatian interests, he should have associated his party with the front organization of a hostile foreign power whose revolutionary violence he abhorred, and whose sympathy for the peasantry was, to put it mildly, questionable. Once again, the initiative passed back to the Radicals. On 6 November, Pašić and Pribičević formed a government, which survived a mere four days before the King dissolved it, just long enough to summon elections for the following February. This administration never even made an appearance before the Assembly, but Pašić took advantage of the situation to extend the Law for the Protection of the State to the Croatian Republican People's Party. In the face of outraged protests from the opposition deputies, who still formed a majority, the CRPP was declared a proscribed organization on 1 January 1925, and its leaders were arrested a few days later.

The elections of 8 February 1925 marked the zenith of the Radicals' grip on the Assembly. They took 142 of the 315 seats, and Pribičević's Independent Democrats 22, compared with the 73 seats won by the Opposition Bloc. The Democrats were reduced to only 37 deputies, with the Slovenes and Bosnian Muslims making up the balance. The Croatian Republican Peasant Party more or less held its ground, winning 67 seats.

These elections were held in an atmosphere thick with accusations of violence and corruption. In a statement to journalists two days later, Davidovic described them as 'a disgrace to our state'. Interestingly, he chiefly blamed Pribičević, without whose prompting, he said, Pašić would not have taken such a path.

Pašić and Pribičević fought the election on the platform of the defence of the state, and when they invoked the memory of the heroic war dead they were not thinking of the Croats and Slovenes killed. Radić's greatest offence in the eyes of the Serbs was his willingness to accept the security won through their sacrifices, whilst rebuking Serbian militarism. In the context of the international situation, the call for a 'disarmed' peasant republic straddling territory stretching from the Adriatic to the borders of Hungary and Austria was a strategist's nightmare. It enraged the military, strengthened the forces at Court favouring a strong hand in dealing with the Croats, and compromised Pašić's efforts (embodied in the Vidovdan Constitution) to build up support for the exclusion of the army from politics. Indirectly, it also destroyed the Democrats, reducing their numbers in the Peoples' Assembly to 37, from 92 in the first round of elections in 1921. This was only partly due to the defection of Pribičević and his fellow deputies. It had more to do with the fact that the Radicals were able to present themselves as the party of all patriotic Serbs, and to establish control of the official Chetnik movement.

The name 'Chetnik' derives from the Serbian word for 'band', and was originally applied to the mountain guerrillas who rebelled against the Turks in the nineteenth century. The title was later appropriated by the militias which emerged during Serbia's clandestine wars in Macedonia and Kosovo, and became incorporated into the structure of the Serbian army during the Balkan Wars, operating in their traditional guerrilla role behind enemy lines during the ensuing years of fighting. The 'Association of Serbian Chetniks "Petar Mrkonjić" for King and Fatherland', founded in 1924 by the amalgamation of two existing associations, was led by Puniša Račić, a Montenegrin who acted as Pašić's hitman in Kosovo. Serb nationalists, including thousands of war veterans, were naturally attracted to the Association, which in its more respectable guise was a useful pressure group for mobilizing the Serbs in defence of 'their' state.

The Pašić–Pribičević 'National Unity Bloc' now had a slim majority in the Peoples' Assembly, but the parliamentary process frequently broke down in scuffles and fisticuffs, and the main business of the Assembly centred on the verification of the mandates of the CRPP deputies, many of whom were still in prison. Radić now performed an astonishing about-turn. From prison, he issued a statement to the Peoples' Assembly on 27 March in which he renounced his republican and federalist ambitions, and offered to work within the Vidovdan Constitution, though his communication to the King (coolly received) spoke of its eventual revision. In language as obsequious as it had been vitriolic in opposition, Radić accepted the authority of the Crown.

Pašić immediately ditched the Independent Democrats, and formed a government (18 July 1925) in which Radić took over Pribičević's old job as Minister of Education, with four other portfolios going to members of the Croatian Peasant Party (CPP), as it was now promptly renamed. However, nothing of substance changed in the conduct of politics. Radić busied himself with his own pet projects for education (he was against too much of it because it spoiled peasant youth), while continuing to berate his Radical colleagues in public for corruption. The Radicals for their part were openly contemptuous of Radić's capitulation, which they ascribed to fear and cupidity in equal parts. In early April 1926, Radić left the government, and the CPP reverted to its traditional opposition role. Four days later, Pašić also resigned, and his alliance with Radić proved to be his last taste of office. He died with the ending of the year, aged 81, from a stroke probably brought on by the King's refusal to allow him to form yet another government.

With Pašić gone, an internal power struggle split the Radicals into three factions. His successor as Minister-President, Nikola Uzunović, headed a series of brief administrations, which lasted in total about 12 months. Radić returned as Minister of Education, and to his old ways of relentless criticism of the government of which he was a member. Long overdue regional elections held during this year – they were originally approved in principle by the Peoples' Assembly in 1922 – exposed the weakness of the Radicals in the main towns of Slovenia, Croatia and Bosnia-Hercegovina. A motion to impeach Božidar Maksimović, the Minister of Internal Affairs, for abuse of his powers was only narrowly defeated in late February 1927, and in mid-March the opposition returned to the attack during the debate on the Budget. No government business could now be settled by normal voting procedures: what was at stake was the legitimacy of the parliamentary system itself.

Elections were called for 11 September 1927 to resolve the crisis, but the results only produced the familiar stalemate. The Radicals took 112 seats (30 fewer than in 1925); the Independent Democrats 22; the Democrats (staging a big revival) 59; the Croatian Peasant Party 61; the Slovene People's Party 20; and a Muslim–Democrat coalition another 20. Velja Vukičević was asked to form a government by the King, who had earlier brought him in to replace Uzunović in April, despite the fact that the majority of Radical deputies favoured Uzunović. With the reluctant support of most of the Radicals and of 17 dissident Democrats, and by splitting the Slovenes and Muslims with offers of ministerial offices, Vukičević assembled an administration, but his position as the creature of King Aleksandar robbed him of any real authority.

This government was instantly confronted in opposition by the formation of the Peasant–Democrat Coalition, which brought together Radić and Pribičević's Independent Democrats. Pribičević was now in the final stage of the personal trajectory that took him from arch-centralist to convinced federalist, in his attempt to secure the interests of the Habsburg Slavs (Croats as well as Serbs) against what he had come to see as a corrupt and self-serving Belgrade clique of politicians. Radić and Pribičević pursued avowedly wrecking tactics in the Assembly, and they were truculent towards those opposition deputies who cooperated to give Vukičević a majority. The government fell in February 1928, when the Democrats withdrew their support. Offered the opportunity to form a cabinet himself, Radić agreed at once, but now the Radicals turned the tables on him by refusing to serve. To break the deadlock, Mehmed Spaho and Anton Korošec, the leaders of the Slav Muslims and the Slovenes, agreed to join a new Vukičević administration – Korošec actually accepted the post of Minister of the Interior, a deeply symbolic gesture on both sides. Radić and Pribičević, unable any longer to represent themselves as tribunes of the non-Serb nationalities, turned their anger upon the parliamentary process itself. In audiences with the King, they stated bluntly that they preferred open dictatorship to the pseudo-parliamentary Vidovdan regime.

The Peoples' Assembly by now resembled the worst stereotype of a Balkan rabble. Radić, always adept in demagoguery and insult, set an example of systematic disruption that prompted Puniša Račić, elected a Radical deputy in 1927, to call for medical opinion to determine whether Radić was unbalanced; and if he was pronounced normal, to be punished to the full extent allowed by the Assembly's procedural rules. The next day, 20 June 1928, amid familiar scenes of disorder, Račić opened fire in the debating chamber, killing two deputies and wounding three others, among them Radić, who died two months later, although initially he seemed to make a good recovery; sufficiently so to maintain his hostility to cooperation with the Serbs.

The Peasant–Democrat Coalition leaders instantly removed their head-quarters from Belgrade to Zagreb, and declared the authority of the Peoples' Assembly void, demanding a federal form of government as the condition for their re-entry into the political arena. The Radicals refused even to discuss the idea. On 6 January 1929, after five months of protracted efforts to resolve matters through a cabinet headed by Korošec, again including talk of the 'amputation' of Croatia, the King proclaimed a royal dictatorship, pending the promulgation of a new constitution.

The ending of constitutional government by royal decree did no more than kill off a moribund system. Very little governing was done during the Vidovdan years, which were largely barren of legislation. There is no profit in trying to pin the blame for the Serb–Croat deadlock on one side or the other. It would be easy to demonize Pašić as a power-hungry manipulator determined to preserve Serbian hegemony at all costs, but equally plausible to argue that Radić's slippery intransigence made dealing with him impossible. Either way, the main point is lost: if the Vidovdan Constitution was the means by which Pašić always intended to impose the will of the Serbs on the new state, then he chose a poor instrument for his purpose. That Pašić was cunning and ruthless in his pursuit of office is not in doubt, but the truth is that real power, effective power, always eluded him. Minister-President for all but three months between 1 January 1921 and 8 April 1926, the longest of his ten admin-istrations lasted just under a year, the shortest four days, and only one of them had a parliamentary majority. Whatever its blemishes, the Vidovdan Constitution allowed the Croatian Republican Peasant Party to emerge, by 1923, as the second largest party in the Assembly, and the absence of its representatives left the opposition, which included many Democrats, seriously depleted. A major cause of the Radicals' domination of government was Croatian absenteeism.

The odds were always stacked against compromise. Parliamentary government was the form in which unification took place, but 'democracy' meant only the right of the founder-peoples to self-rule (samouprava). Given that peoples and territories did not coincide, the system had a built-in tendency towards stalemate. Both Serbs and Croats wanted to be masters in their own house, and the house in this metaphor could not be divided into apartments without a struggle over sovereignty. Invidious comparisons with 'civic' nationalism are beside the point. Liberal democracy of the western type is the contingent product of developed capitalism, and was by definition beyond the reach of all the peasant states of Eastern Europe created at Versailles – there was nothing singular about the first Yugoslavia in this respect. Capitalism guarantees the extinction of the peasantry as a class, but peasants were the stuff out of which parliamentary rule had to be fashioned. Parliamentary government needs voters in order to function, and the parties' appeal to nationalism and ethnic solidarity was a means of drawing the peasantry into the political process.

Serb–Croat antagonisms were not the product of some free-floating, irreducible ethnic hatred inherited from the past. They were a consequence of unification itself. Pašić and Radić did not simply speak for pre-existing 'nations'; they were in the business of creating them. The parties still sat atop a social structure in which the major gulf was not between 'nations', but between peasants and townsfolk. Peasants had no contact and no patience with the fancy ideas and loose ways of the educated urban classes (syphilis was known as 'the gentleman's disease'), flaunting their dandyish clothes, and an education acquired abroad or in the equally remote cities. Villagers lived a communal existence celebrated in the traditional stories and rhythms of the round-dance (kolo), a world apart from the lyrical 'town songs' (gradske pesme) of café society in Belgrade and Zagreb, where they had street lighting and trams. Peasants measured distance by the speed of a cart pulled by draught animals (Belgrade to Kragujevac was two days, with good horses), reckoned the calendar by the succession of saint's days, and few of them owned a bed.[4]

Croatian nationalism fed upon the insecurities and grievances of a peasant society wrenched out of its traditional way of life by war. Thanks to the extension of the franchise to all adult males in 1918, Radić was able to tap a vein of peasant radicalism which might have flowed into revolutionary channels, but was turned by him into a backward-looking agrarian populist movement, resistant to the pressures of political and economic modernization.[5] The structure of the Croatian Republican Peasant Party answered to the fluid, unorganized character of its isolated and mainly illiterate voters. Radić's political style was the whistle-stop tour, mass meetings, street demonstrations. In a society where urban development was at such a low level, and communications so appalling, no other strategy stood any chance of success.

Radić played out the role of political entrepreneur, urging the peasantry into nationalist opposition to Serbia. His courting of imprisonment and exile, his insistence on an autonomous Croatian republic, and his European forays in search of international support, were all of a piece. By demanding what the Serbs could not concede, Radić consolidated his power as the undisputed national leader of Croats of all classes. In this connection, it should be recalled that his party increased its representation in the Peoples' Assembly from 50 to 70 seats in the 1923 elections. Abstention paid off. Conversely, entering institutionalized politics offered no compensatory advantages. The fact is that neither the

Slovenes nor the Bosnian Muslims welcomed the idea of an independent Croatian republic; the first for reasons of military security, the second for fear of the partition of Bosnia-Hercegovina. This is why both groups constantly made their appearance as power brokers within the system, ready in the last resort to ensure continuity of government.

At first blush, it seems forced to draw parallels between Serbian and Croatian nationalism. Serbia had existed as an independent state since 1881, and the Serbs looked back on a century of unifying struggle against imperial dominion, culminating in the Great War. In fact, the position of the Serbs within the new state was precarious. Only after 1903 did Serbia make the transition to mass politics, and take the first steps towards industrialization – by 1910, industry employed just 16 000 workers, in 465 enterprises – an average of 35 each.[6] Warfare stopped this modest progress dead in its tracks, while between the Balkan Wars and Versailles Serbia doubled in size, and its ethnic composition was transformed. The military and political elites of the Old Kingdom now faced the problem of holding down large populations of Albanians and Macedonians, and of subduing a proto-nationalist movement in Montenegro. In order to do this, the support of Serbs everywhere had to be drummed up, in a struggle against demographic realities which translated uncomfortably into electoral arithmetic.

The most important single political fact in the life of the new state was that the two main Serbian parties depended on the vote of the Serbs outside the heartland of Serbdom. In 1921, Serbs made up only 39 per cent of the population, and 56 per cent of all Serbs lived beyond the confines of the Old Kingdom. In the elections to the Constituent Assembly in 1920, the Democrats won two-thirds of their seats outside Serbia, and the Radicals well over half. Pribičević's career is instructive in understanding the dynamics of what might be termed the politics of marginal numbers. He was a key figure in keeping struggling minority governments afloat, because the score or so Croatian Serb deputies he brought to the Assembly were all that stood between Radić and a clean sweep of the vote in Croatia. He was also the dominant figure in the leadership of the Democratic Club, but by taking his followers down the road of centralism Pribičević isolated the Serb liberals around Davidović, foreclosing the possibility that the Democrats might emerge as a party of constitutional reform. He thus also ceased to be a threat to Pašić. In the 1925 elections the Radicals marginalized the Democrats, by recourse to a militant nationalism which played upon the fears and sympathies of dispersed Serb populations.

The new circumstances created by unification introduced a crucial economic dimension to nationalist conflicts. There were of course disparities in industrial development in the South Slav lands, but nowhere had industrialization progressed much, and it was only after 1918 that the division between the *relatively* 'advanced' and 'backward' regions became politically relevant. Austrian and Czech businessmen flocked to their old imperial haunts, bringing expertise and opportunities for investment that sustained Zagreb's early lead in economic recovery. No longer the dim administrative centre of an imperial outpost, dominated by foreigners, Zagreb became a cultural and economic force to be reckoned with in the life of the new state, with its old university and developed civic traditions. By 1928, Zagreb banks held over half of all the country's bank assets, helped by the willingness of the city authorities to pass their own regulations encouraging industry, without waiting for central legislation.[7] In Slovenia, Czech, Swiss and British capital brought a spurt in industrial development, which enabled the Ljubljana assembly elected in 1927 to raise its own local revenues, with a view to by-passing the authority of the Prefect in certain matters of social welfare.[8]

The paradox is that Croatian entrepreneurship flourished behind the defensive wall of a party committed to the installation of a peasant republic. The true beneficiaries of Radić's separatism were not the peasants, whose fortunes changed little, but the urban commercial classes in Croatia's cities, whose activities depended on resisting Belgrade's attempts to control foreign trade. The Radicals retained all their old suspicion of unregulated capitalism, and it was particularly unwelcome to them that Austrian and Hungarian assets made up 60 per cent of the holdings of the Zagreb banks.[9] Whatever he may have said or intended, Radić was godparent to a purely bourgeois Croatian nationalism, a development that may well have influenced his decision to enter the government in 1925. By that time, the level of support for the Croatian Peasant Party was falling away, as normal peacetime conditions were restored, and the peasants went back to minding their own business. The growth in the numbers and social influence of the Croatian middle classes threw up new contenders for leadership, who saw participation in parliamentary politics as an opportunity to capture the levers of power.

It was the Radicals who toiled to shore up the peasant economy and society. Land reform was a lengthy and complex business, but the main pattern is clear. Serbia's rulers had a long history of shielding small-holders from dispossession through debt, and this concern to establish a land minimum passed over into the new state. The protection of the homestead embodied a vision of the peasantry as the backbone of the nation (there was absolutely nothing to choose between Pašić and Radić in this respect), and land reform was obedient to this vision. The scale of the redistribution was quite remarkable: a quarter of all agricultural land was allocated in small parcels to landless families, or to local small-holders, combined with grants to volunteers who had fought with Serbia during the war, to internal colonists (that is, migrants), and to 'optants' left outside the borders of the new state, but who chose to join it. This prime aim of this policy was to alter the balance of local populations in favour mainly of Serbs and Montenegrins loyal to the government, especially in Kosovo and Macedonia.

Land reform amounted to a decision to recreate the traditional basis of social order in an uncertain world. Redistribution broke up large estates (720 of them, comprising 1.25 million hectares, mostly owned by foreigners), reversing whatever impetus existed in pre-war days to commercialized farming, and reinvigorating a smallholding class whose instinct was to seek security in the ownership of a patch of soil.[10] The only source of primary accumulation was the peasantry, but the peasants were now more than ever insulated from market exchanges. If it could be had at all, paid employment was undertaken mainly to supplement the farm income, and credit went mostly on buildings and land, not on improving production. There was no appearance of a kulak class. Peasants produced a surplus only in order to pay what taxes they could not avoid, and to buy a modicum of cheap manufactured goods.

There was no coherent strategy for industrialization. The management of the economy consisted in a self-imposed dependency, an attempt at state-led modernization financed from abroad. The government tried to create the conditions (stabilization and convertibility of the dinar, tariff protection) which would attract foreign loans, but unresolved disputes over existing war (and pre-war) debts made the western capital markets unwilling to lend on a scale needed to finance development on a broad front. These problems were overcome only during 1926–8, by which time the international economy was heading for slump. The single bright spot was the payment of war reparations in gold by Germany, a source of great relief to a state budget that continued to multiply. Foreign capitalists showed little interest in the region, except as a traditional supplier of raw materials and cheap imported foodstuffs. The lion's share of external investment was in the state itself, in the form of the holding of stock, or the servicing of debts. Direct foreign investment in productive activity was sparse, and typically for the benefit of advanced western economies.[11]

The transfer of population from the land was no more than a trickle. The number of insured workers rose by about a third in the 1920s, but they still totalled fewer than 700 000 by the end of the decade. Cottage industries and seasonal work accounted for much of the growth of a monetary economy: the peasant worker, not the proletarian, dominated the structure of wage labour. Urban development was limited, and concentrated around the northern towns and cities. Belgrade's new status as the capital of an enlarged independent state swelled the population by at least two-thirds during the Vidovdan years, to well over 200 000 souls, and Zagreb ran a close second. The fact is, however, that by 1931 only three cities (Subotica was the third) had more than 100 000 inhabitants, and a mere 6 per cent of a total population of 10.7 million lived in towns of over 50 000 people. Urbanism as a way of life meant nothing to the mass of the population in their villages.

The snail's-pace of modernization reflected the powerlessness of a traditional, conservative elite desperately trying to create a unitary framework of government almost from scratch. The first Yugoslavia could well be taken as the limiting case of administrative chaos consistent with the formal existence of a state. The government inherited multiple forms of landholding, six customs' areas, six legal jurisdictions, five currencies, five railway networks and three different banking systems. The resources for state-building were slender indeed. The war destroyed much of what little industry there was, decimated livestock holdings, left the land short of people to work it, and crippled transport networks that in any case were hopelessly inadequate – Serbia's trade northward was strangled until 1921 by the destruction of the only bridge across the River Sava linking Belgrade with the former Habsburg lands.

Despite these problems, by 1926 the economic situation was surprisingly good. Productivity in agriculture had regained pre-war Serbian levels, and the balance of trade was running favourably, helped by a succession of good harvests. However, much of the state's income (which included important monopolies in industries such as petrol, tobacco and salt) went on high levels of military spending and on maintaining a bloated bureaucracy. Furthermore, too much investment was misdirected into unproductive projects – the record in creating badly needed infrastructure, like railway construction – was poor.

Government also lacked the means of administration needed to carry out its tasks. Not that there was any shortage of bureaucrats. Expansion in higher education turned out a growing flood of graduates whose only

real chance of employment lay in securing a job in the state administration. Belgrade was home to an army of officials and state-employed
professionals, who made up a quarter of its population, but the
bureaucracy was of low calibre, and open to corruption. It was also very
lop-sided. By 1927, more than half of all state employees worked for the
Ministry of the Interior,[12] including a Serb-dominated gendarmerie that
had an ugly reputation for strong-arm methods, especially at election
times. But while repression should not be glossed over, neither should
it be exaggerated. Under the Law for the Protection of the State,
individual liberties were always at risk, but there were no mass arrests,
and there were always voices in the Peoples' Assembly ready to raise hue
and cry over electoral irregularities.

Corruption, as much as repression, was the undoing of democracy.
Lack of democratic controls over recruitment to the state bureaucracy
opened the door wide to nepotism, and the ruling elite came more and
more to merge with officialdom, the distinction between the public and
the private spheres blurred. The greatest obstacle to the flourishing of
civil society was the ban on all political activity by state employees,
which silenced the most articulate and educated section of the
population. Officials dependent for their livelihood on the whims of
their superiors made up a network of cliental patronage spread across
the state, which subverted the formal democratic process. The role of
government in the economy also bred corruption of a more obvious
kind. Political life was punctuated by recurrent financial scandals in high
places – Pašić was continually embarrassed by the shady activities of his
son, and himself acquired thousands of hectares of good land in Kosovo
at knockdown prices. Bribery was commonplace, provoking jibes by
critics about the 'Turkish', 'oriental' methods by which the Serbs
maintained their grip on power.

King Aleksandar assumed personal control of his patrimony
determined to overcome by means of energetic leadership and efficient
administration the Serb–Croat deadlock which had paralysed democratic
government. Aleksandar was an enlightened despot rather than a
dictator in the contemporary mould, his self-imposed mission being to
stand apart from all sectional interests, and to symbolize in his person
the 'Kingdom of Yugoslavia', which became the official title of the state
on 3 October 1929. All references to separate peoples, and all the para-
phernalia of nationalist identification, were proscribed – even the army
was forced to yield up its prized battle emblems in exchange for new
flags. The 33 administrative districts were replaced by nine banovinas,
named (except for the Coastal Banovina) after the main rivers, in order

to disinfect them of ethnic or historical associations, with a separate Prefecture of Belgrade. A torrent of royal decrees passed in 1929 included long overdue reforms which replaced the six inherited legal jurisdictions by a single, uniform Code, standardized the tax structure, cracked down on corruption, and rationalized the state administrative apparatus.

The illusion of a fresh start was soon dissipated. Aleksandar could maintain the unitary state only by falling back on the Serb ascendancy, so defeating any claim to supra-national authority. It could hardly escape notice that the carving out of the new banovinas left the Serbs in a majority in six of them, by the expedient of slicing up both Bosnia-Hercegovina and Croatia. In his zeal to root out the sources of nationalism, Aleksandar banned all political parties and organizations based on ethnic or confessional identification, and their affiliated associations, such as sports' clubs. Even religious schools came under threat, but the problem of organized religion proved intractable, because the support of the Orthodox faithful was a central prop of state authority. In 1931 Aleksandar conceded a unified constitution for the revived Patriarchate of Peć, provoking a reaction among the Catholics and Muslims, who feared it was the first step in establishing a state Church. Religion reasserted itself as a marker of ethnic identity, functioning as a surrogate nationalism.

Far from holding the ring, Aleksandar became a symbol of the forces of Serbian centralism and repression. The appointment of General Živkovic, the leader of the 'White Hand' officers, as head of government, was followed by a strengthening of the Law for the Protection of the State, bringing a wave of political trials, police brutality, suffocating press laws and the subordination of the judiciary to Crown control. Many leading Communists were shot, usually while allegedly attempting to escape across the border to Austria, and many more were jailed. Bourgeois opponents of the regime were also ruthlessly dealt with. Pribičević was imprisoned in the name of the aggressive 'Yugoslavism' he once espoused, and was released only into exile (he died in Prague in 1936). Radić's successor Vladimir Maček and two dozen prominent members of the Croatian Peasant Party were put on trial in connection with bombings in Zagreb in December 1929, despite the fact that there was no evidence linking them to the outrage. Maček was acquitted, together with about half of the other accused, but the publicity given to police beatings severely discredited the government. Other Croat leaders fled abroad, including most notably Ante Pavelić, the leader of the Croatian Party of Right, who left to form the fascist Ustasha ('Insurgent') movement in Mussolini's Italy.

Dictatorship achieved almost overnight what a decade of parliamentary government failed to do: it united an opposition that included liberal Serbs as well as Croats, Slovenes and Bosnian Muslims. Internal dissent combined with French diplomatic and economic pressure persuaded the King to promulgate the Constitution of September 1931, which remained in force until the Nazi attack on Yugoslavia ten years later. A bicameral legislature was introduced, with an Assembly containing 306 members (later enlarged to 373) and a much smaller Senate partially appointed by the King, though its seats were never in fact completely filled. The electoral laws required all parties to be registered, and none of the existing parties qualified because of their ethnic links. Furthermore, candidates for election had to collect 60 signatures from every electoral district in the country, plus 200 signatures from the candidate's own district, a hurdle which in practice excluded all except government-sponsored aspirants. Candidates had to foreswear membership of any organization based on religious, ethnic or regional interests, and to promise that they would uphold national unity. The party gaining the most votes automatically took two-thirds of the seats in the Assembly.

Rigged elections for a bogus parliament took place on 8 November 1931. The Serbian opposition, the Peasant–Democrat Coalition, the Slovene People's Party and the Yugoslav Muslim Organization took no formal part in the proceedings, since they were now illegal organizations. Official government statistics themselves record that in the banovinas corresponding (roughly) to Slovenia, Croatia and Dalmatia the turnout was 52 per cent, 55 per cent and 34 per cent, and these figures can confidently be revised downwards in the light of opposition evidence of fraud in the recording of votes. About three-quarters of all the deputies in the new Peoples' Assembly were Serbs. No non-Serb politician of any stature could be found to join the administration formed after the elections, and a token Croat presence was secured only by persuading two veterans of the pre-1918 National Council to dust off their frock coats and join the cabinet, together with two even more obscure Croatian businessmen.

By the beginning of April 1932, General Živkovic had become such a personal liability that the King dismissed him. His successor, who lasted just three months, announced the formation of an official government party called the United Radical Peasant Democratic Party, a farcical amalgam of the names of all the major parties (in 1933 it became the Yugoslav National Party), then resigned in the face of peasant unrest and student demonstrations against the monarchy. Aleksandar was forced to turn to the banned opposition leaders for someone to lead his government. He asked, first, Aca Stanojević, a veteran Radical constitutionalist who had been in the dock with Pašić on a charge of treason in 1899, then Maček, but both refused. The choice finally fell upon Milan Šrškić, a Bosnian Serb detested by the Muslims as an advocate of the dismemberment of Bosnia-Hercegovina. Royal power now rested exclusively on repression, the only active element of government remaining, and the tempo of intrigue and assassination gathered pace.

That Aleksandar was compelled to hawk around promiscuously the most important office of state demonstrates the vicious deflationary spiral of authority in political life. Nobody spoke any longer for the non-Serb nationalities, or for the Serbs either. Many Radicals remained true to their constitutionalist roots, causing a split between supporters of the Yugoslav National Party, and those who wanted a restoration of political rights. Outside Serbia, hostility to the regime was inflamed to the point where, in November 1932, the leadership of the Croatian Peasant Party published the Zagreb Theses (Punktacije), which condemned the royal dictatorship as the culmination of an imposed Serbian hegemony, and recommended a return to the starting-point of 1918. Some weeks later, the Slovene People's Party put out a similar document, and the Bosnian Muslim leaders added their names to it, abandoning the policy of obedience to the state which had brought them nothing but humiliation and disappointment. Maček, Korošec and Mehmed Spaho were arrested and imprisoned, to a chorus of protest from the united Serbian opposition.

Aleksandar's ambition to reform the state single-handed, assisted by men of good-will irrespective of party allegiances, was arrogant and naive, but he also had his share of bad luck. The beginning of the royal dictatorship coincided with the onset of world depression, and the Hoover Moratorium of June 1931 cut off Germany's payments of war reparations. This response to the failure of the Austrian banking system had severe repercussions for the Zagreb banks, which spread throughout the economy. One immediate result was severe cuts in the salaries and pensions of state employees. The impact on the urban classes can easily be imagined, but it was all the more damaging politically because the Slovenes and Croats, having gained most from post-war economic and social advance, also had most to lose. Less developed Serbia rode out the storm better, and the nationalist bias embedded in the land reform programme gave the Serbian peasantry preferential access to state credit.

The full force of the international slump in trade took a little longer to work through to the peasantry. In 1930, a state monopoly (PRIZAD) was created to buy up grain in an attempt to protect the peasants from plummeting world prices, but the grain could neither be sold nor properly stored, and the scheme was abandoned in 1932, at enormous financial cost. The value of exports in 1932 fell by 40 per cent compared with the previous year, and the dreadful winter that followed created a shortage of animal feed, resulting in the destruction of a quarter of all livestock. There was extreme hardship and unrest throughout the country, especially in food-poor areas – peasants ransacked the government grain stores in Prijedor. In March 1933 the government declared a moratorium on all peasant debts, which lasted until late October, and introduced drastic exchange controls. Yugoslavia was broke.

Help was desperately needed from abroad, but France, the traditional lender and defender since 1906, refused to oblige beyond agreeing to a year's deferment of payments on existing loans, in June 1932. The recently elected French government took the view that heavy expenditure on armaments and diplomacy to assure European security by containing Germany achieved no such thing. Yugoslavia was now isolated and subjected to increasing pressure from Italy and Hungary, where Mussolini and Horthy played host to Ustasha terrorists regularly operating on Yugoslav territory. King Aleksandar was forced to pin his hopes for security on a Balkan Pact, signed in Athens in February 1934 by Greece, Romania, Turkey and Yugoslavia.

Bulgaria and Albania were not signatories, but a meeting between Aleksandar and King Boris of Bulgaria in 1933 brought unexpectedly good results. A personal friendship sprang up, and they had a key interest in common, because Boris had reasons of his own for wishing to suppress the Internal Macedonian Revolutionary Movement. But the French connection remained essential to achieving a stable Balkan Entente, and in October 1934, Aleksandar left for an official visit to Paris, travelling by sea. Landing at Marseille on 9 October, he was shot dead by agents with connections both to IMRO and to Pavelić's Ustasha movement, together with Barthou, France's Foreign Minister.

4
Encirclement and Destruction of the First Yugoslavia

In the gardens of Kalemegdan, the old Turkish fortress in Belgrade, stands a monument to the Great War, a massive relief of figures exuding struggle and sacrifice. The inscription commands passers-by to 'love France as she loved us'. This striking memorial is a reminder that, for the Serbs, independence always meant some kind of dependence, reliance on a patron among the great powers. Even when their protector was Russia, Serbs looked to French institutions for models of state-building, and with the coming of the twentieth century France became the main bulwark against the Teutonic threat. The fall of the Romanovs left France preeminent in Serbs' affections. The Serbian army fought its way back into the homeland alongside French troops, and the rivalries between Paris and Rome afforded some degree of protection from Mussolini's Italy.

The eclipse of France as a champion of the Versailles settlement was signalled by the scheme of Laval, Barthou's successor, to persuade Hitler to join with Italy, France and Great Britain in a four-power Pact as arbiters of the international order, supplanting the authority of the League of Nations. This idea was first mooted by Mussolini in March 1933, and it was clear that the price of a French–Italian rapprochement would be paid by Yugoslavia. Laval it was too who forced the Yugoslav government to accept the feeble resolution of the Council of the League of Nations (December 1934), which merely reprimanded Hungary for failing to control Ustasha activities on its territory, and omitted all mention of Italian complicity in the murders in Marseille.

King Aleksandar's death won for him the honoured place as a symbol of national unity which eluded him in life. The genuine mourning expressed throughout the country, even in Croatia, and the uncertainty created by the fact that three-man Regency now ruled in the name of Crown Prince Petar (approaching 11 years old when his father was killed), produced a mood of cautious compromise in the government. Korošec was released from prison to attend the royal funeral, and Maček was amnestied in December, but there was no fundamental change of course or personnel. The cabinet remained in place, except that it was now headed by Bogoljub Jevtić, the young foreign minister, replacing Uzunović. Jevtić had presented Yugoslavia's case against Hungary and Italy at the League of Nations, and was less closely associated with domestic repression and intrigue than his colleagues.

Persuaded that the government's softer line would give him the strong mandate which the fluid political situation demanded, Jevtić called elections for May 1935. It was a gross miscalculation. The government's poodle, the Yugoslav National Party, polled 60 per cent of the votes cast, while the candidate-list fielded by the combined opposition (the Peasant–Democrat Coalition, the Yugoslav Muslim Organization, the Davidović Democrats and a section of the Agrarian Alliance) succeeded in winning 37 per cent, despite the fact that every obstacle, legal and illegal, was placed in their way. However, the electoral law passed in 1933 gave Jevtić more than four-fifths of the seats in the Peoples' Assembly. Disgusted both by the conduct and the manifestly unfair outcome of the elections, the opposition deputies boycotted the Assembly and removed themselves to Zagreb, following the example of the Peasant–Democrat Coalition in 1929. A month after the elections, the three Croat ministers in the cabinet resigned, followed by General Živković and Milan Stojadinović, the Minister of Finance.

The first Regent, Aleksandar's cousin Prince Pavle, now made a surprise move by appointing Stojadinović to head the government, replacing Jevtić, while a number of prominent Serbian hard-liners were excluded from the new administration. What probably prompted the choice was Stojadinović's reputation as a fixer, a man capable of doing deals with his opponents. Prince Pavle, educated in pre-revolutionary Russia and at Oxford, was a stranger to Balkan politics, and must have found it a relief to lean on a cosmopolitan politician with business connections in Berlin, Paris and London – Stojadinović came with a personal recommendation from the British ambassador to Yugoslavia. Prince Pavle also found Stojadinović indispensable as a private banker (Aleksandar had been parsimonious in providing for his kinsman), and they had a personal relationship of sorts, though conducted chiefly through their wives. In one important respect, however, they differed. Prince Pavle was an Anglophile, while Stojadinović opted for cooperation with the Axis powers as a matter of both policy and personal preference.

Stojadinović occupied the post of premier from June 1935 until early 1939. He owed his long tenure to the economic revival he engineered, and to a talent for appearing all things to all men. On taking office, he pledged himself to defend the 1931 Constitution and the unitary state, whilst simultaneously promising democracy, civil liberties, local self-government, and a resolution of the deadlock with the Croats. Educated in Germany, his technical skills were invaluable to Pašić in the early 1920s during the struggle to stabilize the currency, and he applied the same principles of rational management to politics. He was an authoritarian technocrat, no friend to the parliamentary government which had paralysed the state during the Vidovdan years. And like all Radicals, he was a sworn enemy of communism: the government sent aid to Franco during the Spanish civil war, and did all it could to prevent volunteers joining the International Brigade.

In common with much of European public opinion, Stojadinović admired Germany as an exemplar of orderliness and sound government. Hermann Göring visited Belgrade as a prelude to the signing of a commercial treaty in May 1934, in a parade of friendship that promised Berlin's backing against Italy, and Stojadinović worked to foster a relationship which held out the prospect of killing two birds with one stone. Mussolini was trying to tighten the noose around the state whose founding Italy had opposed from the first. The reaction of France and Britain to Mussolini's attack upon Ethiopia, in October 1935, was summed up by the Hoare–Laval plan to dispose of the corpse by dismembering Haile Selassie's possessions. This, together with German re-armament and the re-militarization of the Rhineland, convinced the Yugoslavs that they had nothing to hope for from the liberal democracies. Belgrade was thrown back on a policy of neutrality in a world which allowed none, being dominated by war and preparations for war.[1]

Hitler's plans entailed picking off the states created by Versailles in a certain order, and he found Mussolini's European ambitions a nuisance, because they threatened a premature de-stabilization of the Balkans. Hitler disowned the Nazi plot to incorporate Austria within the Third Reich following the assassination of Dollfuss in July 1934, which brought Italian troops to the Brenner Pass, and Mussolini was encouraged to pursue his fantasy of a revived Roman empire across the Mediterranean.

Hitler wished to build up German military power undisturbed, and Yugoslavia had its uses as an economic satellite. The invasion of Ethiopia gave the Germans their chance. Yugoslavia, always a loyal founder-member of the League of Nations, had implemented the economic sanctions imposed on Italy, at great cost to its own trade, and jumped at Germany's offer to fill the gap.

An agreement reached during another high-level Nazi visit to Belgrade, this time by the German finance minister Dr Schacht, in June 1936, inaugurated a system of barter based on bilateral clearing arrangements which boosted the value of the dinar by around 30 per cent. The effect was to create a secure market for Yugoslav agricultural exports (including industrial crops) and raw materials, keeping the balance of trade in a small surplus. There was also a notable spurt in industrial output (11 per cent annually in the years 1936–41), though, even so, between 1929 and 1939 Yugoslavia's growth lagged behind its Balkan neighbours.[2] The peasants' standard of living improved only marginally, and a poor diet continued to exact a penalty in terms of diseases like rickets and tuberculosis. Yugoslavs ate half the quantity of meat consumed in western countries, and relied on vegetables for two-thirds of their protein.[3] The impact of industrialization on the social structure was minimal (only 5 per cent of an economically active population of 7 million were employed in mining and manufacturing by 1938), but low wages and poor working conditions led to working-class unrest, adding a new dimension to urban political life. The government tried by various devices to head off trouble, such as encouraging workers to join 'approved' trade unions immune from Communist influences, and picking up the threads of the embryonic welfare legislation introduced by early governments under Pašić, but long since abandoned.

Social advance was halting and patchy. No government ever honoured the Vidovdan promise to review the question of votes for women, though urban women did take advantage of improved opportunities in higher education.[4] Education of any kind was a rare privilege. Until the royal dictatorship began to force the pace of change, there was no national system of planning and inspection for education, and shortage of elementary schools kept rural illiteracy rates high. The organization and expansion of the universities into four-year Faculties on the French model brought a surge in student numbers, but they experienced the same old problem of finding secure employment. The economy was too under-developed to support a technical intelligentsia, and the liberal professions could make a living only in the major cities. Teaching was a way out mainly for people of peasant origin, for it was poorly paid and typically entailed a return to the village, from which everyone was trying to escape. The great prize for aspiring young men and women was entry to the Faculty of Law, the springboard to a position in the state administration.

Workers and students contributed a steady stream of recruits to the Communist Party of Yugoslavia, which revived strongly during the later 1930s. Proscribed in 1921, the Party was torn apart by factional struggles, and barely survived the years of police offensives after 1929, when so many Communist activists were murdered. The Fourth Party Conference, convened in Ljubljana during the Catholic Christmas of 1934, numbered just 30 delegates, including one Josip Broz, whose many aliases included the name 'Tito'. Tito had spent almost the exact period of King Aleksandar's dictatorship in prison (he was incarcerated from November 1928 until March 1934), a coincidence that may have saved his life. Aged 42 by the time of his release, Tito emerged to lead a battled-hardened core of Party cadres, who won support by emphasizing practical social questions like wages and unemployment, at the expense of the doctrinal struggles of the previous decade. Stalin's switch (in 1935) to the policy of a Popular Front against fascism also caused the Party to abandon its opposition to the Yugoslav state as an imperialist creation of Versailles, in favour of a federalist framework of government, which was to be the means of solving the nationalities question. This change of heart prompted the formation in 1937 of the Communist Party of Slovenia and the Communist Party of Croatia, though their independence was always largely notional.

Yugoslav official histories state that Tito was appointed General Secretary at a meeting of the leadership at their headquarters in Paris on 17 August 1937, when his predecessor, Milan Gorkić, vanished after being summoned to Moscow. According to later legend, Tito stepped forward to fill his place, the unanimous choice of a Party determined to blaze its own revolutionary path to socialism, thus backdating the Soviet–Yugoslav split of 1948 by more than a decade. What actually went on at this time is unclear in detail, but the main facts can be established, and they speak otherwise. Early in 1935, Tito returned to the USSR, 15 years after leaving it as a liberated prisoner of war, this time as an important guest of the Soviet state, a member of the Balkan Secretariat of the Communist International. Resistance to fascism now took pride of place over world revolution in Stalin's list of priorities, and Tito was quick to pick up on the idea that nationalism was no longer to be treated simply as a bourgeois deviation. During one of his spells in Moscow, in the autumn of 1936, he wrote (under a pseudonym) three articles on the Spanish civil war for the

Yugoslav Party newspaper *Proleter*, expressing confidence that freedom-loving patriots would win the day against Franco.

Despite his own frequent visits to Moscow, Tito survived Stalin's purges (Djilas said of him that he could actually scent danger), which cost the Yugoslav Party about 800 of its most dedicated cadres, including most of the leadership. He next turned up in Split at the end of December 1936, entrusted by the Comintern with the task of 'consolidating' the Party, which was racked by a comradely war being waged inside Yugoslavia's prisons, notably in Sremska Mitrovica, where young militants physically attacked the 'right opposition'. Late in 1938, the Comintern was still contemplating dissolving the unruly CPY (the fate of the Polish Communists). Never one to be seduced by fancy ideas, Tito conducted his own purges, sniffing out Trotskyites and bourgeois deviations with equal dispassion, and his appointment in January 1939 as the interim Secretary of the Party Politburo singled him out as Moscow's trusty lieutenant.[5] When the Molotov–Ribbentrop Pact was signed on 23 August 1939, Yugoslav Communists maintained a disciplined obedience remarkable in a party once renowned for its garrulous sectarianism.

As Yugoslavia drifted into the Axis sphere of influence, Mussolini spoke warmly of the extraordinary improvement in relations between the two countries, and in March 1937 a treaty of friendship was signed between them. The trade sanctions imposed on Italy by the League of Nations were dropped (nobody else had been observing them), but the embargo left a destructive mark on Serb–Croat relations. Trade with Italy never regained anything like its former volume, which hurt Croatia and Slovenia most, while the boost given to the economy by the new links with Germany favoured industries in Serbia and Bosnia-Hercegovina. And since investment was mainly channelled through the government, complaints that the Serbs were being systematically favoured became more and more strident. Croatian intellectuals amassed evidence to prove to the world that Croatia's economic interests were being sacrificed for the sake of a unitary state imposed upon their people.[6]

Stojadinović tried to create a new power base for himself by setting up the Yugoslav Radical Union, which was intended to supplant the Yugoslav National Party as the government-sponsored party. The relationship between them was a peculiar one. Indistinguishable in their aim of maintaining the unitary state, the two parties were locked in a war of attrition for control of the government, and feelings ran so high that in March 1936 a drunken deputy of the Yugoslav National Party tried to shoot Stojadinović in the Assembly. Stojadinović could rely on support for the Yugoslav Radical Union only among a section of the Radicals who were loyal to him personally. Many Radicals and some Democrats were to be found in the ranks of the Yugoslav National Party, while the Davidović Democrats were firmly aligned with the non-Serb opposition deputies in the Assembly. Serb politicians disagreed about all the major issues of the day. Some were in favour of the restoration of constitutionalism, some were adherents of the 'strong hand'; some favoured the developing links with Germany, but many more did not; some believed that it was possible to do a deal with the Croats, others opposed the very idea.

The stability and effectiveness of the Yugoslav Radical Union as an instrument of rule really rested on the willingness of Korošec and Spaho to bring their followers into a coalition with Stojadinović, as a means by which they could protect the interests of their peoples. In return, Stojadinović's first major act as premier was to sign a Concordat with the Vatican, and the following year the Bosnian Muslims received back the religious and cultural autonomy they had lost in 1931. The signing of the Concordat seemed a particularly astute move. Although it still had to be ratified by the Assembly, the government's willingness to concede to Catholics equality of status with the Orthodox Church strengthened the position of Korošec in Slovenia. If given legal sanction, the Concordat would also bolster the authority of the Catholic Church in the battle against communism by allowing religious schools and propaganda work, and be useful in countering the influence of the traditionally anti-clerical Croatian Peasant Party.

Stojadinović had obviously learned something from his mentor, Pašić, who had pursued the same strategy of detaching the Slovenes and the Bosnian Muslims from the Croats, but Pašić was always able, when it mattered, to muster the support of all the Serbs. Now, the Radicals had ceased to be the backbone of government. Disqualified from campaigning as a party, they could only watch as Stojadinović pursued policies many of them detested. His conduct of foreign affairs was the one thing calculated to unite public opinion in opposition throughout Serbia, where the humiliation and atrocities of the Great War were a recent memory, and his attempts to reach accommodation with the Croats could all the more easily be represented as a form of treachery.

The combined opposition formed after 1935 crystallized around a Croatian Peasant Party transformed by Maček into a modern organization in which the urban classes were approaching parity of representation with the peasants (in his memoirs he records that, when asked to nominate local candidates for office, he always suggested young, educated men).[7] Under his leadership the CPP took on the configuration of a bourgeois party, staffed by nationalist intellectuals to whom 'Yugoslavism' was anathema. Unlike Radić, Maček had no great attachment to peasant radicalism, but he knew how to win their support by encouraging the formation of cooperatives, which by 1940 extended to a third of all peasant households in Croatia. He had no profound anti-clerical convictions either, and the influence of Cardinal Stepinac, Archbishop of Zagreb from 1937, added a religious dimension to Croatian nationalism, which Radić had shunned.

After an initial phase of conciliation during which many political opponents were amnestied, the Stojadinović regime came to rely for its survival on political jobbery and a large gendarmerie. Its weakness was exposed when (23 July 1937) Stojadinović brought the Concordat to the Assembly for approval, and it was passed by a small majority (167 to 129 votes). Stirred up by the Orthodox prelates, who excommunicated the ministers responsible for passing the measure, the Serbs flew to the defence of their national church, in a display of mass defiance of government. Their anger was intensified by the strangely coincidental death of their Patriarch, aged only 57, on the very night of the vote: rumour insisted that he had been poisoned by government agents. Stojadinović dared not send the Concordat to the Senate, where he could not be sure of a majority, so it never became law.

The rumpus over the Concordat exposed the cracks in the governing coalition, drawing Serbia's Democrats, Agrarians and Republicans into a formal alliance with Maček's Peasant–Democrat Coalition to form the Bloc of National Agreement, in October 1937. Their manifesto noted that the Vidovdan Constitution was adopted without the consent of the Croats, and that the Constitution of 1931 lacked all moral validity, because it excluded both Serbs and Croats from political life. They demanded a fresh start: the summoning of a Constituent Assembly, and the restoration of parliamentary government, together with civil liberties and the rule of law. The Opposition Bloc was not yet in a position to mount a serious challenge to the government, but the tide of events was beginning to turn against the regime.

The Serbs were angry that Stojadinović was prepared to allow Italy a free hand in Albania, and most of them hated the Concordat. The incorporation of Austria within a greater Germany (12 March 1938), which brought the Third Reich right up to Yugoslavia's borders, was officially greeted in Belgrade with unruffled calm, but public opinion was incensed. When the Serbian opposition leaders protested against the breaking of links with France and the Little Entente, Stojadinović replied that these ties were as strong as ever, and his attitude to the Munich debacle (30 September) confirms the impression of a mind unwilling to grapple with reality. His political memoirs reveal a man susceptible to flattery and curiously devoid of statecraft.[8] He seems really to have allowed himself to believe in Hitler's assurances that Germany had no designs on Yugoslavia, and was particularly beguiled by Mussolini. He rejected the overtures of President Beneš, who visited Yugoslavia during the summer in a last-ditch effort to drum up support, and in an echo of his German backers referred to Czechoslovakia as an 'artificial and hostile' creation.

Stojadinović developed a marked taste for the fascist trappings of power. After meeting with Mussolini, in December 1937, he adopted a version of the Roman salute and took to styling himself 'Leader' of his followers, though not, he said with characteristic equivocation when confronted by Prince Pavle about it, with any wish to emulate the Duce, to whom he had said exactly the opposite. Stojadinović aspired to be Yugoslavia's strong man, and because of it he ended up an Axis stooge. But he did not create a fascist state, and he could not have done. The Yugoslav Radical Union bore no resemblance to a Nazi-type party: it had no mass membership, no national organizational structure. Nor was Stojadinović the stuff of which dictators are made. Even within the Yugoslav Radical Union he failed to command obedience: a dozen deputies were expelled from the parliamentary caucus for voting against the Concordat, and in March 1938 there were open dissensions over the passing of the budget. Jevtić and the Yugoslav National Party were relentless in their attacks on the government, and the 'Old Radicals' strongly disapproved of his pro-Axis foreign policy, as did the military. The Muslims and Slovenes were finding each other's company irksome, and the policy of the 'firm hand' was proving barren. Negotiations to bring the Croatian Peasant Party into government, instigated by Prince Pavle, broke down because Maček would settle for nothing less than an autonomous Croatia, and Stojadinović could not even deliver the Concordat.

After Munich, Stojadinović was forced to call elections to try and strengthen his position, relying on the mixture as before: a propaganda campaign to 'save the state', combined with police pressure to ensure the right result for the government. The elections (11 December 1938) produced 1.6 million votes for the Stojadinović candidates list, considerably fewer than Jevtić's tally in 1935, and 1.3 million votes (45 per cent of the total) cast for the list fielded by Maček on behalf of the united opposition. As a result of the operation of the electoral law, however, the seats in the Assembly were distributed 306 to 67 in favour of the government. The third list, put up by the Serbian fascist Dimitrije Ljotić, polled just 1 per cent of the votes and won no seats at all, in a repeat of the 1935 elections. There were no other contenders to cloud the result, which was both a moral and practical victory for the opposition. Stojadinović formed a second administration, but at the beginning of February 1939 his Slovene and Muslim ministerial colleagues, together with Dragiša Cvetković, a Serb, resigned, stating as their reason the government's intransigence over the Croat problem. Stojadinović's position was now untenable, and he meekly went at the command of the Regent.

The poor showing of Ljotić's Zbor ('Rally') party was good news for Yugoslavia's Jews, who were spared the ugly anti-Semitism suffered by their sister communities elsewhere in Eastern Europe. Their numbers were small (about 65 000 in total), half of them equally distributed among the urban populations of Belgrade, Zagreb, Sarajevo and Skopje, with the rest living in the northern regions in smaller towns. Fewer than 1 per cent of Jews were engaged in agriculture or primary economic activities, and there was no population of orthodox Jewry to attract unwelcome attention, in contrast to the ghettoized Hassidic communities in Poland. To the peasantry, therefore, they were invisible as potential targets of hatred. Although the influence of the Croatian Peasant Party generated an undercurrent of anti-Jewish feeling in Zagreb, no major political grouping singled out Jews for persecution as a matter of overt policy, so that they enjoyed a flourishing cultural and religious life largely unmolested. The Law on the Religious Community of the Jews, passed in 1929, gave the Chief Rabbi (there was only ever one incumbent of the post) a generous state subsidy, and numbers of Jewish professionals rose to prominence in the ranks of the Radical Party, which argues a high degree of assimilation into the political life of the first Yugoslavia.[9]

Younger Jews, on the other hand, were attracted to the Communist Party because of the accelerating deterioration of the moral and political fabric of society caused by the atrophying of democratic institutions, and the penetration of fascist influences from abroad. In 1936, the Federation of Jewish Religious Communities noted the growing frequency of attacks on Jews since 1933. In contrast to the other eastern European states, however, fascism never took hold as a mass movement in Yugoslavia. The most likely vehicle for such a development was the Serbian Chetnik movement, which numbered half a million members by 1938, most of whom had joined after the assassination of Aleksandar, when the Serbs rallied to the defence of the state. The movement had the right pedigree for a fascist following – it was anti-liberal, anti-democratic, anti-Communist, but it was internally divided, and never found a leader or a programme.[10]

It was the Kosovar Albanians who caught the full force of the racial bigotry that surfaced during the 1930s. Murder, dispossession of their land, and cultural oppression had been part of daily life among the Kosovars since the Balkan Wars. The aim now was no longer to keep Kosovo backward and deprive the Kosovars of their language, but to remove them altogether. In 1935, the Turkish authorities offered to accept 200 000 Muslim immigrants from Kosovo. They were described in the negotiations as 'Turks', but the figure exceeded by one-third the total number of ethnic Turks recorded in the 1921 Census, and most of those were already in Turkey. Kosovo's Albanian population was the real target, and expulsions on this scale required a corresponding increase in state coercion. The first step was an edict restricting Kosovar holdings of land to 0.16 hectares (just over a third of an acre) per household-member, unless good title could be proved through documents, which in most instances it could not.[11] This maximum was deliberately selected as insufficient for survival, but it was still too soft an approach for extreme Serbian nationalists.

On 7 March 1937, Vaso Čubrilović, a Serbian historian-Academician at Belgrade University, and a member of the curiously named 'Serbian Cultural Club', produced a policy paper for the government which brought a radical and sinister new approach to the Kosovo question out into the open. In a world where Germany and Russia could move millions of people across continents, he wrote contemptuously, 'the shifting of a few hundred thousand Albanians' would not cause a world war. The piecemeal attempt to rectify the ethnic balance in Kosovo through colonization had failed – he blamed it on the Montenegrin settlers, idle consumers of government 'corn and pensions', too much like the Albanians in their way of life. Now the time was opportune to turn to a policy of systematic coercion. Albanians were to be harassed by every possible means to induce them to leave, including the burning of their villages and town-quarters.[12] Čubrilović, imprisoned as a youth of 17 for his involvement in the murder of Franz Ferdinand at Sarajevo, articulated the fears and stereotypes of diehard Serbian chauvinism, which revived again half a century later (he was still alive to see it – he died in 1990, aged 92). Garašanin's dream of reclaiming Serb ancestral lands would perish at the hands of Albanian irredentism, the security of the state would come under threat, the 'cradle of the nation' would remain occupied by an alien people with a high birth-rate and 'oriental' habits.

In July 1938, Stojadinović initialled a draft treaty with Turkey which provided for the emigration of 40 000 families, many more than the 200 000 individuals originally proposed, but the fall of the Stojadinović government and impending war meant that the treaty was never ratified by the Turkish authorities, and the scheme fell through. The patchiness of the statistics make it impossible to say just how many Kosovo Albanians left their native place during the inter-war years: one can only deal in orders of magnitude. There are sound reasons for rejecting the upper figure 250 000 proposed by some commentators. The alternative 'low' figure of 77 000 may understate the outflow, but is likely to be nearer the true number because it is the product of statistical modelling, not arithmetical guesswork. An estimate of 90 000–150 000 emigrants leaves an uncomfortably wide margin of error, but usefully stakes out the terrain on which the controversy about numbers can reasonably be conducted.[13] The question of numbers in any case should not be allowed to obscure the central point: the government operated a policy aimed at ridding Yugoslavia of all its Albanian citizens and succeeded in forcing tens of thousands of them to go.

Prince Pavle's dismissal of Stojadinović was prompted by the urgent need to make progress in dealings with the Croats, in view of the bleak international situation. Cvetković was appointed to head the government (5 February 1939), and specifically entrusted with this mission, but it was not until 3–4 April that, through intermediaries of the Croatian Peasant Party, Cvetković met Maček in Zagreb for preliminary talks. In the meantime, the Wehrmacht had marched into Prague (15 March), and Slovakia was severed from Bohemia-Moravia to become a German satellite state. On 7 April, Mussolini sprang the trap from the south when Italy sent in an army to annex Albania. Yet even now there was no unseemly haste to conclude a settlement. Negotiations dragged on for nearly five months, and it was not until August 20 that the Cvetković–Maček Agreement (Sporazum) was reached on the status of Croatia, ratified by the Peoples' Assembly on 26 August, just one week before Hitler invaded Poland.

Maček had played a long waiting game, and now his time had come. The Sporazum created an independent Banovina of Croatia, a form of home rule under a Ban responsible to an independent Sabor in Zagreb, as well as to the Crown. The document approving the change was not a constitutional amendment passed by the Assembly and Senate, but a royal decree (Uredba). Its contents were at best ambiguous, in some respects contradictory, and always confusing. Croatia was given full administrative control of a range of social, legal and economic functions, while all powers not enumerated (notably defence and foreign affairs) remained a central prerogative. Article 2.3 then muddied the waters hopelessly by providing that 'matters of particular importance for the general interests of the state' would also be reserved to the Belgrade government. Mining rights, citizenship matters, and internal security were cited as examples, but the category was not a closed one. The source of budgetary receipts was left to be decided, and the relationship between Ban and Crown was distinctly weighted in favour of the latter.

Maček joined the government as vice-premier, together with four colleagues, but Serb–Croat relations were no nearer to the spirit of compromise. A simple head-count shows that Croats were much better represented in government during the 1930s than during the Vidovdan years, but they were mostly nonentities and placemen. A more telling statistic is that of the 165 generals on the active list in 1938, all but four were Serbs, and that Serbs continued to monopolize the key cabinet posts – Interior, Defence and the Premiership. Maček's appearance in government as the head of an autonomous Croatia incensed Serb nationalists, stirred up by the Orthodox hierarchy and the military. The Banovina of Croatia comprised about one-third of the territory of the state and was identified with certain exclusive rights of the Croatian people. The Sporazum also left more than 800 000 Serbs within the Banovina of Croatia, without any guarantees of their minority rights.The Regent appointed Ivan Šubašic as the first and only Ban of Croatia; he was a Serbs' Croat (at least, so it was hoped) who had fought at Salonika, and strongly believed in Yugoslav unity, but it was a feeble gesture that did nothing to appease Serb nationalists.

Only one member of the Cvetković–Maček cabinet was drawn from the Yugoslav Muslim Organization. In-fighting between Serbs and Croats always spelt trouble for the Bosnian Muslims, and it came in the form of a proposal to create a 'Banovina of Serbian Land', with Skopje as its centre, which would incorporate those parts of Bosnia-Hercegovina (the greater share) not already assigned to the Croats. The idea got to the stage of a draft Regulation modelled on the Croatian example, in mid-1940, but was never promulgated. The Slovenes were left out in the cold entirely, denied the autonomy conferred on the Croats, and fearful of what the future might hold. The Slovene People's Party supplied three ministers – Korošec died in December 1940, but his two colleagues lasted until the government fell three months later. The prime concern of the Slovenes was now the security of the state. There were calls for a Banovina of Slovenia, but the overriding interest of most Slovenes was in protection from the Axis powers on their doorstep.

The Croatian Peasant Party was decidedly the strongest party in government (the colourless Cvetković was even less popular in Serbia than Stojadinović), but Maček showed no further interest in the reform of the state. Article 6.1 of the Sporazum spoke of the Croatian Sabor as being constituted through 'general, equal, direct elections with secret voting and minority representation', but no such elections were ever held. Maček owed his position to the favour of the Regent, and he jettisoned his compact with the Serbian opposition to seek a revision of the 1931 Constitution. In the cause of Croatian independence, he had earlier flirted with fascist Italy as a possible sponsor, though stopping short of actual betrothal, and nothing in the brief life of the Banovina of Croatia suggests that Croatian nationalism carried within itself the seeds of liberal democracy. Maček established in Croatia a scaled-down version of the centralist state from which he received authority.

There was perhaps no choice. The Croatian Peasant Party contained both a social-democratic presence and a right-wing element with connections to the Ustasha movement.[14] Maček's single-minded pursuit of Croatian independence at the expense of wider Yugoslav interests can be interpreted as a fear of disturbing the delicate balance of forces among his followers. When asked by Prince Pavle in 1936 whether the Croats wanted the Yugoslav state, he replied 'yes', but within a federalist framework, and this seems to have been his genuine goal. In any case, by the time Maček became vice-premier the international situation ruled out discussion of constitutional reform. Following the Nazi invasion of Poland, Yugoslavia proclaimed its neutrality (6 September), and the government set about strengthening internal controls. An extension of the Law for the Defence of the State established internment camps for political detainees, and the police were even empowered to ban suspects from their own homes.

There was of course no prospect whatever of maintaining a genuine neutrality. France capitulated on 22 June 1940, and Albania was under Italian occupation. Yugoslavia's only chance of escaping hostilities lay in Hitler's protection, which carried its price. Decrees of 5 October barred Jews from engaging (whether directly or by proxy) in the wholesale and retail food industries, and introduced quota restrictions on Jewish students in both universities and schools, though with exceptions for the children of Jews who had fought in defence of the state, a rider that only served to underline the racialist character of the law. The government introduced a series of measures which bound the Yugoslav economy even tighter to Germany, and granted rights to set up German schools which were the counterpoint to the numerus clausus imposed by the state on the children of its own Jewish citizens. The government was weak and deeply unpopular. In December the government disbanded its own creation, the United Workers' Union Alliance, because of labour unrest, as wartime conditions in Europe caused shortages of food and rampant inflation. Ever since Munich a section of the officer corps had been more or less overt enemies of Yugoslavia's foreign policy, and the military generally were hostile to the Sporazum.

This was the moment the Communist Party had been waiting for. The Party had been transformed since the dark days of Aleksandar's dictatorship. The Fifth Conference (19–23 October 1940) was the first major gathering of Communists on Yugoslav soil for 20 years (the Fourth Congress in 1928 had to be held in Dresden), comprising 105 delegates who elected a Central Committee of 29 members, and a seven-man Politburo headed by Tito as General Secretary. All this took place in a suburban villa in Zagreb under conditions of illegality, a testimonial in itself to the Party's organization and security. The delegates were professional revolutionaries in the Leninist mould, young but with much experience of prison and police brutality, and many were veterans of the civil war in Spain.[15] The Politburo line-up included Milovan Djilas, Aleksandar Ranković (both of them with reputations as hard men), and Edvard Kardelj; together with the 'Old Man', as Tito was nicknamed, they had 'Bolshevized' the Party on the Soviet model, creating a formidable clandestine organization numbering well over 6000 members.

At the end of October, Mussolini destroyed the fragile peace in the Balkans by invading Greece, forcing the German army to rescue him from a bodged campaign. Hitler could no longer secure his objectives by stealth, and in November Romania and Hungary were induced to sign the Tripartite Pact, formed two months earlier when Italy joined the existing alliance between Japan and Germany. Bulgaria and Yugoslavia followed suit in March 1941. Cvetković signed on 25 March, in return for non-combatant status and freedom from occupation – a hint that Yugoslavia might get Salonika was thrown in as a sweetener. When the secret deal became known, his government was overthrown by a military coup led by the commander of the air force, General Dušan Simović, on 27 March, which brought Serbian nationalists out on to the streets in a surge of support for his anti-Axis stand. The Regency was dissolved and King Petar II was declared of age, though in fact still six months short of his majority.

General Simović did his best to keep Yugoslavia neutral. Maček was asked to join the new government and he agreed, after stipulating that the Sporazum must stand and that every effort must be made to appease

Hitler. He even offered to go to Berlin to broker a settlement, but it was too late. News of the coup flung Hitler into one of his frenzied rages, in which he declared his intention of settling scores with the treacherous Serbs and of destroying the Yugoslav state. On 6 April 1941, Palm Sunday in the Orthodox calendar, the Luftwaffe reduced much of Belgrade to burning rubble, causing many thousands of deaths and casualties.[16] Within ten days, the resistance of the Royal Yugoslav Army was at an end.

5
War, Civil War and Revolution

Most of the history of the Peoples' Liberation Struggle, as it came to be known in the annals of communist Yugoslavia, remains to be written. For years it was impossible to question the official account of the war as a mass rising against fascism, which contributed significantly to the victory in Europe, and swept the Party into power on a flood of popular support. This founding political myth was designed to divert attention from certain awkward facts. First, Yugoslavs slaughtered each other in greater numbers than they killed the Axis occupiers. Second, the guerrilla war in the Balkans was, from the point of view of grand strategy, a sideshow. Third, the Communist Party seized power at the war's end by force, and thanks to Stalin's patronage.

Even the question of how many were killed as a result of the fighting could not be asked during Tito's lifetime. The official government figure of 1.7 million war dead, submitted in 1946 for the purpose of calculating war reparations, has been shown to be the product of political manipulation. Two recent scientific studies estimate independently that Yugoslavia's war losses amounted to just over 1 million out of an estimated total population in March 1941 of 16 million people.[1] The point is not to belittle the toll of Yugoslav lives, but that it took 40 years for honest arguments about the statistics to become public, because counting the dead raised questions about who suffered most at whose hands.

On 10 April 1941, Croatian fascists rushed to proclaim the Independent State of Croatia (NDH in its Croatian acronym), a week before the formal surrender of Yugoslavia. The NDH was administered under licence from the Axis by Ante Pavelić, formerly prominent in the

Croatian Peasant Party, who assumed the title of 'Leader' (Poglavnik). Pavelić's puppet state was shorn of Dalmatia, but it included Bosnia-Hercegovina, so incorporating 1.9 million Serbs and 0.75 million Muslims, out of a total population of 6.3 million. It then remained only to dismember the rest of Yugoslavia along predictable lines. Slovenia was divided between Italy and Germany. The Italians occupied Dalmatia and Montenegro, from where they controlled a client Albania enlarged by the addition of part of western Macedonia and most of Kosovo. Bulgaria took the remaining (much larger) portion of Macedonia and the Pirot district of Serbia. The Vojvodina was split: Hungary got Baranja and Bažka, while Germany took direct control of the Banat, which was policed by the local population of Volksdeutscher. The wizened remnant of Serbia was entrusted to the collaborationist government of General Milan Nedić, in August.

By this time, Nazi armies were deep inside the territory of the USSR, which transformed the situation in Yugoslavia. With the Germans engrossed in the progress of Operation Barbarossa, a series of local risings broke out in Serbia during the autumn. The victorious Communist Party later claimed most of the credit for this, and although its part in generating resistance has been much exaggerated in official histories, individual Communists were active in placing themselves at the head of armed resistance to the occupation. The entry of the socialist fatherland into the war was greeted with huge euphoria among Party cadres, a blind faith that Nazism would be defeated. The Partizans even controlled the important town of Užice for a time, but they were too weak to hold out against the Germans. As it became clear that the Red Army would not be arriving soon, the Party leaders had to face up to an obvious problem. A successful guerrilla war could be fought only by mobilizing the peasantry, and Serb peasants found a more natural focus of loyalty in the Chetnik resistance movement, led by Colonel Draža Mihailović.

Mihailović took refuge in Serbia's Ravna Gora region, together with a handful of fellow officers who had evaded the fate of the 200 000 soldiers of the Royal Yugoslav Army transported to Axis PoW camps. Mihailović was a staff colonel of no great distinction when Yugoslavia surrendered. There were five Serbian generals in exile in London, and it was not until June 1942 that he was promoted to supreme command of the 'Yugoslav Army in the Homeland'. His authority over the Chetnik commanders was always weak.[2] In keeping with their name and antecedents, the Chetniks were groups of local fighters, partisans in the original meaning of the word. Mihailović was in effect appointed by the exiled government to coordinate the efforts of a number of independent resistance groups, and it was an uphill struggle from the first. The royal officers gave the Chetnik resistance political weight (Mihailović was also War Minister), but its fighting strength was rooted in family, clan and village networks, not a formal system of ranks.

The most prominent pre-war Chetnik leader, Kosta Pećanac, passed straight over into collaboration with the Nazis. The Mihailović Chetniks took to the mountains in rebellion against the Nedić regime (they executed Pećanac for treason in June 1944), but the line between collaboration and resistance was difficult to tread. Urged on by the Yugoslav government in London, Mihailović tried to conserve his forces against the day when Allied landings could support a Chetnik rising. The Chetniks lacked the equipment and training to take on the occupying forces, and in any case it was clear from the outset that the Partizans were their main enemy – it was the Chetniks, not the Germans, who first attacked the Partizans around Užice, at the beginning of November 1941. Mihailović was therefore willing to enter into negotiations with the Nedić regime, and some of his fighters became 'legals', that is, a Serbian quisling force under Nedic, in order to fight the Communists. He was also drawn into 'parallel' actions with Axis troops, coordinated attacks on Partizan units which did not involve relinquishing independent command.

The Chetniks were fighting for the restoration of a royalist Yugoslav state, but just what kind of state was never clear. In the case of Mihailović himself, his war aims were presumably those of the Yugoslav government in London, but the Chetnik ideologue Stefan Moljević argued that the fundamental mistake in 1918 was that the borders of Serbia were not defined, and in 1941 Chetnik maps appeared calculated to appeal to extreme nationalist opinion. Serbia, purged of foreign elements by 'cleansing' (Moljević's word), would make up two-thirds of a reconfigured Yugoslavia, with a rump Croatia and a 'Great Slovenia' accounting for the remainder. Moljević, a key figure in the Chetnik political directorate, seems to have used the term 'cleansing' to refer to the expulsion of Muslims and Croats from Serbian lands rather than to their physical destruction, but the first aim undeniably makes contemplation of the second easier. At least one other Chetnik organization hinted at just such a 'final solution'.[3]

The Partizans, on the other hand, had a genuinely supra-national character. The Communists built up their support by a strict policy of even-handedness between the nationalities and by cultivating non-Communist allies – Partizan headquarters even harboured an Orthodox priest. It helped, perhaps, that the leaders were a mixed bag: Tito hailed from Kumrovec on the borders of Slovenia and Croatia; Kardelj was a

Slovene; Djilas came from Montenegro, as did Moša Pijade, a Jew. Ranković was the only Serb in the inner circle of Tito's lieutenants. But more important was the fact that the Party enfolded its members in a closed world of danger and comradeship in which national differences simply ceased to matter. No extravagant claims need be made for the model character of the Partizans in wartime. The essential point is that the CPY was at least not tainted by association with the racialist massacres of Bosnian Muslims carried out by some Chetnik units.

The Partizans had the organizational strengths the Chetniks lacked. The need for secrecy and strict obedience to orders under conditions of pre-war illegality led to the quasi-militarization of the Communist Party, which proved adept at mobile guerrilla warfare. Tito's forces crossed and re-crossed Bosnia several times during the war, whereas the Chetniks were able to break out of their local strongholds only on the coat tails of Axis offensives. Party discipline, expressed in a puritanical code of personal conduct, was constantly reinvigorated by purges, keeping local commissars responsive to Central Committee orders even when the Partizan movement expanded in numbers far beyond its core of Communist cadres. On the run from the Axis, the Party set up in every liberated enclave the rudiments of civil administration, embodied in 'Regulations' establishing Peoples' Committees, and set the presses to work publicizing the Partizan cause. In addition to the Party newsheets, such as *Borba* and *Proleter*, the Communists took over a pre-war title, *Woman Today*, and made it the official organ of the Women's Anti-fascist Front, founded in December 1942. The mobilization of women turned out to be a remarkable success. Between 15 and 20 per cent of Partizan fighters were women – the Chetniks called them 'whores', in the true voice of patriarchal Serbia.

German reprisals drove thousands of young men and women into the arms of the Partizans. A Wehrmacht directive ordered that 100 hostages should be shot for every German soldier killed, 50 for every one wounded. The readiness of the German commanders to obey (they included many senior officers formerly in Habsburg service), led to one of the most notorious war crimes to capture the popular imagination of the Serbs after the war. Failing to find enough grown men in Kragujevac, the death squads rounded up the older boys of the town gymnasium (there was only one) and shot them (22 October 1941), together with their elderly schoolmaster.[4]

Partizans and Chetniks reacted to total war in quite different ways. The Partizans left the uncommitted civilian population to take their chances, as a way of discouraging collaboration, and attacked the occupying forces wherever they could. Chetnik operations against the Axis started later, were less frequent, and inflicted fewer casualties. The Italians used the Chetniks as a buffer in their own zone of occupation, allowing them to protect Serbs against Ustasha terror attacks and to maintain some kind of civil order. This policy, compounded by the Party's early blunder of 'left deviationism' (that is, mass terror), explains why the Partizans made no headway at all in Montenegro until the spring of 1943. In the areas of the Independent State of Croatia controlled by Italy, Chetniks (about 20 000 of them) actually fought as auxiliary forces, in an anti-Communist militia armed by the Italians and owing notional allegiance to the NDH. Serbia remained a Chetnik stronghold for all but the last few months of the fighting. The Germans oscillated between attack and truce in their dealings with the Chetniks, depending on the fluctuating military situation. They allowed the Chetniks far less rope than the Italians, but Mihailović's men were obviously useful for keeping the Partizans busy and out of the German zone.[5]

After perfunctory initial attempts to organize combined operations against the occupation forces, Partizans and Chetniks settled, from the beginning of 1942, into a struggle to eliminate each other, with the Slav Muslims caught in the middle. The Chetniks recruited exclusively among Serbs and Montenegrins. Serbs from Bosnia and Croatia, young men fleeing from Ustasha killings, also formed the backbone of the early Partizan formations, but the movement did attract support from other nationalities in the later stages of the fighting.

The Independent State of Croatia became the main slaughterhouse of war. Deaths of Yugoslavians from all causes attributable to war numbered 1.027 million, 80 000 of whom died abroad. Of the 947 000 deaths which occurred on Yugoslav soil, 587 000 (62 per cent) were deaths suffered on the territory of the NDH. Most of the remaining victims are accounted for by the 273 000 deaths in Serbia (29 per cent), 250 000 of them in the Vojvodina and Inner Serbia. Montenegro (37 000), Slovenia (33 000) and Macedonia (17 000) complete the territorial distribution of deaths within the borders of Yugoslavia.

Turning to the ethnic distribution of the total number of 1.027 million war dead, Serbs, Croats and Bosnia's Muslims together accounted for 81 per cent of Yugoslavia's war losses (825 000 dead). Serbs bore the brunt of the killing, with 530 000 deaths (52 per cent of the total number of war victims), followed by 192 000 Croats (19 per cent) and 103 000 Bosnian Muslims (10 per cent). Jews and Gypsies suffered the most grievous proportional losses. Four out of every five of Yugoslavia's Jews were killed (57 000 of them), and a third of the Gypsy population (18 000 deaths). The remaining losses are accounted for by the 42 000 Slovenes, 28 000 ethnic Germans, 20 000 Montenegrins, and 18 000 ethnic Albanians who lost their lives.[6]

About 300 000 Serbs perished in Bosnia-Hercegovina and Croatia – one in six of the Serb population, and 56 per cent of the total number of Serbs killed in the war. Pavelić's Ustasha followers treated the Serbs as the Nazis treated the Jews, as vermin to be exterminated. This was not a task imposed by the occupying forces, but sprang out of the Ustashas' own ideology, which incorporated a conception of Croats as a pure Aryan race. The Serbs were classed as racial enemies, and made to wear armbands carrying the letter 'P' for Pravoslavac, 'Orthodox'. The Ustasha commanders carried out their grisly work in the villages and small townships where their control was unrestricted by Axis authority. Their trademark was to descend at night on dazed and defenceless Serbs, who were massacred in their homes, in pits, in forest clearings and in burning churches. Orthodox priests were killed in their hundreds.[7] No attempt was made to keep the killings secret: on the contrary, knowledge of them was intended to instil fear and compliance in the Serb population. Only lack of means prevented the Ustashas from carrying out their genocidal mission by Nazi methods. Although they set up death camps like the infamous Jasenovac, there was no Eichmannesque bureaucracy, no detailed railway timetables or inventories of rolling stock, no neat blueprints of gas chambers. The NDH was run as an economic satellite by the Germans, who were unwilling to divert precious war resources to killing Serbs, and were for this reason opposed to state terror being applied against the Serb population. Powerless to murder all the Serbs, Pavelić decreed that the remainder should be forcibly converted or driven into Nedić's Serbia, where they found asylum of a sort until the Germans sealed the borders in the autumn of 1941.[8]

The National Liberation Struggle also claimed the lives of 192 000 Croats, 172 000 of them in the NDH. It has been estimated that 12 000 Ustasha core members were active when the state was proclaimed in April 1941, and that the Ustasha movement eventually comprised 40 000–50 000 men enrolled in the militias and gendarmerie.[9] Even if we make the simplifying assumption that all of them were killed, 120 000 Croat deaths remain to be explained. There were 170 000 Croatian troops under German command, and they must account for the bulk of deaths during the bitter fighting on the Srem front and in Communist reprisals. But Croats fought on both sides, and by the end of the war made up a third of the Peoples' Liberation Army. Croats joined the ranks of the Partizans, not just for opportunistic reasons when the

Communists seemed to be gaining the upper hand, but because the ideal of Croatian statehood had been irretrievably compromised, both morally and politically, by the criminal character of Ustasha rule. The Communists' promise of a federal state seemed to many Croats the best offer available – the Allies were not going to present them with an independent successor state to the NDH when the war ended.

Those who died included 'left' members of the Croatian Peasant Party; others were rounded up because they had criticized the Ustashas before the war, or simply because they were in the way at a random moment. To his credit, Maček refused to accept office in the Ustasha government and was sent to a concentration camp before being released into house arrest, while a third of the CPP leaders nominated to serve in the Zagreb Sabor in 1942 declined the honour. But Maček nullified the effect of his personal stand by publicly advising Croats not to resist the Ustasha government. The attitude of the Catholic clergy was equally ambivalent. With a few honourable exceptions, they mostly took their lead from Cardinal Stepinac, whose 'blood and soil' patriotism prompted him to welcome the proclamation of the Independent State of Croatia in glowing terms. Stepinac is credited with a deepening sense of private unease and with behind-the-scenes interventions that saved many lives, but his public utterances gave no sign of this repentance.[10]

The Slav Muslims suffered war losses totalling 100 000; three-quarters of them lost their lives in Bosnia-Hercegovina, a further 15 000 in Serbia, 4000 each in Montenegro and Macedonia, and 2000 in Croatia. Some historians have spoken of Chetnik genocide against the Muslims, and certainly not just the numbers alone, but the bestiality of the killings (flaying, boiling alive) convey an intensity of ethnic hatred which suggests a will to exterminate the entire Slav Muslim people. Judgement about Mihailović's personal responsibility for war crimes is complicated by the possibility of forgery in the case of a key document,[11] but the scale of the killings is not a matter of dispute. During the course of a single night, 13 February 1943, 8000 women, children and old men were butchered by the Lim-Sandžak Chetnik forces, a deed recorded laconically in the commanders' own reports. Massacres occurred along the entire line of the borders of Bosnia-Hercegovina with Serbia, Montenegro and the Sandžak, and the roll call of place-names is an all too familiar one: Srebrenica, Višegrad, Goražde, Rogatica.

The Ustasha onslaught on the Serbs initiated the cycle of inter-ethnic butchery, but once it took hold causes and effects intermingled. The presence of some Muslims in Ustasha units could be advanced as a pretext for retaliatory killings which drove even more of them into the arms of Pavelić, but the Muslims generally by no means favoured the Ustasha regime. The official revival of Starčević's old claim that the Muslim Slavs represented the purest stream of Croatian nationhood was a sinister compliment, and attempts to absorb the leadership of the Yugoslav Muslim Organization into the government of the NDH were rebuffed. In their struggle for survival, the Muslims did not conform to any dominant pattern of collaboration or resistance. Early in the war, some members of the Muslim clergy protested vigorously against the ill-treatment of Serbs and Jews, as well as defending their own community from the lawlessness and brutality of the regime. By 1943, others were encouraging their young men to enlist in the Muslim SS division then being formed. Individual Muslim leaders were prepared at times to cooperate with the Chetniks against the Ustashas; sometimes Muslim guerrillas were numerically strong enough to fight without allies, yet others chose to join the Partizans.[12]

Neither Chetniks nor Partizans were ever in any position to engage the occupying forces in head-on fighting. The chronological backbone of the Peoples' Liberation Struggle is formed by the seven major Axis offensives against the Partizans. The first two, launched in September 1941 and lasting until February 1942, set a pattern for the rest of the war. Four German divisions and six (later eight) Italian divisions were joined (in November 1941) by Chetnik formations, and together they chased Tito's forces out of Serbia, Montenegro and the Sandžak to a new temporary base in the Foča triangle, where their borders meet Bosnia and Hercegovina. By mid-June 1942, the Partizans were again on the move, in a north-westerly direction, along the line dividing the Italian and German occupation zones of the NDH. It ran from just west of Zagreb, bisecting central Bosnia, to intersect the northern border of Italian-occupied Montenegro. The line placed the main cities of Banja Luka and Sarajevo within the German zone, leaving the Italians to police the remote and vertiginous mountain country separating the western hinterland of Bosnia-Hercegovina from Dalmatia and the sea.

Italian troops were spread thinly in those parts, and the Partizans were reinforced by a flood of recruits fleeing from Ustasha massacres and German reprisals. The 3000 or so fighters who set off on the march from Foča had increased threefold by the time they arrived in north-western Bosnia, at the beginning of November. Tito seized on this breathing space to summon an Anti-fascist Council for the Peoples' Liberation of Yugoslavia (AVNOJ), in the town of Bihać (26–27 November 1942). The Anti-fascist Councils of Croatia and Bosnia-Hercegovina were also founded at this time, the first to be established for the post-war republics.

It was a typical mixture of bluff and ambition. The Partizans were a magnet for the desperate Serbs of the Independent State of Croatia during their march up-country, and they were now also pulling in an increasing number of Muslims, but they hardly amounted to a major military threat. Even if Stalin was deceived by Tito's fanciful accounts of Partizan strength, he was determined to keep things quiet for fear of offending his capitalist allies. Moscow also rejected the suggestion that a provisional Yugoslav government in the form of a Peoples' Committee should be proclaimed, and so AVNOJ presented itself simply as the parliament of a popular resistance movement.

To the extent that the western Allies took much notice of the Balkan theatre of operations during the first year of the war there, their attention was caught by the Chetniks. Mihailović was the accredited military head of the Yugoslav government-in-exile, and hardly anyone had heard of Tito. The Allied invasion of French North Africa in November 1942, and the defeat of Rommel at El Alamein, changed all that. Yugoslavia was suddenly thrust into prominence as a possible choice for a landing to secure the bridgehead of an advance into occupied Europe across the Mediterranean. The Italians increased their presence in Bosnia-Hercegovina to 16 divisions during the autumn of 1942, to add to the Germans' four, initiating a Third Offensive, an extensive sweep through south-eastern Bosnia and Montenegro, in preparation for an attack on the Partizan stronghold around Bihać.

The crucial Fourth Offensive (January–May 1943), which included Chetnik forces in support of six German and eight Italian divisions, almost trapped the Partizans, but their main force of about 20 000 fighters succeeded in breaking out at the battle on the River Neretva in early March. They penetrated the cordon at a point held by Chetniks, and inflicted severe losses on Mihailović's units, pursuing them all the way back to the Foča triangle, only to be cornered in turn by the Italians and Germans, who launched a Fifth Offensive lasting throughout May and June. Faced by overwhelmingly superior firepower, and outnumbered six to one, the Partizans had to beat the same line of retreat as in the previous summer – back to the safety of central Bosnia, to Jajce, the medieval capital. Once more they had to break out of encirclement, this time across the River Sutjeska, taking appalling casualties: the division escorting the sick and wounded was cut to pieces, and total losses were of the order of one-third.

The crossing and re-crossing of the Neretva was a high point of Partizan heroism in a brutal and exhausting war, and all this commotion behind enemy lines attracted the attention of the British, who in April and May parachuted in liaison officers to the Partizans, personally selected for the job by Churchill. Two of them had his private ear, and they gave Tito a glowing testimonial. Whether their reports caused or only served to justify what followed is unclear, but in any event the decision was taken in September to support Tito and Mihailović equally, and in December supplies to the Chetniks were cut off. The reports would presumably have been less enthusiastic had the authors known that, after breaking out across the Neretva, Tito sent his lieutenants to negotiate with the Germans for a free hand in dealing with the Chetniks, and broached the possibility of common action against a landing by Anglo-American forces. The Communists wanted a Soviet victory in the Balkans which would secure their grip on Yugoslavia, even if that meant keeping the Nazis fighting long enough for the Red Army to arrive as saviours.

Allied landings in Sicily and the Italian mainland (July–September 1943) were followed by the capitulation of Italy on 8 September. Large quantities of Italian military equipment fell into the hands of the Partizans, but even this major windfall was less important than the political eclipse of their rivals. Tito felt assured enough of western support to call a second meeting of the Anti-fascist Council for the Peoples' Liberation of Yugoslavia on 29 November 1943 at Jajce, while Churchill, Roosevelt and Stalin were meeting in Teheran. This time, he forestalled any hesitation by his Soviet backers, who were not represented at the meeting of AVNOJ, by proclaiming a Peoples' Committee as the sole legitimate government of Yugoslavia, and by conferring on himself the rank of Marshal of Yugoslavia. Allied recognition and supplies gave a huge boost to recruitment between October and December, when German estimates put the number of Partizans at 110 000.

The Allies' decision to cut off all support for Mihailović has provoked the charge that Churchill and the western Allies cynically abandoned Serbia (and Yugoslavia) to communism, when they might have saved both by continued support for Mihailović.[13] But even after the Italian surrender, a lot of hard fighting remained to be done in order to defeat Hitler, and independent signals' intelligence indicated that the Partizans were doing most of it in a strategically sensitive area – it was important to keep the Germans guessing about the likelihood of a supporting landing in Dalmatia to cut off the Axis rear. The Chetniks in Serbia were potential allies only on their own soil, then still far beyond the reach of the massive Allied assault required to give a popular rising there any hope of success. Furthermore, it was by no means clear who now represented the wishes and interests of Yugoslavia. King Petar's government in London was torn apart by Serb–Croat divisions, particularly as it became obvious that the Chetniks were fighting for a Great Serbia, whereas the federalist stance of the Partizan leaders seemed to offer a genuine chance of unified resistance to the occupying forces.

Whatever the rights and wrongs of this particular argument, it is beyond question that the Allies' switch of support dealt a terrible blow to Mihailović. The Chetniks were still a force to be reckoned with as the war entered its final months. The Partizan presence within Serbia itself was tiny, just 1700 fighters in January 1944, while the Chetniks numbered between 60 000 and 70 000 on active service, and 10 000 of them were fully armed, according to a British liaison officer on the spot.[14] Never a unified movement, the Chetniks fragmented completely when starved of supplies and Allied political backing. Some of their commanders entered into open collaboration with the Axis against the Communists, so confirming the judgement made about them, while many individual fighters either joined the Partizans or melted away into the civilian population to await the end of the war.

Tito had come a long way in a year. At the Teheran conference it was agreed to give the Partizans all possible military support, including commando operations, and the ideological character of the Partizan movement was now no longer a matter for prevarication by Stalin, who only six months earlier had dissolved the Communist International, so as not to give offence which might delay the opening of a second front. On 23 February 1944, a Soviet military mission was parachuted in to the Partizan HQ located in the Bosanski Petrovac area, and in May the Allies forced the resignation of the Yugoslav government in London. It was a political triumph for the Communist Party of Yugoslavia, but the military situation remained perilous. Despite increased Allied airdrops, the Partizans still had their backs to the wall. The Sixth and Seventh Offensives by German, Bulgarian and Chetnik forces, which lasted from November 1943 until the summer of 1944, again drove the Partizans back into western Bosnia, always their last refuge in extremity.

Even there, on 25 May 1944 (Tito's birthday), German paratroopers almost captured the entire Partizan HQ in an attack on Drvar. Tito was wounded in a desperate escape, and flown out to the tiny island of Vis in mid-Adriatic, made safe by Allied air cover. There he met with Ivan Šubašic, briefly Ban of Croatia in 1939, now the new London premier of Yugoslavia. Šubašic was forced to agree on a mixed government of emigres and Communists, though Tito consented only under pressure from Stalin to accept a monarchist state, until a Yugoslav Constituent

Assembly should settle the question. In the meantime, the Party leadership hastened to lay the foundations of the post-war order, beginning with the State Security Service (13 May 1944), the Department for the Defence of the People (OZNa). Three new regional Anti-fascist Councils for Slovenia, Montenegro and Macedonia were added to those already in existence for Croatia and Bosnia-Hercegovina, foretelling the constitutional form of the communist state.

At a meeting with Churchill in Naples on 12 August, Tito assured his host that he had no wish to create a communist Yugoslavia, but a week later he 'levanted' (as Churchill put it) from Vis to Moscow, where he came face-to-face with Stalin for the first time. A momentous deal was struck. The Red Army was now nearing Yugoslavia, with the spearhead of its advance cutting through Romania and Bulgaria. Marshal Tolbukhin would request permission from the National Committee of Liberation to enter Yugoslav territory, and the task of securing Yugoslavia would be left to the Peoples' Liberation Army, strengthened by the addition of two airborne and twelve infantry divisions provisioned and equipped by the USSR. Belgrade was liberated on 20 October 20, after 11 days of bitter street battles. As Soviet forces hurried on in pursuit of the Germans, Tito had a second meeting (1 November) with Šubašic in Belgrade, at which it was agreed that King Petar (who was not consulted) would not be allowed to return to Yugoslavia, pending a referendum on his future, and AVNOJ was recognized as the provisional government until elections for a Constituent Assembly could be held. During 9–12 September, the first session of the Anti-fascist Assembly (not 'Council') for the Peoples' Liberation of Serbia met and immediately entered into an agreement with the five Anti-fascist Councils to form a Democratic Federative Yugoslavia.

Stalin was distinctly worried about the effect of all this on his western allies, and on 9 October a visit by Churchill and Eden to Moscow resulted in the notorious 'percentages agreement', in which the Central and Eastern European states were to be divided into spheres of influence, with Yugoslavia pencilled in as 'fifty-fifty'. At a meeting with Djilas and Kardelj on 22 November (Tito refused to go), Stalin revealed the deal which had been struck, but the leaders of the Yugoslav Party ignored Stalin's intention to restore the balance in favour of the London government. They held all the cards, as Churchill confessed to Šubašic at the beginning of January 1945. OZNa, the State Security Service, headed by the Party's hatchet-man Aleksandar Ranković, was zealously carrying out Tito's instruction to 'strike terror into the bones of those who do not like this kind of Yugoslavia'. The Peoples' Liberation Army, now numbering about 200 000 troops, was reorganized into four regular army corps on 1 January, and at the end of the month a network of trade unions was installed, the characteristic transmission belts of communist power.

It was all over bar the formalities. When Roosevelt, Stalin and Churchill met again at Yalta (4–12 February 1945), it was agreed that the Tito–Šubašic bargain should be honoured by including in government some of the deputies elected to the National Assembly in 1938, but within Yugoslavia the process of securing the Party's grip on power rolled on undisturbed. The Peoples' Liberation Army was renamed the Yugoslav Army on 1 March, and on 7 March the Democratic Federative Yugoslavia received the accolade of Allied recognition, a full two months before the ending of hostilities in Europe.

The consolidation of power was achieved with great speed and disciplined energy by a Party that now counted 140 000 cadres, against a backdrop of continued fighting. The western areas of Yugoslavia, where the Partizans had spent most of the war, were actually the last to be freed. Bulgaria changed sides on 9 September 1944, and Niš fell to the Red Army on 14 October, forcing the Germans to make their final retreat through Kosovo and Bosnia, so that Sarajevo was not liberated until 6 April 1945, four years to the day after the bombing of Belgrade which began the war. On May Day, Yugoslav troops were still fighting in the battle for Trieste, and it was only on 15 May, six days after VE Day, that the remnants of the Wermacht's Army Group 'E', comprising about 300 000 German soldiers, together with Ustasha and Chetnik hangers-on, surrendered to the Yugoslav Fourth Army, after a desperate battle to break through into Austria. Once again Stalin felt obliged to apply the brakes, in order to prevent the Yugoslavs from precipitating a major crisis with his western Allies over Trieste and Austrian Carinthia.

In August, the founding congress of the Peoples' Front of Yugoslavia marked the beginning of the end of party pluralism, though it took a year or so to complete the interment rites.[15] The Peoples' Front was a monolithic umbrella organization encompassing all others, the peacetime guardian (according to Article 1 of its Statute) of the achievements of the Peoples' Liberation Struggle, and Tito was its President. The elections held on 11 September gave 89 per cent of the vote to the Peoples' Front candidate-list, and the Federal Assembly proclaimed a Republic on 29 November (communist Yugoslavia's National Day). The settling of wartime accounts was already in full swing. One estimate of the number killed by the victorious Communists puts the total at 250 000.[16] Even if the alternative figure of 100 000 victims (and then some more)[17] during 1945–6 is nearer to the truth, it is clear that mass terror ruled the country. Tens of thousands also endured forced marches and labour camps, from where they were put to work on reconstruction of the crippled economic infrastructure.

The Communist Party of Yugoslavia was permeated by the Stalin cult, and determined to follow the lead of the socialist fatherland. In March 1946, the State Security Service (UDBa, the successor to OZNa) was established as a federal force under the continuing command of Ranković, who also controlled cadre policy. The Party itself remained shrouded in secrecy: the names of its members and even of most of the leadership were not published until 1948. The Peoples' Front (PF) was an instrument of centralized control which far outclassed the pre-war royalist bureaucracy, using the workplace as the prime site of political mobilization. All those employed in the social sector (1.7 million by the end of 1947) were automatically enrolled in the PF, as were the members of all the institutions of a counterfeit civil society: trade unions, writers' clubs, professional associations, student organizations, sports clubs. In a series of seemingly endless 'actions', people were dragooned into demonstrations, rallies, and work brigades, in the cause of building socialism.

The sentence of death for treason pronounced by a military court on Draža Mihailović (15 August 1946) was inevitable, but the trial of Archbishop Stepinac in October was a combative new departure in church–state relations in Eastern Europe, a warning to all the religious communities of Yugoslavia. The court sent him to prison for 16 years in October 1946, for collaboration (he was amnestied in December 1957, and died in 1960). At around the same time, the young Alija Izetbegović received a two-year prison sentence for his activism in the 'Young Muslims', who were committed to the defence of their cultural and religious traditions in Bosnia. Twelve months on, the Peoples' Front was being purged of subversive elements (the remaining bourgeois democrats and their rump parties), and it was really only a matter of time before 'imperialist traitors' were discovered within the Party itself. Beginning in April 1948, 37 middling Party functionaries, 30 of them Slovenes, were tried and condemned; 11 of them were executed. What gave these trials a particularly macabre tinge was that all of the accused were survivors of Dachau, and they pointed the way to more systematic purges to come.[18]

The Party's claim to legitimacy in the new state was not wholly unfounded, and not everyone found its power intolerable, especially at first. Young idealists (some of them from abroad) joined in the projects for postwar reconstruction. Hardship was universal, but could be ascribed to the huge destruction inflicted by the war, and local initiatives sprang up everywhere, which together with United Nations Relief and

Rehabilitation Administration (UNRRA) aid (the most bountiful in Europe) rapidly brought the restoration of economic activity to something near pre-war levels.[19] The Partizans had to some extent made good their claim to represent all nationalities. Some 46 000 Croats died fighting in their ranks, and there was a Communist-led resistance movement among the Slovenes, who suffered much at the hands of both the Italians and the Germans. The fact remains, however, that neither the Croats nor the Slovenes wanted communism, especially since the 'Red Terror' claimed so many of them as victims: 50 000 Croats and 18 000 Slovenes (including 8000 handed back to Tito by the British) are estimated to have been massacred.[20]

The Serbs did not choose communism either, as the strength of the Chetnik movement demonstrates. The Party was indifferent to the ethnic allegiance of its class enemies, and one source suggests that 60 000 victims were taken from Belgrade alone.[21] Nevertheless, Serb hegemony reasserted itself, initially through the prečani Serbs and Montenegrins who dominated the military and security forces. Serbia did not have its own republican Party organization at the war's end – the foundation of the Slovenian and Croatian 'branches' of the Party in 1937 was an ad hoc response to particular circumstances, as was the creation of a notionally separate Macedonian representation in 1943. At the beginning of May 1945, the Communist Party of Serbia came into formal being and immediately established its place as the most powerful within the federation. This was not just a simple reflection of demographic facts. Belgrade's position as the capital of the new state (Djilas' suggestion to remove the seat of government to Sarajevo was dismissed on the grounds that the city lacked the necessary infrastructure) drew many thousands of Serbs and Montenegrins into the huge federal bureaucracy, creating an avenue of social promotion far less accessible to other nationalities.

Serbs were unwelcome in Kosovo, in whatever uniform. The Party never commanded the support of more than a couple of dozen Albanians during the early years of the war, and Mihailović was equally unsuccessful in recruiting there. And since the Communist Party of Albania (founded in November 1941) was organized and dominated by the Yugoslav leadership, no impetus to national communism could come from that source. The question of an independent Albania could not be aired, and a fortiori the status of Kosovo, because the Yugoslav Party leaders assigned to themselves the pivotal role within a future Balkan communist federation, which would include Albania, Bulgaria and Greece, an idea that was actively encouraged by Stalin.

As a consequence, the Italian surrender provoked the formation of a 'Second League of Prizren' by Kosovar Albanians, fearful that the union of Kosovo and Albania would be undone, and the Germans quickly declared Albania an independent state, within the borders established by Mussolini. The expulsion of Serbs and Montenegrins from Kosovo intensified, and by the spring of 1944 an estimated 40 000 of them had been displaced since 1941. The Kosovar Skenderbeg SS Division, though mostly ineffective as a fighting force, terrorized the Slav inhabitants. There was some belated support for the Partizan movement in the final stages of the war, but most ethnic Albanians in Kosovo (including the Communists among them) looked to Albania as their homeland. As it became clear, in late 1944, that the Communist Party of Yugoslavia would take power, a mass rising in Kosovo required the intervention of the Yugoslav Army and UDBa to put it down, in fighting that lasted well into the summer of 1945.[22]

In contrast to its dismal showing in Kosovo, the Party scored a great success in Macedonia by placing itself at the head of an indigenous partisan movement there and contriving to maintain its control later. The main problem facing the Yugoslav Party was to break the attachment of Macedonian Communists to the Communist Party of Bulgaria. The second meeting of AVNOJ (29 November 1943) set the tone by affirming the separate status of the Macedonian nation within a federative Yugoslavia. Tito's emissary, Svetozar Vukmanović-Tempo, and his Macedonian lieutenant, Lazar Koliševski, were able to capitalize on the growing antipathy towards rule from Sofia, which after March 1942 instigated a policy of centralized control, contradicting initial promises to respect Macedonian autonomy. They skilfully fudged the issue of unification of the three regions of Macedonia – Vardar (Yugoslav), Aegean (Greek) and Pirin (Bulgarian) – and so managed to persuade nationalists that their best chance lay with Yugoslavia, especially in relation to Greece, where civil war broke out in December 1944.

The reason for this delicate manoeuvring was that the tiny Communist Party of Macedonia (800 members in 1943; still only 1450 at the liberation) was in no position to dictate terms. The Anti-fascist Council for the Peoples' Liberation of Macedonia (ASNOM) established on 2 August 1944 (the anniversary of Ilinden in 1903) had as its President the resistance leader Metodi Antonov (nicknamed 'Čento'), who headed a phalanx of Macedonian nationalists, and the Čentoists took up an anti-Serbian position over a number of issues, including a refusal to accept back Serbs who had fled during the war. There was also a marked unwillingness among Macedonians to fight outside their own territory. Units of the Macedonian Partizan brigade mutinied in late November 1944 when ordered to the Srem front, asking instead to be sent to Salonika, the undisputed capital of Macedonia in the eyes of unificationists.

By April 1945, when ASNOM was reconstituted as the Peoples' Assembly of Macedonia, the Communist Party of Yugoslavia had brought the situation under control. Koliševski now headed a republican government saturated by a huge influx of Party members (there were by this time more than 6000 of them), operating through the Macedonian Peoples' Front. Čento lasted until March 1946 as the President of the Assembly, but he was reduced to a figurehead by the bureaucratic machinations of the Communists in the government. He was shortly afterwards sentenced to 11 years' forced labour, and his followers were subjected to arrests and executions – though just how many of them is not known.[23]

In one respect, however, Macedonian nationalism threw up a problem which the Party could not ignore: the question of the status of the Macedonian language. If, as Dr Johnson remarked, languages are the pedigrees of nations, then the Slav inhabitants of Macedonia were by any reasonable linguistic criteria part of the Bulgarian nation. The codification of colloquial Macedonian, approved by ASNOM as the official language of the Macedonian state (ASNOM's phrase), was the work of a Commission for Language and Orthography, whose recommendations were accepted officially on 3 May 1945. The construction and dissemination of a distinctive Macedonian language was the medium through which a sense of Macedonian identity was to be fixed. The dialects chosen as the norm were far more akin to standard Bulgarian than to Serbian, but that was irrelevant to its political uses as the vehicle for the invention of an entire national tradition, in which (as so often in the Balkans) the question of language dominated. The past was systematically falsified to conceal the fact that many prominent 'Macedonians' had supposed themselves to be Bulgarian, and generations of students were taught the pseudo-history of the Macedonian nation. The mass media and education were the key to this process of national acculturation, speaking to people in a language that they came to regard as their Macedonian mother-tongue, even if it was perfectly understood in Sofia.[24]

The Constitution of 31 January 1946 proclaimed a Federative Peoples' Republic of Yugoslavia embodying six constituent republics, each having the right to secede. This right was as illusory as in Stalin's 1936 constitution, on which it was modelled, since the five constituent peoples (Serbs, Croats, Slovenes, Montenegrins and Macedonians) were deemed to have sunk their claims to a separate existence by acceding to the new state through their wartime struggles. There was no attempt to make the boundaries between the republics coincide with the ethnic map. Bosnia-Hercegovina was left intact, and the Sandžak, which arguably should have been attached to the republic, was given to Montenegro. Serbia resumed its traditional role of policing the ethnic Hungarians and the Kosovar Albanians: the Vojvodina and Kosovo-Metohija were subsumed, although with a notionally autonomous status, within the Republic of Serbia. The Srem was divided north–south between Croatia and Serbia, but Croatia's share (which included Vukovar) still contained substantial Serb enclaves, and nothing could be done to separate the large Serb minorities from the Croats in the rest of Croatia.

Establishing the constitutional principle of absolute equality between peoples and republics was the Party's way of wiping the slate clean. The lines drawn around the republics were conceived as essentially administrative divisions, with no thought of giving them any real independence. The problem of nationalism was, for the moment, contained. The essential task now, in the eyes of the Party leaders, was to force the pace of industrialization, to create the material preconditions of a socialist Yugoslavia which would transcend ethnic and national jealousies, already blunted (as they believed) by the common wartime struggle against the Axis. The Five Year Plan adopted on 28 April 1947 (Marshall Aid was rejected in June) set grandiose targets for growth. Wholesale nationalization of the economy the previous December paved the way, including the seizing of all foreign assets. Industrial production was scheduled to increase by a factor of five and agriculture by 150 per cent; 200 major investment projects were planned, together with the doubling of the skilled labour force needed to run them.

The Plan was a Soviet-style blueprint for the construction of socialism, and the Party intended to control all the resources – material, cultural, and political – needed to transform a peasant society into a communist industrial state. Boris Kidrič, the Moscow-trained Slovene member of the Politburo in charge of the Plan, took it as axiomatic that the surplus for investment would have to come from the peasantry, to be realized through the otkup, the forced delivery of grain at fixed prices. The peasants, naturally enough, resisted (apart from anything else, it was what the Germans had been doing until recently), and arrests of 'kulaks' became so widespread as to force the government to declare an amnesty in order to save the 1947 harvest.

One of the earliest decrees (August 1945) expropriated peasant holdings over 25 hectares, and holdings of more than 45 hectares where leasing or hired labour were involved, part of a bundle of measures directed against capitalists and wartime enemies (notably banks, churches, German nationals and collaborators). Half the 1.57 million hectares of expropriated land was distributed to individual peasants – 43 per cent of them landless – in very small parcels averaging 3 hectares, favouring those who had supported the Partizans – it was, in its own way, a repeat of the inter-war colonization programme.[25] The wider propaganda campaign to soothe the peasantry failed completely. Although the hallowed name of 'zadruga' was adopted to try and tempt the peasants into cooperatives which retained an element of private ownership, they stayed away. Rebellions, hundreds of arrests, and the execution of a number of ringleaders was all the Party had to show for its efforts, when the severe drought of 1950 brought the collectivization drive to an end.[26]

For the moment, the Party was disinclined to force the issue. Communist rule in Eastern Europe was by no means secure during 1946–7. Yugoslavia was reliant on UNRRA assistance to rebuild the economy, and trade links with the West remained too valuable to jeopardize. Among the Party leadership, the question of the correct line on the peasant question led to serious arguments – after all, Lenin had sponsored the New Economic Policy. Andrija Hebrang, the dynamic leader of the Croatian Liberation Movement moved sideways by Tito at the end of the war for nationalist leanings, urged a policy of gradualism from his powerful position as chairman of the Economic Council until replaced by Kidrič, and there were others of the same mind. There were also problems of trade relations with the USSR. The Yugoslavs could not understand why two joint ventures signed in 1946 were implemented to their great disadvantage, and they refused further cooperation. Stalin was soothing: when the Five Year Plan was scheduled to come into force; he offered investment credits (never paid), a gesture which confirmed the Yugoslavs' readiness to believe that these problems were the fault of the Emperor's servants.

In other respects, relations with the Kremlin seemed to be blossoming. In September 1947, the Cominform was founded, nominally a forum for international cooperation between seven Communist parties of equal rank (Hungary, Czechoslovakia, Romania, Bulgaria, Yugoslavia, France and Italy), but intended by Stalin to replace the Comintern as an instrument of Soviet foreign policy. Zhdanov set the tone of the inaugural meeting with a keynote address about the division of the world into two power blocs and the threat from western imperialism. Kardelj and Djilas represented the Communist Party of Yugoslavia, and Belgrade was selected as the centre for the publication of the Cominform's in-house periodical, *For Lasting Peace and Peoples' Democracy*. All of this confirmed the Yugoslavs' view of themselves as first among equals in Eastern Europe, and Stalin's favoured allies.

Stalin was displeased by their presumption, and the Soviet-Cominform presence in Yugoslavia became a cover for espionage by Beria's MVD (Ministry of Internal Affairs). Although Stalin feigned shock when the Yugoslavs complained, Tito's regional ambitions had no place in Moscow's plan for the future of the Balkans. It was assumed in Belgrade that Yugoslavia would swallow Albania (this was the advice Stalin gave to Djilas on one occasion),[27] and Tito's plans also included the incorporation of Bulgaria as a constituent republic of Yugoslavia, together with a united Macedonia, to form a Balkan communist federation. Tito did not seek Moscow's prior approval when he reached agreement with the Bulgarian leader Georgi Dimitrov to begin the process of uniting Pirin and Vardar Macedonia (August 1947), and immediately sent in teachers and publicists from Skopje to promote the Macedonian language. Dimitrov had no intention of allowing Bulgaria to become a seventh republic under the control of Belgrade, but he had no objections to his country playing a major role in a South Slav federation that encompassed a unified Macedonia, that is, including its Aegean portion.

Stalin wanted quiet in the Balkans. The Americans were back in Europe with the Marshall Plan and Truman's promise to defend Greece and Turkey, so that Yugoslavia's active support of the Greek Communist Party in the civil war was becoming positively dangerous. In February 1948, at a meeting in Moscow, Stalin demanded that Yugoslavia and Bulgaria should form a federation on his terms. Isolated (even within his own Party) by nationalist opposition to his deal with Tito over Pirin Macedonia, Dimitrov capitulated, but the Yugoslavs (Kardelj and Djilas again) refused. Meeting on 1 March, the CPY Central Committee made this decision known to Stalin, who recalled all Soviet military and civilian advisers from Yugoslavia on 18 March. Two days later, France, Britain and the US decided the fate of Trieste unilaterally by assigning the city to Italy, without any protest from the USSR. On 27 March, the Soviet Central Committee sent a letter to their Yugoslav counterparts, accusing the CPY of anti-Soviet propaganda (Trotsky's name was mentioned in this connection), and the letter was copied to all the members of the Cominform.

Charge and counter-charge flew back and forth for three months. The Yugoslavs refused to submit to the adjudication of the Cominform, and repudiated the Soviet position entirely. Hebrang and Sreten Žujovic, a Serb in the Politburo, wanted the two sides to talk in Belgrade, but were expelled from the Central Committee in mid-April for having allegedly communicated secretly with the Soviet ambassador. The deadlock could not be broken. On 20 May, the Yugoslavs reiterated their refusal to attend a meeting of the Comintorm and instead published in the press their intention to call a Party Congress, the first since coming to power. On 3 June, the government had to raise an internal loan of 3.5 billion dinars (slogan: 'Truth Will Conquer') in order to stave off bankruptcy. There was an atmosphere of real emergency as more than 2000 delegates gathered in Belgrade (21 June) for the opening of the Fifth Congress of the Party, the first since Dresden in 1928.

6
The Long March of Revisionism

On 28 June 1948, the Cominform states issued a Resolution in Bucharest expelling the Communist Party of Yugoslavia. Instigated by Stalin and Molotov, the attack was timed to disrupt the final stages of the Fifth Congress, and bring Tito to heel by calling on rank-and-file members to put an end to the 'Turkish-terroristic regime' of their leaders. The political map of Eastern Europe was being redrawn, though this was not yet clear even to the principals in the drama. The Party continued to acclaim the Soviet Union as the leader of the people's democracies[1] in the struggle against capitalist imperialism. Compliments were lavished on Stalin personally, to whom Congress sent fulsome comradely greetings. For more than a year the CPY lived in limbo, ostracized by the socialist camp but hoping for a return to normality. Stalin was unrelenting. On 29 September 1949, he revoked the treaty of friendship and cooperation between Yugoslavia and the USSR, and it was clear that he meant business. In secret session, the Federal Assembly declared a state of national emergency and prepared to resist invasion.

Inside a month, on 25 October, Yugoslavia was elected to a seat on the Security Council at the United Nations, after Kardelj had put the question of Yugoslav–Soviet relations before the General Assembly, which gave full support to the Yugoslav position. The break with the Kremlin was completed by a second Cominform Resolution, issued in Budapest in November, couched in all the deranged rhetoric of Stalinist vilification. The text of the Resolution compared the 'Tito–Ranković clique' to Hitler, and condemned the Party elite as 'spies', 'murderers' and 'enemies of the Yugoslav people' for having completed the transition from bourgeois nationalism to fascism. The show trials of leaders in

Albania, Hungary and Bulgaria, where Deputy Prime Minister Kostov was executed on charges of 'Titoism', made it plain to the Yugoslav leaders that their only choice was between resistance and liquidation.

Not surprisingly, they chose resistance; surprisingly, it succeeded. Stalin blundered because he judged the CPY by the standards of his own emasculated Bolshevik party machine. The Fifth Congress still represented the armed peoples of wartime. Nearly half of all Party members were peasants, and a third were workers. The delegates to Congress were drawn overwhelmingly from this mass base, and more than half of them were veterans of 1941, while most of the remainder had been active in the ranks of the Partizans. The Party hierarchy stood firm, and set about consolidating their control. UDBa unleashed a ruthless cull of the political bureaucracy. Out of a total Party membership of half a million, some 60 000 were expelled and 12 000–13 000 imprisoned, for alleged Cominformist leanings.[2] More than 200 000 state functionaries were removed or transferred from their posts, half of them during 1950 alone. The camps on the notorious Goli Otok ('Barren Island') were filled with victims of the purges. The crisis was all the more threatening because Cominformist sympathies were strong in the military, particularly in the Soviet-trained air force. Tito won his battle against Stalin, but it took a Stalinist purge to do it, and the struggle left its repressive mark on Yugoslav society for decades.

In January 1949, the Party decreed the speeding-up of the collectivization of agriculture. This was not simply, perhaps not even primarily, a gesture to appease Moscow. The leadership was determined to squeeze out of the peasantry the resources needed for survival, and to go it alone, but it was an impossible ambition. By the end of 1947, Yugoslavia was exchanging half of all exports and imports with the Soviet Union. The collapse of the Five Year Plan combined with a renewed military build-up led to a protracted period of war communism. Pay differentials all but disappeared and rationing was introduced to ensure an adequate distribution of food to the population, regulated according to the physical requirements of work. As the crisis dragged on, the Party was compelled to move towards accommodation with the capitalist powers. Washington's policy of Soviet containment was by 1950 clearly formulated, and Yugoslavia fitted perfectly into it. Military and economic agreements were signed with the US, the first step in a bilateral relationship which began with bank loans, and extended through food aid to an agreement (in November 1951) on military cooperation. During the same year, hostilities with Austria and Germany were at last formally terminated, and a three-power conference in

London (the US, the UK and France) awarded Yugoslavia a US$500 million grant-in-aid, which was crucial in kick-starting the crippled economy. By 1955, Yugoslavia had received US$1.187 billion from the United States, distributed equally between economic and military aid, and another injection of US$420 million from UNRRA.[3]

Internally, there was no real move toward liberalization, but the Party did conclude a tacit truce with peasants and workers. The collectivization drive was allowed to fall into abeyance (it was not formally abandoned until 1953), and the peasants were also relieved of part of the burden of forced sales of their produce at state-controlled prices. The control of the industrial labour force was de-militarized, and socialist honorifics such as 'shockworker', and 'hero of socialist labour' disappeared. Repressive employment laws were abandoned, like the one that empowered commissions to suspend notices given by workers and to levy fines for ignoring prescribed quitting procedures. As the economy began slowly to improve, the government took care to build up a network of egalitarian welfare measures that spread the benefits throughout the social sector (peasants were excluded). In 1952, for example, child allowances were increased by a factor of 14 – as late as 1956, a skilled worker with one child still got a quarter of his income from this source.

The Sixth Congress, held on schedule in November 1952, marked the end of the first phase of international realignment. The Party had won itself some breathing space which was used to celebrate a new version of official marxism based on the management of industry by workers. According to Djilas, the idea germinated while he was re-reading *Capital*, was taken up in a half-hour discussion in a parked car with Kardelj and Kidrič, and was then put to Tito, who immediately grasped its significance. Within the space of two months the first workers' council was installed, on 31 December 1949, at a cement factory near Split.[4] It is likely that Djilas seriously misjudged the enthusiasm of his colleagues for doctrinal niceties, but the slogan 'Factories to the workers' was undoubtedly a convenient ideological stick with which to beat Stalin. On 27 June 1950, Tito personally sponsored the Basic Law on Workers' Councils in the Federal Assembly, which was approved unanimously, amid tumultuous applause. The Assembly then passed a resolution urging that the withering away of the state should begin at once. Marx would have enjoyed that.

The charge against Stalin was 'bureaucratism'. In *Socialist Democracy*, published to coincide with the Sixth Congress, Kardelj noted, in an unmistakable echo of Trotsky, that the 'executive apparatus' in the USSR had produced an 'independent bureaucratic caste with special social interests' in opposition to the interests of the working masses. Yugoslav socialist democracy, by contrast, rested on the principle of 'direct democracy' (neposredna demokratija), embodied in workers' councils. Freed from the dead hand of bureaucracy, productivity would soar, carrying the proletariat along the road towards a communist society governed by associated producers, as envisaged by the founders of scientific socialism. Congress voted to re-style itself the 'League of Communists of Yugoslavia', reviving a name redolent of the authority of Marx and Engels, and the People's Front was replaced by the Socialist Alliance of Working People of Yugoslavia, which abandoned the tactics of mass political mobilization that dominated political and social life in the early post-war years.

The doctrine of 'self-governing socialism' became the orthodox discourse of political life under Titoism,[5] but the problem remained of translating it into a programme of economic and political reforms for which there was no historical precedent, and only sparse hints in the Marxist-Leninist theoretical canon. Lenin's occasional remarks about the relationship between the Bolsheviks and the soviets in the USSR, and Marx's writings on the Paris Commune, were ammunition enough for the attack upon Stalin, but they hardly amounted to a blueprint for monoparty pluralism in practice. UDBa, fresh from its purges of Cominformists, maintained a vigilant watch for signs of nationalist or liberal deviations. As Kardelj warned, more democracy did not mean more parties.

The Party was in fact by now thoroughly bureaucratized, saturated by the interests and ethos of officialdom. In spite of the purges, between 1948 and 1952 membership grew from 500 000 to 750 000. The new recruits were overwhelmingly drawn from the ranks of the state administration, with a leavening of the intelligentsia, while the proportion of peasants plummeted from about a half to a quarter. With collectivization off the agenda, the Party no longer needed a major presence in the countryside. 'Primitive communism' was out of fashion, the revolution was complete. The place of the peasant activists (some of whom in fact 'disappeared' from the statistics through upward mobility) was taken by those social groups having an interest in stability and gradualism within the new order. The new Party man in authority was typically a non-combatant who joined after the war.[6]

The work of the Sixth Congress was given institutional shape by the new Constitution of January 1953, which proclaimed the communes as the basic political and administrative unit of self-governing socialism. The communal assemblies incorporated a bicameral system: a political chamber elected by universal suffrage, and a chamber of producers composed of representatives of the workers' councils. The elevation of the commune to the place of honour was another calculated appeal to the untainted sources of libertarian Marxism. It was also the means by which 'direct democracy' was tamed and made safe. Beyond the level of the communes, elections were in fact indirect. Delegates to the communal assemblies decided who should sit in the republican assemblies, which in their turn elected representatives to the Federal Assembly. Through its control of elections and candidate lists, the central Party machine operated as gatekeeper to all positions of authority, at every level of society – even the workers' councils, Djilas recalls, were packed with UDBa nominees.

The Party also had to ensure that the new decentralized structure of administration remained obedient to central authority. Conflicts between rival Communist bosses posed a far greater threat than a disaffected but powerless citizenry.[7] The creation of a large number of communes (well over 400 of them) was a way of dispersing power among a plethora of local elites, but the communes were too small to constitute viable units of planning. Inevitably, the large municipal authorities running the major towns and cities, and the governments of the republics, would tend to accumulate any coordinating functions shed by the federal bureaucracy. The danger was that disputes between regions and republics might open the door to nationalism. To forestall trouble, the constitutional powers of the Chamber of Nationalities were drastically lopped. During its existence as a constituent body within the Federal Assembly, the Chamber of Nationalities had never shown any signs of life; now that there was a chance that it might be used for airing disputes in public, it lost most of its formal authority.

There was a revealing about-turn in the management of the economy. As part of the constitutional settlement, nearly half the funds for investment in new industry were transferred from the federation to the republics. Within months this decision was rescinded, and plans to reform the banking system along market lines were shelved indefinitely. Instead, a system of fiscal planning was adopted, which set the ratio between personal consumption and savings using a formula culled from Marx's *Critique of the Gotha Programme*. This formula was then applied at every level of accounting, including the individual enterprises, so that the federal administration determined the pattern of national expenditure right down to the last dinar, administered through a General Investment Fund.[8]

The intention was to reduce the republican governments to adminis-
trators of centrally determined policies. Feuding between Serbs and
Croats continued to simmer. On the eve of the Sixth Congress, Miroslav
Krleža, a distinguished Croatian novelist, addressed the Writers' Union
on the need to free the arts from the paralysis of socialist realism. Krleža,
who had a close if sometimes stormy relationship with Tito, was
prominent in the 'Croatian' wing of the Party between the wars, and the
apparatchiki feared the spread of cultural nationalism among intellectuals and youth. The July 1953 issue of the Party journal *Komunist* carried
a heavy warning against nationalist deviations within the ranks. It was
no coincidence that the Party was having trouble with the Catholic
hierarchy in Croatia, and in November, clear against the trend of foreign
policy, the Yugoslav government broke off relations with the Vatican.

Conflicts within the political bureaucracy came to a head when Djilas,
one of the 'gang of four' at the apex of power, turned the attack upon
Stalin against his own comrades. In a series of articles published in the
Party daily *Borba* between October 1953 and January 1954, Djilas
advanced the ideas that were to become the basis of his book *The New
Class*. Communist monopoly of political power, he argued, created a
ruling bureaucracy, neither capitalist nor socialist in character, but
embodying elements of both: a new social formation, 'state capitalism',
was emerging. The conclusion Djilas drew from his analysis was that the
dogmatism and conservatism of the bureaucracy could be broken only
by allowing the formation of independent workers' political associations. His colleagues were aghast at this heresy, not least because they
had helped to propagate it. A plenary meeting of the Central Committee
(16–17 January 1954) expelled Djilas from the Party. Kardelj, who gave
the keynote speech derided his writings as a 'mish-mash of anarchism
and bourgeois-liberal forms' which objectively entailed the restoration
of capitalism.

Although a majority of the Central Committee refused to adopt the
language of some hard-liners, who spoke of Djilas as 'an enemy of the
people', the reform process took a severe knock. The USSR was making
overtures of friendship, and Soviet–Yugoslav rapprochement required a
demonstration that Yugoslav revisionism had strict limits. Tito therefore
decided on a 'final accounting' with liberal-bourgeois tendencies, a
subject which was the gist of his speech to the first session of the Federal
Assembly elected under the new constitutional arrangements, on 29
January 1954. The key to the delicate balance of forces within the CPY
was the benevolent neutrality of the Kremlin. Unless normal relations
could be restored with the USSR, Yugoslavia would be pushed further

into the arms of the capitalist states, which nobody in the Party wanted. The death of Stalin created a climate of compromise, but it took a good two years of careful manoeuvring by both sides to heal the breach. By the middle of 1954 the Executive Committee of the League of Communists pronounced itself satisfied that the Soviet Union had come to respect the Yugoslav path to socialism, but reserved its position on top-level talks, and unanimously rejected the suggestion that Yugoslavia should rejoin the Cominform. Despite this rebuff, trade with the USSR was resumed, and in June 1955 Khrushchev and Bulganin arrived in Belgrade to cement a renewed friendship.

The Bolsheviks' Twentieth Congress (February 1956) seemed to confirm that all was now well. The sensational attack on Stalin in Khrushchev's secret speech, the formal acknowledgement of different roads to socialism, and the posthumous rehabilitation of many Yugoslav Communists, persuaded the leadership that an accommodation might be reached, and this impression was confirmed when in April the Cominform was dissolved, so that in June Tito travelled to Moscow to sign a joint statement which affirmed the need to respect the richness of forms which the building of socialism might take. Diversity, the Moscow Declaration said, was a source of strength to the international communist movement, and promised that relations between the two parties would be conducted on the basis of comradely reciprocity between free and equal partners.

The Yugoslav Party leadership was therefore in no particular hurry to force the pace of change at home, and it was not until September 1955 that the substantive legislation devolving authority to the communes was passed. It took the appearance of Red Army tanks on the streets of Budapest to put the steam back into revisionism. Once more confronted by Soviet imperialism, official reaction in Belgrade to the invasion of Hungary was characteristically hair-splitting. The Party condemned the first intervention of Soviet troops to put down a popular rising against the Rakosi regime; on the other hand, the second, undertaken at the request of the 'legitimate' Hungarian government, was adjudged justified by the need to avert a civil war fomented by Horthyists and the west. The response precisely reflected the Party's own delicate position. The right of communist governments to find their own path to socialism did not include the right of their peoples to choose not to go down it.

This time Yugoslavia was better prepared to meet the threat from Moscow. Buttressed by western aid, the economy was in relatively good shape, and for some time Yugoslav diplomacy had been moving closer to the Third World. This policy was consolidated when, in June 1956,

Tito, Nasser and Nehru signed a declaration on Tito's private Adriatic island resort of Brioni. They condemned the division of the world into competing power-blocs, calling for disarmament and for the channelling of economic assistance to the underdeveloped nations through the United Nations. The next year, Yugoslavia staged the First Self-Management Congress, a huge political showpiece attended by more than 2000 delegates representing some 6000 workers' councils, and by over 100 representatives of workers' organizations in 21 different countries. The theme of the Congress was economic reform, and it was another affirmation of Yugoslavia's independence. Attempts by the USSR to repair the damage caused by the invasion of Hungary cut little ice. Kardelj and Ranković travelled to Moscow in November 1957 to take part in the fortieth anniversary celebrations of the October Revolution, but they refused to sign the Twelve-Party Declaration produced by the other socialist states at the conclusion of the proceedings, which called for a restoration of ideological unity. The Soviet Union promptly revoked an agreement to build an aluminum plant in Yugoslavia, and reduced trade links.

The reply of the League of Communists was the adoption of the historic Programme of the Seventh Congress, held in April 1958, two years behind schedule.[9] The Party gathered in Slovenia, the most westernized of the republics, to set out in comprehensive form the principles of self-governing socialism. Lenin was identified as the last true heir of revolutionary communism – Congress particularly approved his dictum that Marxism was not a 'finished and inviolable' body of doctrine. All the democratic elements of the Leninist vision were reasserted, all the rest left out. As the vanguard of the proletariat, the Party must defend and consolidate the proletarian revolution, but it must simultaneously embody the burgeoning socialist consciousness of the masses. The withering-away of state power could not be made to wait upon economic development or the education of the masses by the Party. On the contrary, only the Party and people together could construct the moral and material basis of socialism. The function of the Party was not to exercise power on behalf of the working class (Stalin's error), but to nurture the forms of direct democracy appropriate to a self-governing society.

The Programme went out of its way to stress that 'Yugoslavism' did not represent an attack on national languages and cultures within the federation, but rather was a simple acknowledgement of a Yugoslav identity emerging alongside existing national allegiances. In an updated version of his pre-war (1937) book on the Slovenian national question,

Kardelj distinguished between bourgeois nationalism and the nationalism of the phase of socialist transition, which he described as the 'democratic consciousness' of historically differentiated peoples. By making the distinction, Kardelj rejected the conception of nationalism as nothing but an expression of capitalist social relationships, and the timing of the argument is the key to understanding the form it took. Yugoslavia was under strong Soviet pressure to rejoin the socialist international fraternity, and the idea of a 'Yugoslav socialist nation' was essential to the argument in favour of independent paths to socialism. By the same reasoning, only reactionary nationalism could exist inside the borders of Yugoslavia. Kardelj was careful to deny that the republics had any 'progressive' economic function: they could not constitute a 'nation', which he defined as the political form in which the development of the capitalist productive forces took place. With the strengthening of self-governing socialism, bourgeois national antagonisms were being progressively transcended by an attachment to 'Yugoslav socialist consciousness'.

The claim had no basis in reality. The hardening of the Party line after the dismissal of Djilas was followed by the first of a series of secret trials of Croatian students for nationalist activities. The leadership began to push the idea of 'Yugoslavism' harder and established a Council of Cultural-Educational Associations to coordinate cooperation between the nationalities at the federal level. The Party by this means engineered an agreement signed in Novi Sad (December 1954), in which representatives of these associations from Serbia and Croatia declared that Serbian and Croatian were one language. This attempt to promote cultural integration through committees spread alarm, and did nothing at all for 'brotherhood and unity'. In Kosovo, Ranković ruled with an iron hand. In July 1956, UDBa put on trial nine men on trumped-up charges of spying for Albania, apparently with the real motive of discrediting the Communist leadership in the province. In May 1959, 2000 Croatian students took to the streets of Zagreb in a demonstration of nationalist solidarity, and national sensitivities were prickly everywhere.[10]

In the face of mounting resistance, the notion of 'Yugoslavism' was quietly laid to rest – it was indispensable in foreign affairs, but too burdened with historical memories of Serbian centralism for domestic consumption. This was a momentous shift in policy. A sign of the new realism was that the Census of 1961 recognized 'ethnic Muslims' as a national minority (narodnost) for the first time. This move was to defuse tensions in Bosnia – previously the Muslims had overwhelmingly chosen to record themselves as 'Yugoslavs' by default, so as to avoid identification with either Serbs or Croats. The concession was an indication of a weakening of centralism. The Party leaders, Tito foremost among them, continued to voice a continuous stream of nagging about the spread of national chauvinism, especially among young people, speaking ominously of 'unhealthy', and 'anti-socialist' elements at work in society. However, the fact was that the Party was too disunited to contemplate a major crackdown on nationalism, because the leadership was split over the question of economic reform.

At the time of the Seventh Congress, Yugoslavia was enjoying a period of sustained economic growth. Well over a million new jobs were created in the social sector during the years 1952–60, so that (except for a brief hiccup in 1955) employment rose by between 6 per cent and 11 per cent annually. For the first time in the history of the Yugoslav state, the problem of rural over-population was being overcome. Industry, however, remained inefficient: while employment increased on average by 7 per cent every year between 1952 and 1961, labour productivity rose by only 2.6 per cent annually. There was no market in producer goods, nor in social capital, nor in labour, which was paid for on a more or less uniform basis of skills, at rates determined by the state authorities. The fixed and working capital of enterprises remained state property, and – because it treated the costs of production as given – the system did nothing to reward economies in the use of resources. This decentralized-administered form of economic management also encouraged the building of 'political' factories, as regional Party bosses vied with each other for power.

International developments were crucial in shaping the course of economic reform. Relations with the socialist states continued changeable, subject to sudden freezes. In September 1960, Tito made a high-profile visit to the United Nations fifteenth anniversary celebrations (he stayed for a whole fortnight), rubbing shoulders with world leaders. He was immensely influential within the Non-Aligned Movement at the UN, and as a consequence the League of Communists of Yugoslavia was the only Communist party in the world not invited to a conference of leaders, representing 81 countries, held in Moscow in December. China, ideologically still aligned with the USSR, was a vitriolic critic of Yugoslav revisionism. Tito repudiated the charge, made at the conference, that Yugoslavia had deserted the world socialist movement, and named the Chinese as the instigators of the slander.

The snub to Yugoslavia appears to have swung the balance suddenly in favour of an ambitious reform programme. The recession which set in at the turn of the decade forced the Party to confront the problem of injecting elements of the market into the system. Hurriedly adopted only a week before the Moscow conference took place, the Social Plan for 1961–5 envisaged the promotion of Yugoslavia from an underdeveloped to a medium-developed industrial state. This was to be based on an average annual increase in labour productivity of 7 per cent, which would secure a 50 per cent rise in personal consumption, and fund a generous extension of expenditure on schooling, housing, health and welfare. Another key target was the balancing of exports and imports, in the context of a 75 per cent growth in the volume of trade. Yugoslavia accordingly applied for associate membership of GATT, and obtained promises of short-term credits to the tune of US$275 million to cover existing deficits for western imports. A condition of both was a devaluation of the dinar and the cutting of the tariffs protecting Yugoslav industry.

The success of the Plan depended on making enterprises more efficient, and able to compete in world markets. Collectives acquired greater control over the distribution of their net income, and they were free to regulate matters such as hiring and firing, labour discipline and the setting of pay schedules. Under the system introduced in 1952, the wages' fund of the enterprises was fixed according to a complicated framework of pay tariffs agreed between the firm and the state authorities, based upon job evaluation and skills. Any increase in incomes above this level attracted a steeply rising scale of tax. In 1961, therefore, pay tariffs were formally abandoned. Important though these changes were in principle, their effects were muffled by the continued grip of the state authorities on prices, and by the fact that the proportion of income retained by the enterprises remained unchanged, at about 40 per cent. Even so, this limited reform produced a rapid growth in inequalities which disadvantaged the backward areas of the federation. The government responded with a levy on 'windfall income'. Firms able to take advantage of the new trading conditions were required to contribute to the federal coffers a sum equal to 30 per cent of their profits, accompanied by a promise that this penal tax on high productivity would be removed when less profitable enterprises had adjusted to reform.

There was anxiety, too, about the fact that responsibility for drawing up pay schedules now rested with the self-management organs in enterprises. The question was whether manual workers in low-profit firms could exert enough influence on the workers' councils to defend their living standards; and even if they succeeded, there was the danger that the collectives might swallow up all the enterprise income in wages, leaving nothing for reinvestment. Within 18 months of its inception the Plan had been effectively abandoned. Wages were frozen, and the process of creating income differentials between skills, which was such a marked feature of the old pay tariffs, was put into sharp reverse. Between 1962 and 1965, the Party and trade unions mounted a major campaign to intervene in the distribution of enterprise income, and to stem the zeal of some collectives for shedding labour, which was causing a sharp rise in unemployment, and led to the first wave of emigrants to find work abroad, mainly in West Germany.

Such dithering only succeeded in creating the worst of both worlds. Competitive enterprises forged ahead, generating expectations of higher standards of living which were continually dashed by bureaucratic interference designed to soften the impact of market forces on the economy as a whole. At the same time, ailing firms raised their wage rates in line with others, knowing that they would invariably be bailed out by local elites fighting for the survival of their 'own' industry and commerce. In this they were greatly helped by another innovation of the Plan, which transferred responsibility for allocating short-term loans from the three state banks in Belgrade to a network of communal banks. This move, intended to ensure the more rational allocation of resources by bringing lenders and borrowers together at the local level, backfired badly. The banks were instantly absorbed into the existing communal elite structures, and used to fund local growth. The volume of credit doubled in two years, adding to the inflation caused by dearer imports resulting from the devaluation of the dinar. Industrial prices rose sharply, and even more so the cost of living.[11]

The problem for Party unity was that Serbia was the main agent and beneficiary of the decentralized-administered system of economic management. All the republics, except Serbia and Montenegro, were net contributors to the federal budget, with Slovenia and Croatia accounting for more than half the total. Serbia gained massively, contributing 29 per cent, but taking well over two-thirds of receipts. In terms of investment, Bosnia and Macedonia fared quite well, but again Serbia stood out, receiving over 40 per cent of the federal purse. Croatia and Slovenia maintained rates of return on investment two to three times higher than the rest, and they complained that they were financing an economically irrational and wasteful policy of equalization, which in fact favoured Serbia, not the most backward regions of the federation.

Friction was exacerbated by the underlying question of who was footing the bill for the federal bureaucracy at the centre of this redistributive web, and for the Yugoslav People's Army (YPA), which probably consumed a higher proportion of national wealth than any country in the world, as western subventions dried up. Serbs were disproportionately represented in the federal state apparatus, they made up at least two-thirds of the YPA officer corps, and a similar proportion of the State Security Service (UDBa). Obviously, proposals for economic reform could not be disentangled from the nationalities' question and raised prickly issues about the control of central institutions. Reform also entailed accepting the risks of economic and political penetration by capitalist states, the source of the advanced technology and export markets needed to sustain high-productivity growth.

The hard-liners within the Party therefore opposed any increase in the power of the collectives to control investment decisions. It was one thing to concede a measure of budgetary autonomy to local elites appointed and controlled by the central Party machine, quite another to give ground to managerialism, or betray any weakness in the face of demands to strengthen the powers of the republics at the expense of the federal administration. Opposition to reform crystallized around the commanding figure of Aleksandar Ranković, People's Hero of the Liberation Struggle, and Tito's heir-apparent. Ranković combined his republican power-base in the Serbian League of Communists with the offices of chief of UDBa and Organization Secretary of the central Party apparatus. He also controlled the Foreign Ministry, through his power of appointment of ambassadors, and by means of an extensive network of personal supporters, underpinned by UDBa surveillance methods. His aim was to maintain the centralized power of the Party, organized around Serbia as the centre of gravity of the Yugoslav federation.

Confrontation broke out in March 1962 under cover of a routine meeting of the Central Committee held in Split, in a parallel secret session later described by Tito as a broadened sitting of the Executive Committee, though no documents exist recording this unofficial 'plenum'. Everyone present, of course, knew about the illegal activities of the secret police – their objection was that they themselves had been put under surveillance. (It emerged that Kardelj, who was aware that his phone had been bugged, assumed this had been done on Tito's orders, a telling comment on the state of comradely relations within the Party elite.) Discounting the more sensational later accounts of what went on at this meeting, two things are as certain as they can be: the Serbs came under fierce attack from the others present (especially the Macedonians); and Ranković was forced to back down.[12]

Since the history of the period remains largely conjectural, it is difficult to say how the balance of forces between reform and reaction lay at any particular moment, but the battle-lines within the Party ran between the 'old guard' and the technocrats. At this time, about 40 per cent of the League of Communists held membership dating from before the Sixth Congress. For most of these Party veterans, reform represented a threat to careers based on an understanding of the rules of the game operating in a system grounded in centralized political patronage. They were Ranković's natural constituents: industrial managers in declining branches of the economy, typically skilled workers by origin, the army of middling officialdom threatened by the dismantling of the federal administration, and local Party officials, alarmed that attempts to democratize the League of Communists would destroy personal networks of influence built up through years of uncontested office.

For their part, the reformers looked to mobilize the support of the Communist technocracy. The years following the Seventh Congress saw the wholesale social promotion of the rising generation of younger, professionally trained Party members to important positions in the economy and the administrative bureaucracies. Support for economic reform was strongest among trade union and managerial circles in advanced industry, and these groups made it their policy to push their nominees into the economic chambers of the elected assemblies, where they found it easier to bring their influence to bear than within the Party machine itself. Interestingly, Ranković seems to have conducted his campaign through the Executive Committee of the Serbian League of Communists, which was packed with his own cronies, avoiding confrontation in the Central Committee where the professional and entrepreneurial elite was better represented.[13]

However, the contest within the Party can only be partially understood as one between ideologues and technocrats, first and second generations of leaders. The Titoists also had to play the dangerous game of altering the balance of power between the republics. Nationalist rivalries were embedded in the system. Any shift towards the market would inevitably alter the balance of power within the federation in favour of Slovenia and Croatia. On the other hand, Ranković's dogged policy of the 'firm hand' was equally spiked with difficulties. The underdeveloped republics and regions had an interest in the possible economic benefits of centralism, but a monolithic, authoritarian League of Communists was perceived as a vehicle of Serbian domination within federal institutions. Meanwhile, an unreformed economy left untouched the fundamental problem of regenerating the industrialization drive. Both sides tried to keep their disagreements under wraps, and the struggle ran its protracted course amid deafening official silence, but public rumour ran riot.

In April 1963 another new Constitution announced the transition of Yugoslavia from 'People's' to a 'Socialist' republic. The Preamble spoke of the 'sovereign rights' of the working people and the nationalities making up the Federal Socialist Republic of Yugoslavia, exercised through both federal and republican institutions, and protected by a newly established Constitutional Court. This complicated formula denied sovereignty to the republics as territorial entities, whilst opening the door to a degree of polycentrism in the governance of the federation, by allowing them to enter into agreements on specified social and economic questions without federal interference. There was much talk, too, of 'the working class organized as the state', by bringing 'working people' into the assembly system, and introducing new rules on the rotation of offices. Like all Communist constitutions, this one had a mainly propaganda function – the management of the economy was left untouched – but it was an important moment in the battle for control of the Party.

The constitution conferred the new office of Vice-President of the Republic on Kardelj. He was its main author, and the honour was a sign of Ranković's increasing isolation within the elite. Relations between Ranković and Kardelj had been strained for years – a persistent rumour circulated that Kardelj blamed his colleague for failing to prevent an attempt on his life in 1959. Kardelj favoured decentralization, and his preferment was a clear public indication that Tito was leaning towards economic reform. The international situation was delicately poised. The USSR was sliding towards the neo-Stalinism of the Brezhnev era. Tito had no wish to offend Moscow, for reasons of both strategy and ideological conviction, but nor could he countenance being pushed into siding with the hard-liners, and so becoming a hostage to the Kremlin – one of the charges later made against Ranković was that he had entered into secret negotiations with the USSR. Personalities must have played an important part. Unlike the grey, shadowy leaders of the Soviet satellite states, Tito was used to moving easily in the rarified circles of international statesmanship, representing socialist Yugoslavia to the world, and he was a star of the Non-Aligned Movement. Ranković epitomized the authoritarian face of Yugoslav communism, the anonymous bureaucratic establishment. Tito was always a reluctant reformer. A lifetime of training made him put his trust in the Leninist form of party-state organization as the only secure guarantee of Communist power, but faced by the choice of going on or going back, Tito decided to take a gamble on reform.

Meeting in early December 1964, the Eighth Congress of the League of Communists endorsed the principles of market socialism, though accompanied by a maze of contradictory qualifications about the role of the Party in controlling inequalities, and heavy warnings against ideological and nationalist deviations. Congress also took the important decision that in future the congresses of the republics would be held in advance of the federal gathering. This procedural change was the clearest signal yet that the Party was set to reform itself in line with the constitution. Vladimir Bakarić, the doyen of the League of Communists in Croatia and Tito's closest associate in the republic, gave a number of interviews to the press in the months leading up to the Congress, in which he stressed that centralism was crippling the development of the federation. Bakarić was also a convinced opponent of nationalism, and he argued that nationalist tension in Croatia was not the work of reactionary Ustasha elements, but bred out of growing resentment caused by the disintegration of the old economic system. If the Party wished to bring nationalism under control, economic growth and a redefinition of the constitutional status of the republics was the answer.

Bakarić exemplified the real strength of the reform movement. His Communist-Partizan credentials were impeccable, and he spoke the language of class, not of nation. His attack upon 'unitarism' was couched in terms of the weaknesses of the decentralized-administered economy, while insisting that the authority of the League of Communists must be maintained by other means. This technocratic, incremental approach to change was decisive in creating a coalition in favour of reforms to which the Party was already in principle committed. The reformers could claim with complete justice that they were the authentic voice of official Marxism, champions of self-governing socialism in the battle against bureaucracy.

Open hostilities broke out in the spring of 1965, when the Serbian League of Communists came under attack in the pages of *Komunist*. Ranković stepped up his use of the security apparatus (UDBa) to discredit or remove opponents. According to later accounts, even Tito's villa and offices were bugged, a fact revealed to him by courtesy of the army's counter-espionage service (KOS). Here too nationalism seems to have played a telling part, since both the Minister of Defence and the officer responsible for the KOS operation were Croats – without this split within the security forces it is difficult to see how Ranković could have been brought down. The balance of power between the military and UDBa now began to alter in favour of the army High Command, and remained that way for the next 20 years or so.[14]

In June, Tito held talks with the Soviet leadership in Moscow, and while he was there the Federal Assembly in Belgrade brought in the first of a series of economic reform measures. This was the very moment at which the Kosygin plans for economic reform in the USSR were in the process of being shelved, and the Soviet leadership had to be reassured that Yugoslavia was not straying into the capitalist camp. Ranković immediately began to organize resistance to the implementation of reforms proposed by the Central Committee – strangely enough, he it was who broke the discipline of democratic centralism. When it came to a showdown, Ranković found himself up against the collective authority of virtually the entire top leadership. A year of intense in-fighting finally drew to a close when, in July 1966, the celebrated Brioni Plenum of the Central Committee relieved Ranković of all Party and state offices. Eighteen years after the break with Moscow, Yugoslavia's hard man was gone from the scene.

7
Reform – and Reaction

Getting rid of Ranković was the easy part of the reformers' task. The real problem was how to create a stable system of inter-republic bargaining without undermining the power of the central Party machine. They still had no experience to guide them. The rhetoric of the Seventh Congress about distancing the Party from power had absolutely no basis in reality. The rulers of Yugoslavia would have fitted comfortably into two buses,[1] and the role of the League of Communists as the 'ideational vanguard' of self-governing socialism was notoriously a farce – among the public at large, Communists had a well deserved reputation for careerism and corruption.[2]

As a beginning, in October 1966, the two functions on which Ranković's power had rested were separated. Control of the central Party organization became the collective responsibility of a newly created Presidium of 35 members, while control of cadre policy, *including* UDBa except for a residual federal arm, was devolved to the republics. The Executive Committee was initially reduced to 11 members, but then promptly enlarged by the co-optation of the republics' party secretaries, bringing the total membership to 17. The aim was to put a stop to the seeping infiltration of government by UDBa nominees, and to develop the Presidium as a check on the power of the Executive Committee, which had run the country without opposition for the past 20 years. Membership of both bodies was therefore forbidden, and rules governing the rotation of offices were introduced to prevent the covert exercise of power through strategic bureaucratic networks.

There was a new tolerance of freedom of expression, though TV and radio remained more restricted than print, and satire was always more acceptable as a form of social criticism than serious investigative journalism. Even within the Party itself there was a wide circulation of heterodox ideas drawn from bourgeois social theory, and official marxism came under attack from the radical New Left, whose ideas were focused in the output of the journal *Praxis*, part of the movement sweeping through the universities of Western Europe. An ideological carnival broke out, in which nationalist currents surfaced, putting the Party back on guard.

The fall of Ranković encouraged Matica Hrvatska, the official Croatian cultural organization, to organize a celebration of the 130 years since the birth of Illyrianism. It was perhaps an odd number to choose, and the Titoists were displeased when, in March 1967, a group of Croat intellectuals (including Krleža, a member of the Croatian Central Committee) repudiated the 1954 Novi Sad language agreement. They complained that the Serbo-Croatian dictionary then in preparation relegated Croatian variants to subordinate status, and was part of a general tendency to promote Serbian as the 'state' language. This was a very sensitive issue, because it raised questions about the treatment of Yugoslavia's other official languages (Macedonian and Slovenian), and about the policy with respect to minorities. A reply in kind came from a group of Serbs (including a member of the Serbian Central Committee), who accepted that Croatian was a separate and equal language, but, by the same reasoning, demanded full cultural and linguistic independence for Serbs living outside their own republic.

The Party's response was sharp, and all those involved on both sides were disciplined, but the episode did not prevent the passing of the first Amendment to the 1963 Constitution, on 18 April, which restored the Chamber of Nationalities to the Federal Assembly. However, the previous day Tito brought his great personal authority to bear in a speech to Communists in Belgrade, to caution them against 'petty-bourgeois liberalism and confusion in the ranks of our intellectuals ... which might paralyse the League Communists, or turn it into an organization without ideas in which every member just pays his dues and does as he likes. The Communist Party [*sic*] is the vanguard of the working class, and its role will for long be an important one.'[3] It was a clear warning that the time had come to close ranks within the Party, for by this time economic reform had flung Yugoslavia into turmoil.

By the end of 1965, every third enterprise was operating at a loss. The legislation that came into effect in August aimed to create a capital-intensive, high-productivity manufacturing industry, capable of placing its goods on world markets, and to diversify investment into neglected branches of the economy, particularly agriculture and tourism. Subsidies to industry for domestic sales were ended, together with the differential exchange rates applied to various branches of economic activity, and the dinar was allowed to float against the US dollar. The proportion of the net income disposed of by enterprises was raised from about 40 per cent to about 70 per cent, in order to encourage innovation and savings. The effect of these changes was to smash the stable, egalitarian patterning of income distribution characteristic of the period of decentralized-administered economic management. Huge disparities in income appeared between enterprises, and between different branches of the economy, while the per capita income of the advanced republics began to show a runaway rate of increase compared with the less developed regions of the federation.[4]

The main victims of reform were industrial workers. During the period 1964–7, real incomes are estimated to have risen by 29 per cent, but these gains were very inequitably distributed. Most households suffered a severe drop in living standards. The report by a trade union commission into the causes of the major dock strike at Rijeka in 1968 revealed that workers were facing the prospect of cuts in pay and benefits amounting to a third of their real incomes. One Croatian textile firm tried to adjust to competitive trading conditions by cutting all incomes by 20 per cent, upping production norms and tightening labour discipline. Such drastic measures were commonplace, yet during the four years following reform the cost of housing rose by 154 per cent, food and clothing by 80 per cent. Official estimates calculated that reform would produce a one-off jump in the cost of living of about 25 per cent, but this figure had already been substantially exceeded within a matter of months, and by the end of 1966 an additional rise of 23 per cent had been recorded.[5]

The Party was by this time completely cut off from grass-roots support. In 1962, peasants and workers ceased, for the first time, to form an absolute majority of members. Workers occupied fewer than one in five of the leadership positions within the League of Communists even at the level of the communes; in higher state and Party organs their representation was negligible. In 1966, workers made up about 30 per cent of Party members, but supplied two-thirds of its defectors. Faced with swingeing wage cuts, workers rebelled against the self-management system, which had fallen into the hands of managers. Enterprise directors were able to control their collectives through cliques of key activists, with top management typically hijacking the Party and trade union organizations within the firm. Workers lacked the information necessary to influence the self-management organs, which were packed with administrative and managerial personnel. In the rash of strikes which broke out in the post-reform years, shopfloor workers invariably chose to bypass the workers' councils, preferring to set up their own strike committees.[6] The Party was confronted by a potential working-class revolt, which lacked only the means of organization to turn it into a formidable political force.

The intelligentsia was also hit very hard, producing strikes by teachers in Ptuje and Osijek, court officials in Lazarevac, doctors in Kraljevo and medical personnel in Ljubljana. The professional stratum resented the conspicuous consumption of the new elite of finance communism, with their round-the-world travel, second homes and luxury consumer goods, paid for with desperately scarce hard currency. The new breed of business leaders created by market socialism were able to put their own price on their services, and it followed that the political bureaucracy would take its cut. The government's own statistics reveal that, by 1971, 43 per cent of the mass of personal incomes came from sources other than regular employment, most of it accounted for by the fees and honoraria which 'leadership personnel' paid out to each other.[7] All this was in addition to the customary perks which had always been the been in the gift of communist officialdom: access to quality housing at knock-down rents, jobs for children, and the like. Gross nepotism in appointments, fraudulent currency deals on foreign markets, gambling with enterprise funds on the London Stock Exchange – a whole gamut of scandals in the press highlighted the problem of accountability in the management of social wealth.[8]

For the mass of the population, the psychology of everyday life was dominated by the problems of poverty, emigration and unemployment. By the end of the 1960s, an estimated 20 per cent of working-class and peasant households lived on the margins of existence, while another 70 per cent barely made ends meet.[9] Even professional families needed two earners to maintain the standard of living that suddenly became the norm after so long living in a scarcity economy, but jobs were harder and harder to come by. The unemployment rate doubled (from just over 6 per cent) between 1966 and 1970, even though during this period the figures ceased to include first-time job seekers without experience or qualifications. The situation would have been much worse but for the fact that, by 1970, a million Yugoslavs were working abroad, mostly in West Germany. A quarter of all employed Yugoslav citizens were now working for capitalism, about half of them with formal occupational qualifications, and less than a fifth of their earnings was being repatriated. It was an expensive waste of skills, and it had socially demoralizing consequences. Few of the exiles entertained serious hopes of an early improvement in the Yugoslav economy, and the problems of split families became a thriving sub-specialism of the social sciences.[10]

Economic reform was highly variable in its regional impact. To take one politically sensitive indicator: between 1965 and 1974, the index of registered unemployed 1974/1965 (1965 = 100) was 179 nationally. In Serbia, Bosnia, and Montenegro the figures were 216, 258 and 312 respectively; in Macedonia the index was 1216; in Slovenia and Croatia unemployment actually fell. At the same time, the more developed northern regions (including Inner Serbia and the Vojvodina) were exporting labour abroad, and within Yugoslavia there was also large-scale migration, as unskilled workers gravitated to the urban centres from the rural hinterlands, where they became internal 'guestworkers', living in hostels and rented rooms away from their families, while continuing to send money home.

The question of whether to press on with more radical changes split the Party once more. Younger, professionally trained industrial managers were dissatisfied with economic reform because it did too little. During 1965 (the reform year!) the state authorities issued almost 1000 decrees regulating enterprise affairs, and nearly as many again in the following 12 months. The scope and capriciousness of interventionism made rational strategies for management impossible. The banks issued regulations at odds with those of the state authorities, and charged usurious rates of interest for their monopolistic services. Directors of profitable enterprises also typically found themselves exposed to strong pressures from local elites trying to influence personnel and incomes' policies, or demanding help for ailing firms. Planning was impossible in such quirky conditions. The rights of decision-making vested in the enterprise collectives were subject to constant outside meddling. Employees wanted prosperity and job security, not empty self-management rights, and it was not rare to find effective bargains whereby the director was left to get on with it, without much reference to the formal structure of authority – the director of a major engineering firm in Niš conducted all meetings of the workers' council in a room without chairs.

Managerialism acquired a voice in academic journals and the press, especially in Croatia and Slovenia, where it had strong institutional support within the system of higher education. A spate of academic studies appeared, arguing that democracy and efficiency in industry were two sides of the same coin, because the existing system shielded incompetent and corrupt directors. The answer was to make top managers the contractual servants of the collectives, who would play a role similar to shareholders in western firms. This would have required the surrender by local elites of their control over managerial appointments and over the socio-political organs within the enterprise, with independent trade unions for workers.

In late 1967, at the request of the Croatian Sabor, the Federal Executive Council (FEC) undertook an extensive review of economic policy. The Croats took their stand on the decisions of the Eighth Congress, which promised changes in the control of economic policy in favour of the 'direct producers', that is to say, the enterprises. This form of 'bottom-up' decentralization was quite different in its political implications from the efforts by the Party to construct mechanisms for consultation and agreement in which resources were first centralized, and only then distributed on the basis of criteria agreed by the members of the federation. The Croats wanted an end to the allocation of social capital at federal level, except for aid to the underdeveloped regions, arguing that only by breaking the continued grip of bureaucracy on the economy could reform achieve its stated goals. Frustrated by the delaying tactics of the FEC, they went public (28/29 May 1968) while negotiations were still in progress. This was followed by a campaign in the mass media to drum up public support within Croatia, and the confrontation also marked the beginning of the recurrent tactic of blocking federal decisions.

Less than a week later (3–4 June), student sit-ins and demonstrations, widely supported by their teachers, broke out in the four main university centres, following the example of the New Left in Western Europe. In Belgrade the students declared themselves members of 'Karl Marx's Red University': in Zagreb they chose the name 'Socialist University of the Seven Secretaries of SKOJ' (the Communist Youth League). These disturbances owed a lot to mundane grievances, and the authorities did not allow themselves to be goaded into overreacting, once it became clear that the police could confine the students to the campuses. The student radicals were fiercely anti-capitalist, and Tito's opportunistic genius turned their attacks on the 'red bourgeoisie' to his own advantage. He interrupted a meeting of the Presidium to make a televised speech (9 June), which was later, in a crowning touch, published in *Praxis*. To the nation at large he acknowledged that it was time for unity and action, and in that the students were right. To the students he addressed a homily about the dangers of spontaneous demonstrations becoming infiltrated by unhealthy elements (Maoists were mentioned more than once), and advised them to return to their studies, which they did on the very same evening. It was an impeccable piece of political theatre.

Whether unity and action were supposed to advance the cause of reform or reverse it was left unclear, because the Party was still in two minds, but the problem was settled by the Soviet-led invasion of Czechoslovakia in late August. The effect was to create a welcome surge of genuinely popular support for the Party, as Tito roundly condemned the Brezhnev doctrine, rallying the forces of reform. The new-look Presidium and Executive Committee already embodied the principle of parity of representation for the republics, and further changes now followed to give this essentially cosmetic innovation some operational bite. Amendments VII–XIX to the 1963 Constitution, passed in December 1968, reserved defence, security and foreign affairs as the domain of the federal government, while decisions affecting social and economic development were to pass to the constituent members of the federation. These now included not only the six founding republics, but also the Vojvodina and Kosovo-Metohija, which became 'autonomous provinces' within Serbia, giving them the right to their own flag and to proportional representation in all state organs. Each of the federal units was to provide the chief officers of state in turn.

This was a radical break with the history of the Yugoslav state, but for some Kosovars the concession was not enough. Violent disorder broke out in Kosovo and spread to Macedonia, fired by the slogan 'Kosovo Republic'. The reaction of Serb nationalists faintly foreshadowed the events of 1981. Dobrica Ćošić, an eminent novelist and member of the Serbian Central Committee, spoke for them all, predicting in melodramatic terms that the change would re-ignite the hunger of the Serbs for their ancestral homeland. Kosovo Serbs complained of persecution and discrimination, and the army was sent in to restore order, but the reformers were strong enough to hold their ground. Ćošić was removed from his position on the Serbian Central Committee, and Kosovo's constitutional gains were confirmed by the Serbian Assembly in January 1969. The detested Serbian addition of 'Metohija' also disappeared from the title of the province.[11]

Amendment VIII confirmed the Chamber of Nationalities (after 1974 it was called the Chamber of Republics) as the constitutional partner of the Socio-Political Chamber within the Federal Assembly, with enlarged powers and the right to meet separately. The 1963 Constitution made the Council of Nationalities a subordinate, occasional body within a single Federal Chamber. It now became responsible for introducing legislation, and the principle of majority voting was rejected. The republics and provinces acquired a virtual veto over matters within their jurisdiction, because of the stipulation that agreements had to be unanimous. These changes swung the balance of power away from Serbia, which had always been able routinely to muster a majority in party-state forums, thanks to the incorporation of Kosovo and Vojvodina, and the cousinly relationship of Serbia and Montenegro.

Within this intricate system of checks and balances, the Titoists intended to play the role of power brokers. It was therefore necessary to bring in new blood sympathetic to reform. As promised at the Eighth Congress, the republican parties (excepting Bosnia-Hercegovina) held their congresses during November and December 1968, in advance of the all-Yugoslav Ninth Congress, and were allowed to nominate their own candidates for offices. By the time of the Ninth Congress, the Party had recruited over a quarter of a million new members, a third of them workers, and 80 per cent aged under 25. Half of this increase, 10 per cent of the total membership, occurred in the six months following the invasion of Czechoslovakia. The Party bosses took their chance to make a clean sweep of the old guard in the republican leaderships, unblocking the channels of promotion to the younger generation: 90 per cent of the delegates to the Ninth Congress were newcomers, and 80 per cent of them were under the age of 45.

These changes had no impact on the conduct of politics at the level of the communes, nor were they intended to. There was no systematic purge of Rankovic supporters at the lower echelons of the League of Communists, and the structure of local elites was left undisturbed. They might play musical chairs to conform to the rules on rotation, but it made no difference to their collective grip on affairs. The machinery of decision-making in the communes remained inaccessible to the ordinary citizen. The Party Secretary, the President of the communal assembly, officials of trade unions and the Socialist Alliance, the directors of important enterprises, combined in an informal network to exclude the general public from all but parish-pump debate. Reform was exclusively Party business, and it needed delicate handling.[12]

These precautions were not enough. The notion of a federalized Party was a contradiction in terms, yet reform was producing just that effect. Providing a forum for bargaining between the constituent members of the federation was not the same thing as getting them to agree on policy, and the tidy separation of powers between the federation and the republics proposed in constitutional theory was unworkable in practice. The question of how the economy should be run was bound to raise disputes about the proper limits of federal authority. Quarrels broke out over the control of convertible currency reserves, and over the related question of the allocation by Belgrade of rights to trade with foreign countries. Croatia was especially aggrieved – four-fifths of the Adriatic coast, with its lucrative tourist industry, lay within the republic, yet Croatia was the biggest single exporter of labour abroad.

The governments of the republics became primarily concerned to foster the growth of their 'own' economies, and the lurch towards autarky was rapid. A prominent academic close to the reformist wing of the Party noted as early as 1968 that social capital was to a great extent 'territorialized', with foreign capital 'territorialized' to the greatest degree of all, ring-fenced in the hands of the federal authorities in Belgrade.[13] Time and again the advanced republics returned to the issues of aid to the underdeveloped regions, monetary policy, reform of the banking system, international trade, complaining that the system was inequitable and squandered the resources they did most to earn. Slovenia and Croatia were restive about what they saw as Serbian centralist machinations, and they were especially critical of the role of the Yugoslav National Bank in the allocation of investment resources. The banks took over where the General Investment Fund left off, and their control assumed the same bureaucratic character – in manufacturing industry, for example, the enterprises had to hand over all their profits to be re-allocated in the form of credits. At no time did the enterprises control more than 40 per cent of resources for new investment, and by 1971 the proportion was just over a quarter, actually less than a decade earlier.

Reform released a relentless assault on communist economic dogma. Among the ideas floated were free-trade zones (Rijeka was proposed as an entrepôt for Middle East oil going to Central Europe); the issue of shares in enterprises to private and corporate investors (this proposal infuriated the student leaders of 1968); the setting up of GG-enterprises ('GG' being the acronym for 'groups of citizens') exempt from the severe restrictions imposed on private employers of labour; the suggestion that takeovers by enterprises should be allowed (strongly favoured by the advanced republics). There was also pressure to encourage peasant agriculture and the self-employed worker (privatnik). After all, as the President of the Slovenian federation of trade unions enquired acidly in a press interview, what was so immaculately socialist about limiting private enterprise when hundreds of thousands of Yugoslav workers were being exploited by foreign capitalists?

The apparatchiks also noted with increasing chilliness the emergence of what Party-speak called 'big systems', formed by the merging of firms into industrial and commercial conglomerates which dominated their regional economies. The directors of these giants were now making decisions of a scale and complexity which outstripped the ability of lower-level Party forums to exercise effective control over their activities. Rather, the reverse was happening. The new Communist entrepreneurs subordinated the Party and its affiliated organizations within their bailiwick to their business interests. The key institutional innovations here were the drastic reduction in the large number of communal banks, in favour of fewer and larger ones; and the creation of a network of 'chambers of commerce' (privredne komore) to coordinate investment policy. The machinery of power was being lubricated by money, not driven by Party directives.[14]

By the time of the Ninth Congress (March 1969) the tide of reformism was already on the turn. In his speech to delegates, Tito insisted on the need for the strongest possible central leadership 'in view of the current political situation in the world, and the need for more decisive action against all deviations'. On his initiative, the Central Committee of 155 members was replaced by an enlarged Presidium of 52 members, including three from the Yugoslav People's Army, and the Executive Committee made way for a new Executive Bureau composed of 14 representatives elected by Congress – one from Kosovo and the Vojvodina; two from each republic. The renewed concentration of power within the Party had its ideological correlate in Kardelj's attack on the power of 'technocracy', his theme being that economic reform had created conditions conducive to 'capital-relations'. As Marxist analysis, it would not perhaps have scored very high marks, but the message to Congress was plain enough. Voices silenced by the fall of Ranković were heard again, calling for a return to the Communist virtues of equality and austerity, coupled with demands for the restoration of Party discipline and pointed references to the growth of 'dinar nationalism'.

The delegates to Congress had only just dispersed when the so-called roads' affair erupted in Slovenia, in June 1969. The Slovenes complained of discrimination by the federal government in the distribution of an important loan to Yugoslavia by the World Bank, in violation of an inter-republican agreement. For the first time, the government of a republic openly opposed a decision of the Federal Executive Council, backed by hints of secession, and it required the personal intervention of Tito and Kardelj to persuade the Slovenes to back down. The Croatian leaders also became increasingly outspoken in their criticisms of centralism, and they allowed these quarrels to surface in the press. Specific complaints about the blocking of economic reform became entwined with a more overtly political confrontation, which focused attention on the two federal institutions most closely identified with Serbian hegemony: the Yugoslav People's Army and the security forces.

As a matter of policy, an 'ethnic quota' system kept the High Command evenly balanced between Serb and Croat officers, with Montenegrins and Muslims making up the remaining third or so of staff officers. However, Serbs and Montenegrins made up about 80 per cent of junior officers and NCOs, and at least two-thirds of the State Security Service.[15] Policing was also a very sensitive matter because Serbs were disproportionately represented in the police in areas of mixed populations. In Kosovo, Serbs had a virtual monopoly of policing, though the subject remained taboo even in the most liberal phases of reform. In Zagreb, Serbs made up 57 per cent of the municipal police force, but only a quarter of the population of the republic. In its issue of 17 June 1970, the influential Zagreb weekly *Vjesnik u Srijedu* ran an article which raised the question of the nationalities' bias within the defence forces, and recommended greater control of defence policy within Croatia.

The Croats were constitutionally quite within their rights in bringing the matter up. A National Defence Council was set up in 1968, the first step in a reformulation of defence policy endorsed by the National Defence Law of February 1969. The stated aim of this legislation was, in accordance with Leninist principles and the declarations of the Seventh Congress, to give greater weight to the 'armed people' as a second echelon of national defence. The Yugoslav People's Army would remain a federal responsibility, but the organization of the Territorial Defence forces would fall to the republics, whose militias would have to bear the brunt of any future partisan war. The YPA commanders were not opposed to this development – the Soviet invasion of Czechoslovakia forced them to confront the fact that reliance on the regular army would not be enough in the event of attack. What raised the hackles of the military and the Party elite was that the debate had been taken into the public arena.

Even more alarming was the development of a major schism within the leadership in Serbia. At a meeting chaired by Tito in October 1971, as the Croatian leadership crisis was coming to the boil, the President of the Serbian Assembly attacked the Secretariat of the Central Committee of the League of Communists of Serbia for persistently frustrating attempts to implement economic reform.[16] The Serbian party organization was itself split. As a result of the campaign to oust Ranković, the Serbian leadership now contained some of the most vociferous technocrats, who urged the creation of a few large, export-led, efficient corporations as the spearhead of economic growth, with managers freed from endless political interference. From the point of view of the Party's central apparatus, this was a very serious development. If Serbia, the bastion of centralism, threw its weight behind further liberalization, reformism would run out of control.

Matters came to a head when the top leadership of the Croatian party (Miko Tripalo, Savka Dabčević-Kučar and Pero Pirker) lost their grip on the situation in their republic. What began as a cautious mobilization of public support ended with the infiltration of the republican party machine by sympathizers of Matica Hrvatska, which almost overnight acquired the contours of a mass, nationalist opposition movement, with its own weekly newspaper commanding a readership of 100 000. The Croatian leaders were now riding a tiger. Tito warned of the danger during a visit to Zagreb in July 1971, and so it proved.[17] At a top-level meeting convened on 22 October to discuss a new, consolidated constitution (the number of Amendments now totalled 41), the Croats declared that what was on offer was a barely acceptable minimum. They reiterated their opposition to economic centralism, and demanded control of their own reserves of foreign currency. The nationalist-led students of Zagreb University (the Communist student leadership had been ousted in April) went on strike in support of this latter demand in November, and refused to call off their action when ordered to do so by the cornered Croatian party leaders, who were forced to step down.

Meeting on 1–2 December 1971 at Tito's hunting lodge in Karadjordjevo in deepest Serbia (a pointed piece of topographical symbolism), the Twenty-First Session of the Presidium of the League of Communists set in motion a rolling purge, beginning with about 1000 Croatian party-state functionaries, then moving on to deal with other republics. The Macedonian party chief Lazar Koliševski led the line of penitents. Ever since the Fifth Congress of the League of Communists of Macedonia in 1968, the Macedonian leadership had been pressing for a relaxation of the sacred doctrine of democratic centralism, arguing that it made no sense to keep it if the whole point of reform was to produce inter-republic consensus. Writing in the Party newspaper *Borba*, Koliševski admitted that this had allowed the impression to develop that Macedonia 'was not wedded' to Yugoslavia. The Slovenian party leaders, headed by Stane Kavčič, were dismissed after a confession of errors which included 'separatism' and a wrong approach to the Non-Aligned Movement, Tito's favourite international cause.

The Serbian party leadership refused to go quietly, and Tito therefore took on personally the job of setting their house in order. A letter from the Presidency and Executive Committee of the Party, dated 29

September 1971, warned all members that the decisive moment for the future of Yugoslav socialism had arrived, and Serbia's entire top brass (about 80 in number) was assembled in Belgrade for an informal meeting which dragged on for four days (9–12 October). Tito's target was the liberal-technocratic wing of the leadership, and he singled out Marko Nikezić for attack, asking sarcastically how it was that the Italian and German press were so well informed about the differences between the 'progressive' Nikezić and the 'conservative', indeed 'virtually Stalinist', Tito, matters which could have been learned only from 'our own people'. Nikezić and Latinka Perović (the President and the Secretary of the Serbian League of Communists) had to resign, followed by the Secretary of the Belgrade party organization, and the President and Secretary of the Vojvodina's League of Communists. In the end, the total number purged in Serbia very nearly matched that of Croatia.

It was the end of reformism. The content of Tito's attack (a rather rambling condemnation of the concentration of economic power in Belgrade, which fed 'nationalism and hegemonism') was incidental to its tone and purpose. His allusions to the 'hostile press abroad' were supplemented by references to 'petty-bourgeois' influences within the Party, and to 'the class enemy'. It was a blast directed against the cosmopolitan smart-asses of the big cities, for whom the Party was an irrelevance. Tito identified Belgrade, Zagreb and Ljubljana as all harbouring 'little groups, particular milieux able to dominate things', exerting 'incredibly strong pressure' on leadership personnel. Belgrade's mass media took the full force of his attack: obsession with democracy without regard for its true content had opened up the press, radio and TV ('which should be in our hands') to the enemies of socialist Yugoslavia, aided and abetted by judges guilty of 'overinterpreting' the law to their advantage – he lamented the lack of a revolutionary judiciary appropriate to a country developing amid the throes of revolutionary pains. The speech was a throwback, loaded with the threadbare imagery of revolutionary struggle. Unsurprisingly, it drew precious little by way of support or self-criticism from his audience, but the reaction seems to have surprised Tito, who gave up in disgust and unceremoniously adjourned the meeting.[18]

Seen from the opposite angle, the attack was a reassurance to the Communist bosses of small-town Yugoslavia that their day was not over yet. Ranković's silent supporters out in the sticks had to be mobilized, if a centralized Party structure was to stand any chance of survival. It was also an admission that a strong central authority was linked to the fate of the Serbs. Serbs made up well over half the membership of the League of Communists while Croats numbered fewer than one in five, with no other nationality even reaching double percentage figures, and the disparities were increasing. In Montenegro there was virtually no change in the leadership as a result of the purges. In Bosnia, the leadership not only survived intact, but three Bosnian Muslim federal functionaries were removed from office for 'fractional' activities, after accusing the party bosses in Sarajevo of 'undemocratic relations' and a 'firm hand' approach.[19] The purges in Croatia completed the jigsaw, shoring up the waning political influence of the minority Serb population in the republic.

Serbia's new leadership accepted the Titoist deal on Kosovo, which combined a minimum of political liberalization with the promise of more money to counter the backwardness of the province. Kosovo's great extractive economic potential promised large revenues, and development would be financed mainly by contributions from other republics to the federal Fund for the Underdeveloped Regions. And since Kosovo was an autonomous part of Serbia, not a republic, it meant that cadre policy was overseen by Belgrade. This explains the absence of substantial opposition within the Serbian party to the rapid increase in the recruitment of Albanians into the Kosovo party and police after 1974 (the local Serbs and Montenegrins took a different view). Liberalizing in form, centralist in operation, it was the kind of reformism which the conservatives in Belgrade could accept. Ethnic Albanian leaders in Kosovo would implement policies advantageous to Serbia in the name of 'brotherhood and unity', and Tito was welcome to take the credit.

The Party was reorganized yet again. A new and strengthened Executive Bureau was introduced, with its own Secretariat, the rule of democratic centralism was reasserted as the first principle of political life, and cadre commissions were set up to scrutinize all candidates for office. An ideological offensive began in the form of centres of 'Marxist studies' attached to central committees at all levels and in large work organizations. The Party cell structure was revived in the state administration and the non-productive sector, where it had not functioned for years. The purge extended to include the mass media, publishing houses, cultural organizations and the economy. Those in 'leadership' positions (a legal category corresponding to the Soviet nomenklatura) who were suspected of a lukewarm attitude to the Party were weeded out, and the advertisements for such jobs now incorporated the condition that candidates must demonstrate their 'moral and political suitability' for appointment. A sustained recruitment drive (briefly) raised the proportion of workers within the Party from under 30 per cent to 40 per cent, and worker activist groups at communal level were promoted as a means of influencing elected bodies.[20]

The crackdown damaged lives and blighted careers, but it was not a reaction in the sense of trying to put the clock back, so much as an attempt to stop it ticking altogether. Croatia was not made a scapegoat, nor an excuse for the 'unitaristic revanchism' which Bakarić warned against publicly on numerous occasions. Economic reform could not be simply reversed. The end of austerity released the pent-up consumerism of people accustomed to running the gauntlet of hard-faced customs' officers to smuggle in jeans and rock-tapes from Trieste or Munich. They became fond of saying of their neighbours in Romania, Bulgaria, even Hungary, 'We are like America for them.' JAT, the state airline, ran weekend cheapies to London, where the visitors shopped with hard currency scraped together at great but willing sacrifice, and a new Belgrade–Sydney direct run linked Yugoslavs with their relatives in Australia. Popular culture soaked up spaghetti Westerns, the Rolling Stones, *Love Story*; the evening streets emptied when an episode of *Peyton Place* or *The Forsyte Saga* was showing on television. Alone among the communist states, Yugoslavia was represented in the Eurovision Song Contest, and in a way it summed up the new order emerging.

The trains bringing the guestworkers home for New Year were stuffed to the roof with all manner of scarce consumer goods, and as often as not they arrived in the ultimate status symbol, a Mercedes or BMW. Domestic industry responded. Car-ownership took off with the establishment of a Fiat subsidiary (Zastava) in Kragujevac, which even found some custom in western markets. Yugoslav brand names sprouted in the production of washing machines, fridges and household appliances, snapped up to fill the homes built or refurbished in the construction boom fed by foreign earnings and the greater availability of bank credit. Television advertising appeared for the first time. The Yugoslav film industry competed with western cinema for audiences, turning out movies of high quality, and TV was forced to brighten up its act. People were bored by the interminable news bulletins reporting Tito's travels or the latest meeting of the Central Committee; tired of Partizan war epics, Yugoslav travelogues, old cartoons for the children. They wanted western sit-coms, serious cultural programmes – anything but the pap they had been fed for so long.

Maybe it was beefsteak socialism, but it conferred legitimacy of a sort on a regime which dared not rely on the ballot box. The reformist horse had already bolted, and the 33 Constitutional Amendments introduced in the summer of 1971, which confirmed the jurisdictions of the republics, were not rescinded. Instead, the five inter-republic economic committees responsible for formulating policies were downgraded, and subordinated to a central Coordinating Committee, where the Party elite could keep an eye on developments. Most important of all, the collective state Presidency (introduced in 1971) was also retained, as decisive proof of the Party's benign intentions towards the autonomy of the republics. The Presidency was composed of one member from each of the republics, and one each from Vojvodina and Kosovo, with the office of President rotating to each of the constituent members of the federation annually.

Yet when the dust settled after two years of frenetic activity, the problem of striking a balance between federalism and centralism was no nearer a solution than before. The new Constitution adopted in January 1974, and the Tenth Congress of the Party in May, sent out contradictory messages, which restated but could not solve the problem of reform. The Constitution reaffirmed the principle of equality between the constituent members of the federation, but also referred to the 'leading role' of the Party (Preamble VIII), without specifying how it was to be reconciled with the autonomy of other institutions – the section entitled 'The Foundations of the Socio-Political System' made no mention of the League of Communists at all. Congress took up the same themes with an opposite emphasis, laying stress on the need for taut Party discipline, and stressing the role of Communists in 'guiding' the work of socio-political organs. Within a newly restored Central Committee of 166 members, the Yugoslav People's Army was allotted 15 seats, as many as Kosovo and the Vojvodina, making the military the 'ninth partner' within the federation, and the holding of multiple offices in Party and state organs was once again permitted, although not of executive functions.[21]

The Party's central apparatus did not however take back control of cadre policy, and the right to parity of representation for the federal units within the ruling bodies of the League of Communists was confirmed. Control of officialdom (*including* most State Security Service personnel) passed to the republics. Shorn of the centralized means of administration, the Party elite had nowhere else to look for support. There was no basis for a restoration of Party authority in any other class of the population. The intelligentsia needed the Party only in the sense that a membership card was a ticket to employment and social ascent. The Party offered nothing, not even material security, to the working class whose revolutionary vanguard it claimed to be. The Yugoslav People's Army and the residual federal arm of the SDB were the only institutions left which the Party leaders could rely on to enforce their will. No doubt it was the contradiction embedded in the system that prompted the inclusion in the Constitution of a provision which suspended the rotating collective Presidency of the Federal Republic in favour of Tito, who became President for life. Only the Founder could make it all work.

The 1974 Constitution was the longest in the world (at 406 Articles it just nosed out India), but it was followed in 1976 by another blockbuster, the Law on Associated Labour, sometimes referred to (by its friends) as the 'workers' constitution'. The Party's aim was to restore its links with the working class by creating 'basic organizations of associated labour' (BOALs), previously known under the more prosaic name of 'economic units', the smallest entities established within enterprises for the purposes of accounting and decision-making. By 1973, nearly half of all Yugoslav enterprises employed more than 1000 people. Even firms employing fewer than 500 people frequently had second-tier self-management organs; in bigger enterprises, second (and third) levels of self-management were normal. Study after study had shown that workers had little influence on major decisions within collectives, so the new BOALs were headed by their own director, and special Courts of Associated Labour were set up, to which workers could refer disputes. The sole effect was to insert another layer of bureaucracy into system already choked by red tape.[22] Strikes remained illegal.

These two overblown pieces of legislation epitomize the fundamental flaw in the system: they conferred every right except freedom of political association, the only one that mattered. Introducing the Law on Associated Labour, the President of the Federal Assembly (it happened to be Kiro Gligorov, the Macedonian party leader) assured his audience that 'it overcomes the need to decide social questions, or to speak of political authority, outside the sphere of associated labour'. His panegyric, presumably composed with the assistance of some handy primer on Marx, hailed a decisive step in a Yugoslavia's maturing socialist order, based upon 'social contracts' concluded between 'self-managing interest groups' (SMIGs), which were in principle quite distinct (Article 51) from the state administration. Citizens could in theory influence decision-making as voters, as members of work collectives, as members of a dozen or more socio-political organizations – health services, pension funds and public utilities, for example, were all formally open to representation from interested parties. It was the bureaucrat's dream of a perfectly ordered society, a system of rule by committees.

Critics had another word for it – 'SMIGocracy'. From the point of view of grass-roots politics, the 1974 Constitution was simply business as usual. The first priority of the reformers had always been to quarantine the reform process from the sources of collective action outside the Party, whether rooted in class or nationalism. An eye-witness account of political life at ward level reveals a system stifled, not by repression, but by sheer tedium, with presiding officials using all the techniques of bureaucratic manipulation to rule the public permanently 'out of order'.[23] The battery of citizens' voting rights was the butt of endless jokes ('I self-manage, you self-manage ... they decide'). When the authorities imposed a levy on incomes in aid of the victims of an earthquake which struck Banja Luka, they even managed to invent the Orwellian word 'self-contribution' (samodoprinos) to cover the case.

It was all part of a general descent into obfuscation. Cowed by the purges, the mass media ceased to let light and air into public political debate. Official marxism parodied itself, and paralysis gripped the academic study of society. In 1975, *Praxis* was closed down – not by the method of frontal attack, but ostensibly as a result of the 'self-managing' decision by the printers not to handle such subversive material. The intellectuals around *Praxis* were representative of an older generation of intellectuals, who took Marxism seriously. The role of social criticism now became the preserve of the 'establishment' political intelligentsia, with its institutional base in the faculties of Law, Economics and Political Science, which typically incorporated the schools of Journalism. Higher learning was a well-trodden path to elite status, and there were handsome rewards waiting for those able and willing to elaborate the platitudes of politicians into something resembling social theory. The field was not exclusively dominated by Party hacks, but any overt challenge to the Yugoslav socialist project carried heavy penalties, including, in some cases, imprisonment.

Ideological blinkering had a terrible effect on the management of the economy. According to Kardelj, Yugoslav socialism had now moved into the era of 'mass planning', with the Federal Executive Council setting prices according to complex criteria based on 'social contracts' between self-managing interest groups.[24] In fact, the fate of a system driven neither by markets nor by central planning was the 'feudalization' of the economy. The law forbade takeovers by enterprises, and the advanced republics could have no conceivable interest in propping up their rivals within the federation. By the end of the 1970s, two-thirds of all goods and services were being exchanged within republics, and only 4 per cent of investment resources were jointly owned by firms cooperating across republican boundaries. The republics actually traded abroad more readily than with each other.[25] Yugoslavia was in hock to foreign lenders, and Yugoslavs working abroad were keeping the home fires burning as inflation ate away at real incomes (in 1972 their remittances already accounted for 13 per cent of all personal spending),[26] but many were now being sent home, and unemployment was rising.

Quarrels over the Fund for the Underdeveloped Regions continued to fester. This residual economic centralism was deeply resented by the advanced republics, because it was ineffective and poured money into regions dominated by Serbia. The north–south gap widened inexorably, and so did the disparities between urban and rural life. The 'Green Plan', launched in 1973 to attend to the needs of peasants as a means of stimulating growth, brought about much higher levels of investment in agriculture, but too belatedly to undo the consequences of 30 years of neglect, and the limitation of private holdings to 10 hectares was not abolished until 1990. As a consequence, Yugoslavia failed to develop an efficient agricultural export industry, and the peasant economy benefited more from expanding tourism and emigrants' remittances than from official policy.[27]

The Eleventh Congress (June 1978) marked another change of heading in the Party's zig-zag course between reaction and reform. The purges had gone too far, bringing back into positions of power hard-liners who had no idea how to run an advanced industrial economy, and no use for democracy, even within the Party. Despite endless chatter about democ-ratization, the composition of the Federal Executive Council after the Tenth Congress contained much the same old faces who had ruled Yugoslavia since the war (the wartime leaders were very young by the standards of peacetime political careers) and of the 23 members elected to the Party Presidium by the Congress, only three were newcomers – the remainder had accumulated an average of three four-year mandates apiece. Career politicians also continued to dominate the representative assemblies: during one electoral period in the 1970s, a quarter of all delegates had held four or more four-year mandates.[28]

A sobering assessment of the weaknesses of the Yugoslav economy was provided in a study published by the World Bank in 1979.[29] The authors criticized the duplication of plant; the practice of firms expanding their activities using resources unsecured by assets; fraudulent record-keeping which included unsaleable stocks as a profit item, or counting bad debts as income. Foreign investors began to take note. Warnings were also coming from within the party-state establishment. Writing in *Politika* (7 September 1978), the head of the Social Accounting Service (the federal Treasury department) pointed out that in the first half of the year nominal incomes in the productive sector rose by 30 cent, but that a third of this increase was attributable to what he delicately termed 'easements in the accounting system'. He also noted a related anomaly, that a third of all basic work organizations were still operating at a loss.

In plain language, 13 years after the introduction of economic reform every third enterprise was keeping afloat through a combination of political patronage and cooking the books. Government spending ran well ahead of the growth in real incomes, increasing the burdens of an industrial base already suffocating under the weight of bureaucratic superstructure, and fuelling the galloping inflation caused by the weakening of the dinar. By the end of the 1970s, Yugoslavia was importing three times by value more than it exported to western markets, while the Comecon states were by far the most important destination for Yugoslav goods, and increasingly so. In 1978, the US$1 billion earned by tourism, and the US$2 billion sent home by Yugoslavs abroad, just cancelled out the current trade deficit – a coincidence which underlines the extent of Yugoslavia's dependence on capitalism.[30]

This was precisely the reverse of what reform was supposed to achieve. What was needed was not a lengthening of the list of criteria for setting prices, but competition to drive unprofitable firms out of business. The problem was not that economic reform failed to discriminate between firms – there were numerous local success stories – but that fortune favoured the feckless at the expense of the bold. Profitable firms were milked dry to counter the inequalities generated by reform, and the redistribution process itself required the multiplication of bureaucracy.

International loans and reckless government spending masked the problem for a while. During the 1970s Yugoslavs, or rather the lucky ones, lived well beyond their means: it was the golden age of the little weekend retreat (vikendica), holidays in Bali, car ownership and savings in the bank. The beneficiaries were two-income, white-collar families, working in banking, the professions or the state administration (incomes in the productive sector were unfavourable at all equivalent levels of qualification). Most people were far less fortunate. Total employment in the social sector rose from 3.6 million in 1970 to 5.8 million in 1980, but by then the bubble had already burst – productivity showed only half the rate of increase and inflation was running out of control. The unemployment rate was 14 per cent in 1978, and the structure of the labour market had changed very much for the worse. In 1957, two-thirds of those looking for a job found it within three months; in 1967, this situation was reversed, with two-thirds still looking for work after three months; in 1977, 40 per cent of unemployed had been registered for more than a year. Skilled workers returning from abroad (300 000 of them) had swelled the ranks of the jobless, together with graduates of a higher education system that had registered a sixfold increase in 20 years, reaching 400 000 students in 1978. Unskilled labour by now made up less than half the total of unemployed persons.

The changes made to the Party statutes by the Eleventh Congress amounted to an admission that reaction had gone too far. For the first time, the rule of democratic centralism was diluted, and the Executive Committee of the Presidium disappeared as a distinct Party organ. The search was on for a formula to deal with what was now more or less openly acknowledged as the succession problem. Congress itself could not agree on what was to be done, and it was left to Tito to propose in November the annual rotation of all Party and state offices (the 'Tito initiative'). Each republic would be given a quick turn at the controls, and so none would be able to dominate the others. This required yet more constitutional reforms, which were still in the pipeline when Yugoslavia disintegrated. What traces of authority still clung to Party rule were concentrated in Tito as life President, supported by a cult of personality which had always been vigorously promoted, not least by Tito himself. Every republic contained at least one town prefixed with his name, and his stern photographic portrait hung everywhere. In 1972, and again in 1977, Tito was awarded the Order of National Hero for a second and third time, recalling the mythic days of the national struggle against Nazism. Hollywood obliged by turning the retreat by Partizan forces across the Sutjeska into a big-screen epic, starring Richard Burton and the usual cast, but virtual reality was all that was left. Although the aged core elite retained their grip on office, the substance of their power was gone.

With the death of Kardelj (February 1979) and the long-ailing Tito (May 1980), the League of Communists lost the two remaining stars of the revolutionary generation. The collective heirs to the state Presidency, led by Lazar Koliševski, escorted Tito's cortege to his mausoleum on Dedinje, a select suburb of Belgrade, with scores of heads of state and hundreds of foreign dignitaries following on behind. Cynics in the cafés said they had only come to collect what was owing to them, and they were not far wrong.

8
The End of Titoism

The history of the League of Communists can be written as a series of leadership crises, as the Titoists fought to strike a balance between centralism and devolution. Three new constitutions in 21 years, and endless tinkering with the party-state machine, testify to how hard they tried. There is of course more to the record than a catalogue of failures. Communist rule transformed a peasant society into a middling industrial power without the gross deformations of Stalinism, and in that respect Yugoslav socialist democracy delivered on its promises, but it was the failures that mattered in the end. 'Market socialism' never existed, if by that is meant a stable allocation of authority between the Party and self-managing enterprises operating on a profit-and-loss principle for their survival. 'Direct democracy' was always an empty slogan. Economic ruin, and the absence of a democratic framework within which the federation could evolve, killed off the second Yugoslavia. For so long held up as a model of socialism with a human face, Titoism disintegrated amidst the bloodiest nationalist wars seen during the fall of communism in Eastern Europe.

The eight-man state Presidency installed in May 1979 (the last appointments during Tito's lifetime) included, in the 'hot seats': Vladimir Bakarić (Croatia); Sergej Kraigher (Slovenia), an architect of the 1965 reforms but out of top-flight politics until he filled the vacancy left by Kardelj; Fadil Hoxha (Kosovo), a former Partizan commander and staunch opponent of Albanian nationalist separatism; Lazar Koliševski (Macedonia), Tito's oldest ally in the republic; and Petar Stambolić (Serbia), who had sponsored the rise of Nikezić, but replaced him as Tito's choice to bring Serbia into line in 1972. Together with figures like the hard-liner Stane Dolanc, a Slovene with a long record of service at the heart of the Party's central apparatus, and Stipe Šuvar from Croatia, a sociologist-politician known for his fundamentalist approach to ideological questions, these veterans took as their slogan 'After Tito – Tito'. They came without distinction of republic, and the leading role of the Party looked safe enough in their hands.

Within a decade they were all ousted by a younger generation of leaders whose power was rooted in their native republics, and who spoke in the idiom of nationalism. To say that Tito 'clamped the lid down on nationalism' and that his death led to a 'resurgence' of nationalist rivalries, does not go far towards explaining what happened. It was simply a question of whether the man or the system would be the first to succumb. His East–West balancing act, the key to Titoism as a structure of power, was overturned by changes in the world political order. Tito's non-aligned strategy died with him. Held in Havana, the Sixth Conference of the Non-Aligned Movement (September 1979) gave him a glowing testimonial, but barely survived Cuba's determination to give the movement a pro-Moscow direction, just when the USSR, courted by Tito as a counterweight to western financial penetration, had invaded Afghanistan. The second Cold War was in the making, but this time around it was no longer possible to play the dog-eared card of persuading the capitalist states to pay the tolls along Yugoslavia's independent road to socialism.

Yugoslavia's economic development was heavily underwritten by western subsidies during the 1950s, and later by western loans. The difference was that loans incur interest, and have to be repaid. Developments in the international economy left Tito's successors with an impossible burden of debt. In 1971, Yugoslavia owed US$4 billion; in 1975, US$6.6 billion; in 1978, the figure was around US$11 billion; by 1983, US$20.5 billion and rising. Titoism's Indian summer during the 1970s fatally delayed action to limit the damage caused by structural problems in the economy. Tito's personal indifference to hard economic questions did not allow them even to be posed – incredibly, it was not until 1983 that the extent of Yugoslavia's foreign debts was officially acknowledged.

As the economy spun out of control, deadlock set in. The republican leaderships fought each other to protect their own territorial power-bases from the consequences of a drop in standards of living estimated to be in the order of 30 per cent, as consumer prices rose by 36 per cent annually between 1980 and 1983, and then by 67 per cent during the following 12 months. A quarter of all families were below the poverty line in 1984, and spending on basic food items accounted for two-thirds of most household budgets.[1] Shops appeared displaying goods priced in western currencies, and advertisements for the sale of housing typically began with 'Offered for sale to returnees', meaning actually 'only guest-workers with hard currency need apply'. In the underpasses and rail termini of the big cities, a thriving black market in foreign notes sprang up as people tried to escape the inflation-racked dinar economy. After a decade of growing affluence, everyone had to get accustomed to shortages again. Long lists of everyday items – cooking oil, detergents, soap, paper products, even that indispensable staple of Yugoslav social life, coffee – would disappear from the supermarket shelves. Petrol was the most expensive in Europe, when you could get it, and restrictions on car use were frequent. Workers often remained unpaid for months at a time, and most pensioners were reduced to near destitution.

Governing circles sent up a chorus of calls for economic reform, but (except for a few months in 1991) it never came. The experiment of 1965 had been abandoned, and there was no enthusiasm in any quarter for a repeat performance. Whatever their differences, the leaders of all Yugoslavia's republics were men and women who had made their careers by advancing through the League of Communists, their power grounded in the operation of a non-market economy. They were apparatchiks, not closet capitalists. The differences between them centred on the question of implementing the 'Tito initiative' launched after the Eleventh Congress. In the past, consensus had been bought by giving everyone a bit more, with the federation footing the bill by borrowing abroad. The dire situation in which Yugoslavia now found itself required re-central-ization, a strong federal authority able to enforce the fiscal and monetary discipline necessary to reassure western creditors, and to redistribute the social costs of economic collapse in order to keep the federation together.

Despite the watering-down of the doctrine of democratic centralism, Party discipline was strong enough to compel unity in top Communist forums, where decisions were taken on the basis of majority voting. The problem lay in persuading the governments of the republics to carry out policies which hurt them. Each of the eight constituent members of the federation, six republics and two autonomous regions, wielded a veto in the Federal Executive Council over all matters except defence, foreign affairs and security (these ministries were subordinated directly to the state Presidency). Tito was scarcely buried when (in June 1980) Slovenia's liberal premier was replaced by former security policeman, in order to enforce federal import restrictions hitting the republic's industry,[2] but the move only magnified tensions within the leadership. Slovenia's hard-liners found themselves isolated within their own political bureaucracy. The strengthening of federal powers meant the surrender of elements of republican sovereignty granted in 1974, and the re-creation of a centralized Party machine with authority to override dissent.

The Slovenes were having none of it. For the first time in the history of the Yugoslav state, Slovenia, rather than Croatia, stepped forward as the main opponent of centralism. Ljubljana is separated from Belgrade by virtually the entire east–west span of Yugoslavia, about 450 kilometres, and by a further 300 kilometres from Skopje, passing near Priština towards the end of the journey, using the main trunk routes. Trieste is just up the road, Vienna a half-day's drive away. Germany and Italy were now peaceable members of the European Community, an economic attraction, not a military threat. An ethnically compact republic, with no substantial minorities to complicate the issue of national allegiances, Slovenia was also the economic powerhouse of the federation, the main primary export earner. By the time of Tito's death, 1.9 million Slovenes, or 8 per cent of the population, accounted for 16 per cent of Yugoslavia's gross material product and a third of its foreign currency earnings. As the mounting economic crisis began to put paid to years of rising prosperity based on separate development, Slovenian separatism took an anti-Yugoslav turn. The Slovenes emerged as relentless critics of all federal institutions, and as advocates of confederal arrangements in which Slovenia would have a privileged place.

Serbia's leaders, headed by Ivan Stambolić (the nephew of Petar Stambolić) tied the question of economic reform to the constitutional status of Kosovo and the Vojvodina. They wanted the re-incorporation of the two autonomous provinces within a unitary Serbia, the project that Slobodan Milošević was to carry through in 1989 by force. There was some justice in the Serbs' claim, expressed in the so-called 'Blue Book' of complaints presented to Tito in 1977, that the near-equal federal status of the republics and the provinces left Serbia in an anomalous position. The Constitution of 1974 gave the Vojvodina and Kosovo each a vote in the state Presidency, leaving Serbia with just one vote out of eight. Both provinces were represented in the Serbian assembly, but there was no corresponding voice in the two provincial assemblies for those Serbs living in Inner Serbia. Alone among the republics, Serbia was divided constitutionally, and because it was the capital, Belgrade was excluded from federal aid for investment in infrastructural projects. Serbia was saddled with many deficit enterprises, including notorious political white elephants like the huge steelworks at Smederevo, and unemployment in Belgrade was running at about 25 per cent, as migrants flocked there in search of work.[3]

Elsewhere, the situation was even worse. Kosovo had fallen further and further behind the developed republics during the post-reform years, and parts of Bosnia were now experiencing de-industrialization. Both of them were regions where Serb interests and sentiments were heavily engaged, and in both cases a typically Titoist compromise had been arrived at. In Kosovo, the leadership of the provincial League of Communists was allowed to pass into the hands of ethnic Albanians who applied the Party line in exchange for a voice in federal affairs. In Bosnia, the Communist Muslim leaders won concessions on the question of the national status of their community, but cooperated with the Serbs and Croats to ensure the same disciplined attachment to 'brotherhood and unity'. It was in Kosovo that the compromise first broke down, and Kosovo became the burial ground of the Yugoslav ideal.

Early in March 1981, a student protest against poor conditions at Priština's university campus escalated into a street demonstration. Two weeks later, disturbances erupted again, on the occasion of the torchbearers' relay organized annually by the Socialist Youth Alliance to celebrate Yugoslav unity, and this time thousands of industrial workers came out onto the streets in support. Tanks were sent in, but the revolt spread to other towns. Kosovo came under a curfew, and a state of emergency was declared. Calls for a 'Kosovo republic' brought in the security forces, in a major operation to quell the province, and the air was thick with ominous references to 'fascist' and 'Cominformist' agitators working to undermine Yugoslavia's security. At a press conference (6 April) Stane Dolanc told foreign journalists that two members of the SDB (formerly UDBa) had been killed, together with nine demonstrators, two of them by bullets fired from their own side. As Minister of the Interior (after 1982), Dolanc was chiefly responsible for allowing the security forces to operate unchecked in the province, and six years later he revealed that 1500 people had been tried for serious crimes against public order and the state, another 4500 for lesser offences.[4]

Kosovo illustrates the maxim that revolutionary situations build up when hopes of improvement are raised, only to be frustrated. The reforming years bore fruit in the founding of Priština University as an autonomous institution (1970), and the Constitution of 1974 established Kosovo as a constituent member of the federation, freeing the province from its immediate subordination to the Serbian assembly in Belgrade. Within the provincial party organization Albanians made significant gains: by the end of the 1970s they made up about 70 per cent of the membership, and a similar proportion of the provincial police (but not of the SDB, which was in the hands of Serbs and Montenegrins). Economic development limped far behind. Most of Kosovo's 1.2 million Albanians lived in extended families engaged in traditional peasant farming on smallholdings. Only 12 per cent of the total population had jobs in the social sector, and the unemployment rate was three times the Yugoslav average, at well over 40 per cent. It was a case of uneven development on a grand scale.

Investment in the province was directed towards heavy industry such as the mining of coal and minerals, electricity and ferrous metallurgy, which were capital-intensive and generated few jobs. Furthermore, the prices charged by these industries were kept low in order to supply the rest of Yugoslavia, so that wages and conditions were poor. The miners of Kosovo, concentrated in a few large enterprises (about 19 000 of them worked in the huge Trepča complex alone) were in the forefront of industrial unrest, and always willing to ally themselves with student protests. The students numbered some 24 000–30 000 in 1981 (estimates vary), and few of them had any hope of finding work. The very fact that the right to instruction in Albanian had been won limited their chances of moving into employment outside Kosovo, even if jobs had been available, because the only domain in which Albanians used the Serbo-Croatian language (and even then of course only men) was during their military service. It was therefore not very surprising that their discontents should take a political turn, in the form of demands for a separate republic.

The reaction of the government was swift, drastic, and totally bungled. The activities of the State Security Service (now known as the SDB) in Kosovo ignited mass Albanian resistance. Although the precise extent of their involvement can only be surmised, it is clear that the ferocious and misguided policy of sustained repression in Kosovo originated in the role of the federal arm of the SDB, and of military counter-intelligence (KOS), in putting down the revolt. These agencies were primarily concerned with terrorism and foreign subversion, and were the last remaining covert arm of repression available to an attenuated Party central apparatus. They fomented trouble through the use of agents provoca-teurs and infiltrators, in order to discredit moderate Albanian opinion. By mendaciously equating demands for a separate republic with irredentism and 'counter-revolution', the government tried to justify its harsh repression, but the severity of the punishments inflicted on the demonstrators, many of them teenagers, stirred up fears of a return to the bad old days of Ranković's rule. Sentences of 10–15 years' jail were commonplace for those convicted (as they invariably were, once accused) of political offences or violence against the security forces. What Serbs were again beginning to call Kosovo-Metohija became in effect occupied territory.

The Party maintained a rigid constitutional line that harked back to the mentality of the first Yugoslavia. The Kosovar Albanians were not a constituent people (narod) of the Republic of Serbia or of Yugoslavia, but a 'national minority' (narodnost), a branch of the Albanian people which had its own state outside Yugoslavia (the ethnic Hungarians in the Vojvodina being an analogous case). This legalistic quibble ignored the fact that the Kosovars were a minority only within Serbia as a whole; within Kosovo itself they made up nearly 80 per cent of the population, which at 1.6 million was not far short of Slovenia and Macedonia, and outnumbered the inhabitants of Montenegro by four to one. The remaining pillars of centralism, the Party elite, the Yugoslav People's Army and the federal security forces, were completely unmoved by such arguments. Vaguely worded though it was, the Constitution of 1974 included provision for the secession of sovereign peoples from the federation, and demographic trends suggested that Kosovo would soon (like Slovenia) become an ethnically homogeneous territory.

If Kosovo became a republic, Serbia would lose a province rich in natural resources as well as nationalist associations, but that was only part of a much bigger problem. Bosnia was the strategic key to the integrity of the federation, and was the location of most of the Yugoslav armaments' industry, linked to Serbia's ailing heavy engineering base. The ethnic coalition that ruled in Sarajevo would fall apart if the Serbs came under threat of Albanian secessionism. But it was not just the Serbs who wanted to cordon off Kosovo. Croatia would be drawn into the conflict in Bosnia. Macedonia had a large Albanian minority (427 000, 21 per cent of a total population of 2 million in 1991), Montenegro also contained a sizeable Albanian population (about 10 per cent), and was home to many Muslims who had migrated from Bosnia.

The other republics were glad to let well alone, and so the situation in Kosovo became defined by default as Serbia's internal security problem. The news blackout imposed following the declaration of a state of emergency in Kosovo prevented critical coverage by media on the spot, so that rumour and anecdote drove out reasoned public debate. By smothering the sources of public information, the federal authorities played straight into the hands of Serb nationalists. The cloak-and-dagger atmosphere that enveloped Kosovo encouraged perceptions of the riots as the work of seditious elements in the pay of Tirana, linked particularly to the Kosovar Albanian intelligentsia. Why else would the security forces be there for so long? It followed (surely?) that the Serbs in the province were under threat from enemies of the state.

In Croatia, still under the hard-line leadership brought in after 1972, the authorities had problems of their own, as the Catholic Church became an outlet for the nationalist resentment fuelled by the purges. Mass rallies to celebrate religious occasions, and clashes between the Catholic hierarchy and the authorities over the wartime activities of Cardinal Stepinac, were the backdrop to a campaign to prosecute nationalists, including Franjo Tudjman. Tudjman, a Partizan veteran and a former Major-General in the Yugoslav People's Army before his reincarnation as a nationalist historian in the 1960s, had already served one term in prison for his views, in 1972. In a book published abroad, and in English, in 1980, Tudjman again set out the familiar nationalist case that Bosnia-Hercegovina was by historical right and geographical logic an integral part of Croatia. His former Communist associates chose not to leave the book in obscurity (there was probably a strong element of revenge at work in the whole affair), and he was imprisoned for maliciously misrepresenting Yugoslavia abroad, in February 1981. The former editor of *Hrvatski Tjednik* in the days of the 'Croatian Spring', and the student nationalist leader of the proscribed Party of Right, also got jail sentences.

Still struggling to contain the situation in Kosovo, the Party was dealt another nasty blow by General Jaruzelski's military coup, in December 1981, when Poland defaulted on its international debts. Western infatuation with Yugoslavia had ensured a continuing stream of credit to shore up the economy, led by West Germany, but now lenders began to see East European communist governments as a bad risk. The crushing of the Polish Solidarity movement also presented the Yugoslav government with a major test of its legitimacy, which it failed. Official reaction in Belgrade was decidedly muted, and the force brought to bear on a tiny public protest revealed the state of Party thinking on the subject of democratic rights to peaceful demonstration. Yugoslav workers had to be deterred at all costs from re-enacting the mass protests in Gdansk and Radom, and prevented from forming alliances with the intelligentsia.

One particular target of repression were the academics associated with a new journal, *Praxis International*, founded in Oxford in 1981 as the avowed successor to the proscribed Yugoslav *Praxis*. Meeting in private, though not in secret, to address subversive philosophical topics such as 'The Nature of Needs', they fell foul of officialdom because of their international reputation, and because their jobs (which some of them lost) gave them influence within the universities. Students were a problem for the authorities: the situation in Kosovo had parallels everywhere. The Yugoslav student population in 1956 numbered 54 000; by 1969 the figure was 240 000; by 1978, 440 000. Most of the expansion occurred in the social sciences, which grew two and a half times faster than technical subjects during the 1970s, because it could be done on the cheap. Mass education was a way of siphoning off entrants to the labour market. Even so by 1985 younger people with higher educational qualifications made up an absolute majority of the unemployed, and the unemployment rate had passed 16 per cent. In any given year, only about one in five students graduated within the prescribed minimum of four years of study. Most of them took six or even seven years to complete, by which time they were in their mid-twenties.

For an activist minority, 'student politics' meant the real thing, not a nursery for the smooth transition of the intelligentsia into elite positions. Student newspapers were an important ingredient in the opposition press, often being left for free distribution on the pavements of the main city centres. The passive majority of students took what occasional work they could find, hoping that things would take a turn for the better, but the events of 1968 had shown what could happen, and Kosovo rammed the lesson home. Higher education was anything but an ethnic melting pot. In Croatia and Slovenia, 95 per cent and 93 per cent of graduates in 1978 were educated in their ethnic republic; elsewhere the figure hovered around 85 per cent. In Belgrade and Zagreb, the student leaderships oscillated between 'left' Marxist and nationalist positions, and there was a danger that one or the other might take hold, linking up with working-class activists fighting the corruption and incompetence of the self-management system.

Anyone who expressed heterodox opinions too noisily, or was brave enough to take a stand against injustice in public, ran the risk of persecution, but the republics were left to police their own dissidents, and there was nothing elsewhere to rival the scale of repression in Kosovo. Indeed, the deep-rooted conflicts within the Party led to a loosening of ideological surveillance in the post-Tito years, especially in Serbia and Slovenia. Freedom of expression remained circumscribed (Kosovo, nationalism and official corruption were themes best avoided by prudent editors), but the various factions within the political bureaucracy were often quite willing to air by proxy the disputes that Party discipline ought to have confined to its own closed forums. In any case, a literate, urbanized population could hardly be kept in the dark about the growing crisis around them, especially as so many people had extensive contacts abroad. The serious press came out strongly against the suppression of Polish workers by their 'own' state, and also broke the news of Yugoslavia's debt crisis. Television and radio were always more constrained in their reporting, because they dealt with current affairs, but the toleration of 'responsible' journalism still gave greater scope for critical comment and analysis.

In the run-up to the Twelfth Congress (26–29 June 1982), the Party itself came under public attack from a retiring member of the Croatian Central Committee, Peko Dapčević, a distinguished Partizan commander who had sided against his own brother in the struggle against the Cominformists. He raised again the recurrent argument that self-governing socialism was incompatible with the doctrine of the dictatorship of the proletariat, and that therefore the Leninist form of Party organization breached the Constitution.[5] This could never have appeared in print in Tito's time. The Party was in deep disarray, a spectator of the economic crisis, unreformable and unable to control events. Working-class representation was at an all-time low of 17 per cent, and the trend towards the decline in membership in the advanced republics continued. Attempts at the Congress to restore the balance of power in favour of the central Party apparatus were defeated: a commission set up to examine proposals to strengthen the Central Committee by allowing the republics the right only to nominate, not elect, their candidates for office, could not be induced to recommend the change, leaving the republics with their rights intact.[6]

In order to be seen abroad to be doing something about the economy, the leadership brought to the Twelfth Congress proposals for a set of radically deflationary measures, as part of a long-term 'stabilization programme' on which a special Commission headed by Sergej Kraigher was due to report. Congress reluctantly adopted these proposals, but the Federal Assembly rejected them right up to the eleventh hour. It was the incoming President of the Federal Executive Council, Milka Planinc, appointed to head the Croatian party leadership after Karadjordjevo, who delivered Yugoslavia to the western bankers. As she told the Federal Assembly, there were no other options left. Prodded by a pro-Yugoslav American lobby, the IMF and a consortium of private lenders assembled a loan package, which came with stringent conditions, including a quarterly devaluation of the dinar against a 'basket' of western currencies.[7] Yugoslavia's current trading account recorded a small surplus the following year, and the effort was rewarded by further credits.

Structural reforms, on the other hand, were effectively shelved for good. The Kraigher Commission had already been at work for the best part of two years when its final conclusions appeared in print in May 1983, the last of a 15-part series devoted to various aspects of the economy. Constituted in the autumn of 1981, the Commission was made up of some 300 politicians and experts, and their deliberations ran to four volumes. Astonishingly, in their initial survey (1982) of the problems faced by the economy, the authors claimed that Yugoslavia had found in the institution of 'social property' the answer to the contradictions that bedevilled capitalism and state socialism. All that remained was to translate the theory of self-governing socialism into practice![8] Little wonder, therefore, that the Commission failed to promote a serious programme of economic reform, and actually encouraged Party dogmatists to mount their ideological high horse in defence of Yugoslavia's sovereignty against their capitalist paymasters.

Planinc appointed Admiral Branko Mamula, a Serb from Croatia, as Minister of Defence in her administration, and he began promoting a number of his fellow prečani Serbs to top jobs, flouting the strict rule of maintaining an ethnic balance in first-echelon military appointments. He also wanted to reverse the thrust of the National Defence Law of 1969, to bring the Territorial Defence forces under closer control by the Yugoslav People's Army.[9] In Slovenia, a youth counter-culture began busily deflating the Partizan myth by mocking it. One crowd-catching band (called Laibach, the original Austrian name for Ljubljana) caused a sensation by flaunting fascist symbols on stage and actually drew support from *Mladina*, the Slovenian Socialist Youth newspaper, which was beginning to make a name for itself as a damaging critic of central government. The Slovenian leaders looked on, unwilling to compromise their standing by strong-arm methods in defence of a system which was cutting their republic off from its western economic hinterland. In the autumn of 1982, the federal authorities imposed border tolls, new duties on domestic consumer items brought home by guestworkers, a substantial 'exit tax' on foreign travel, and restrictions on the disposal of foreign-currency accounts held by Yugoslav citizens in the country. Tito had once boasted that Slovenia's frontiers were the most open in Europe, but they were now slamming shut.

While Stambolić controlled the party machine in Serbia, nationalism found no voice in official political circles, but there too it welled up through society. Nationalists blamed Tito and Kardelj for putting the Serbs at the mercy of the other nationalities through their policy of devolving power to the republics. Ranković became the posthumous champion of the Serbs, who had kept the Kosovar Albanians in their place. Although Ranković's death was given little coverage in the media at the time, the bush telegraph brought out thousands of mourners to follow him to his grave (20 August 1983), many sporting the traditional Serbian peasant cap and singing patriotic songs, interspersed with shouts of 'Kardelj stitched him up' (Kardelj ga namestio).[10]

Serb poets, publicists and novelists celebrated romantic national themes in a flood of publications, but Serbia's leaders did nothing to check the drift towards cultural chauvinism, which would have been simple enough, since it had a clearly defined institutional base in the Serbian Writers' Club and the Serbian Academy of Sciences and Arts. The strong anti-Muslim strain in Serbian literary culture surfaced again with the publication in 1983 of *The Knife* by Vuk Draškovic, a novel set in the time of wartime Ustasha massacres, in which Muslims murdered Serb children on Christmas Eve. The Orthodox clergy also felt confident enough in the changing mood of officialdom to raise their voices in support of the Kosovo Serbs, after decades of avoiding trouble. A full-blown metaphysics of nationalism preached the doctrine of Kosovo as the Holy Land of the Serbs, a 'heavenly people' (nebeski narod) whose soul resided there in perpetuity.

Revisionist history was a major conduit through which nationalism entered the public domain. Even reputable historians tended to lose their heads when it came to Kosovo, and there were others not so reputable. The essential facts about emigration from the province were readily available. Using Serbia's own official statistics, the Belgrade weekly *NIN*, on 24 September 1984, reported that 112 600 Serbs and Montenegrins had left Kosovo between 1961 and 1981, an unremarkable figure in the context of the massive population shifts associated with industrialization, and one easily explained by the economic and social attractions of northern Serbia. Nationalists saw only the fact that the Serb presence in Kosovo was dwindling fast (from 18.3 per cent in the 1971 Census, down to 13.2 per cent in 1981), and complained that the Serbs had been continuously hounded out of the ancient lands of Tsar Dušan.[11] To this theme of exodus was added hysteria about differential fertility rates. During the 1971–81 inter-census period, the natural population increase in Kosovo was 31.57 per thousand, compared with 6.35 and 3.73 in Serbia proper and the Vojvodina, a contributory factor in pushing up the proportion of ethnic Albanians from 74 per cent to 77.4 per cent. Stories spread of the martyrdom of Serbs in Kosovo, forced from their ancestral hearths by intimidation and the rape of their women, those who remained drowning in a rising sea of backward Muslims, who were using their high birth rates as a deliberate means to separatist ends.

The 'Islamic threat' was also invoked to justify repression in Bosnia, where the hard-line alliance of Muslim, Serb and Croat party leaders, which had kept Bosnia the least vulnerable of all the republics to charges of nationalist deviations in 1972, broke down. Within the Bosnian Muslim community, a split developed between the Communists who had done so much to advance the cause of national recognition under Tito, and the adherents of cultural Islam, who deplored the loss of national identity caused by the weakening of religious values among their compatriots. In Sarajevo, a police offensive launched in March 1983 against alleged Muslim 'fundamentalists', led to the trial during the autumn of 13 Islamic intellectuals, among them Alija Izetbegović, whose defence of religious freedom won him a two-year prison sentence as a young man, in 1946. This time he was sentenced to 14 years, for the contents of a scholarly treatise on Islam and the state written a decade earlier, and two of his co-defendants got terms of 10 years.[12]

The unity of Bosnia's leadership was by this means publicly reaffirmed, but it was clear that the Bosnian Serbs were restive, and that they had allies in high places – it is inconceivable that the Party elite was not privy to a political trial of this kind. The Serbs in Bosnia had experienced a reversal of their earlier demographic preponderance over the Muslims: in 1961, Serbs made up 43 per cent of the population, Muslims 26 per cent; by 1981 the figures were 32 per cent and 40 per cent. This situation was largely caused by emigration, rooted in the same cumulative problems of underdevelopment that afflicted Kosovo. Many Serbs (and Croats) moved out in the boom years to try their luck in their respective ethnic republics – for the Muslims, of course, Bosnia was their ethnic republic. The Bosnian Serbs who stayed put owned just over half of all land in private cultivation in 1981, compared with the Muslims' 28 per cent – a legacy, this, of the inter-war land programme. The Serbs made up the peasant element in the social structure of Bosnia, while the Muslims were mainly educated townspeople. Like their kin in Kosovo, the Serbs were backwoodsmen, easy meat for nationalist demagogues like Radovan Karadžić and Milošević, who milked the ideology of the peasant 'folk', offering them paternalistic reassurance that they had not been forgotten.

The Party leaders were caught in an authoritarian trap of their own making. The return to the 'firm hand' objectively pandered to Serb interests, and antagonized the non-Serb nationalities, but without appeasing Serb nationalists, to whom the 1974 Constitution was an affront which had to be undone. Caught in the crossfire, the Party tried to revive the barren and repressive 'Yugoslavism' abandoned twenty years earlier. In early October 1983, Stipe Šuvar launched a vicious attack on Slovene and (especially) Serb intellectuals. With the recent death of Vladimir Bakarić, Šuvar had become the foremost figure of the Croatian Communist hierarchy in federal circles, and he inherited Kardelj's position as guardian of the Party's theoretical purity. Credited with saying that the problem of intellectual dissent could be solved by 'a platoon of good soldiers' (he was Croatia's Minister of Education at the time),[13] Šuvar now set the propaganda department of the Croatian Central Committee to work collecting excerpts from 186 authors published over a period of two years. The fruits of this labour were presented to a symposium held on 23 May 1984 in Zagreb, the citadel of Titoist orthodoxy, attended by 140 painters, writers, film and theatre directors, journalists, and the like. The purpose was to alert them to the 'unacceptable messages' disseminated by a 'petty-bourgeois cultural counter-revolution'.[14] It was the dying roar of senescent Titoism, which for all its quasi-democratic trappings abhorred all talk of 'bourgeois rights'.

The accompanying crackdown claimed a mixed bag of victims, among them Vojislav Šešelj, arrested for advocating the partition of Bosnia between the Serbs and Croats – in the light of his later career, there is a certain black humour in the fact that his case was taken up by Amnesty International. A Serb from Sarajevo (and yet another ex-Communist zealot), Šešelj was the first to express in public the demand for a Great Serbia, but his time had not quite come, and he went to prison in September 1984. In April, the arrest of a group of dissidents after a talk by Djilas in a private flat prompted a score or so of Serbian intellectuals, led by Dobrica Ćosić, to form a Committee for the freedom of expression for all nationalities, and the liberal face of Serb nationalism attracted the support of some eminent figures among the Serb *Praxis* scholars. Dissident groups had little in common, but they did share a complete blindness to the national rights of Kosovar Albanians, and there were some surprising converts to the cause of the Kosovo Serbs – even Djilas harboured an unexpectedly sentimental view of the place of Kosovo in the Serbian national psyche.[15]

The destruction of Tito's reputation was by now well advanced. The publication by the historian Vladimir Dedijer of a huge biographical corpus on his old comrade, in 1981, set off a process of academic reappraisal that cut his hero down to size. It was followed two years later by a book dealing with the negotiations with the Germans concerning possible cooperation against the Allies, in March 1943. Tito's Partizan companion and later second wife, Jovanka Broz, was subjected to an official investigation into her inheritance of his enormous assets – houses, yachts, islands – which were now reclaimed as 'social property'. Censorship continued to operate, but it was weakening. In 1985, two scholarly works, one on Yugoslavia's war losses, the other attacking the Party's suppression of opposition parties in 1945, had to find western publishers. In the same year, a history of the war in Yugoslavia, portraying Mihailović and the Chetniks in a sympathetic light, came out in Belgrade under the auspices of the Serbian Academy of Sciences and Arts. The author was expelled from the League of Communists amid a mighty fuss, but two years later it appeared in a second edition.[16] The press also began to feature populist 'exposures' like the humiliation of Djordje Martinović, a Kosovo Serb who had to have a broken beer bottle removed from his anus, allegedly as the result of an attack by two masked Albanians. The case caused such a furore that it was twice debated in the Federal Assembly.[17]

A draft Memorandum of the Serbian Academy of Sciences and Arts, leaked to the press in October 1986, gave a systematic and lucid summation of the various currents of Serb nationalist resentment. The Memorandum alleged that Serbia had been divided into three parts and made to carry the burden of development for the federation as a whole, a reproach that was linked to the demand for a revision of the 1974 Constitution. In Section 6, the tone of the document changed abruptly, as the authors moved on deal with Kosovo as the epitome of Serb suffering. They declared that 'The physical, political, legal, cultural genocide of the Serb population of Kosovo and Metohija is the greatest defeat of the freedom struggles Serbia has waged from Orašac 1804 to the 1941 rising', claiming that 200 000 Serbs had left the province during the previous 20 years, and that 500 000 of them had been driven out from the time of the Great Migration of 1690 to the Balkan Wars of 1912–13. Their grievances were not confined to the Kosovo question, but ranged over the whole Titoist conspiracy to foster every nationalism except their own. Kosovo would have to be recovered for a third time, if the Serbs were not to lose all they had died for since their epic First Rising.[18]

It is unlikely that the publication of the Memorandum at this particular moment was pure coincidence – it had been in circulation for well over a year. In May 1986, Slobodan Milošević was chosen to succeed his patron, Ivan Stambolić, as head of the Serbian party organization, in obedience to the rules on rotation of offices. However, Milošević was not yet ready to adopt the nationalist manifesto of the Academicians as his own, preferring to wait and see what turn events would take. As long as

Serb interests could be served by Šuvar's kind of 'Yugoslavism', it was better not to provoke conflicts with the other republics, but even in Croatia changes in the republican leadership were beginning to leave the hard-line Croatian federal functionaries isolated. Following the appointment of a pragmatic technocrat, Ante Marković, as leader in 1982 (he headed a big Zagreb engineering firm in the 1960s), the government of Croatia began to address urgent questions of economic reform. The same process of rotation that brought Milošević into the political foreground in Serbia, ousted or sidelined a number of the 'class of 1972' in Croatia, and Marković took a place on the Croatian presidency.

In April 1986, Milan Kučan emerged as party boss in Slovenia. Like Miloševic, Kučan was a product of a younger generation of Communist leaders in the republics (they were both born in 1941), but he rose more rapidly, and his career included substantial experience of federal politics. Although a reformer, Kučan was a staunch Party man who hung on after the purges in 1971, and he was again near to the centre of power in Slovenia when, in January 1985, Stane Dolanc rebuked Slovene talk of a federation of sovereign republics making up Yugoslavia, which would allow Slovenia to find a place in Central Europe. Whether the Slovenian leaders actually believed in such a possibility at the time is open to doubt, but after 1986 Kučan and Milošević embarked upon a kind of personal duel which ended only with the declaration of independence by Slovenia six years later.

The Thirteenth Congress of the Party, held in mid-July 1986, was notable only for the success of Serbia, even before it opened, in securing the appointment of a special commission, from which the other republics were excluded, to investigate the legality of sales of land by Kosovo Serbs, which were suspended until 1990. There was virtually no discussion of the situation in Kosovo, and it quickly became evident that the incoming President of the Federal Executive Council, Branko Mikulić (replacing Planinc), had no intention of using the breathing space she had won to press for economic reform. The modest recommendations of the Kraigher Commission were buried, and the Party retreated into an ideological dream world of a return to its glory days, choosing this moment to attack the IMF for its 'interference'. And so the drift towards chaos continued. In the period 1982–6, the number of officially recorded strikes rose from 174 to 696, and reached a total of 1570 in 1987. By 1988, average real incomes were two-thirds of what they had been a decade earlier.[19]

The warming of relations between Washington and Moscow was by now reducing the security importance of Yugoslavia in western calculations, and the knowledge that the Party was not going to reform the economy deprived the federal authorities of their only other strong card, the ability to borrow money abroad. In the summer of 1987, Yugoslavia's credit-rating hit zero when the 'Agrokomerc' scandal erupted. 'Agrokomerc' was an agricultural combine located in a Muslim area of north-western Bosnia around Bihać, employing 13 000 people, which went bust when it was discovered that the director, Fikret Abdić, had financed his empire by the use of unbacked promissory notes. The Zagreb weekly *Danas* (1 September) brought together a number of prominent contributors to discuss the affair, including Abdić, who proved totally unabashed. 'Agrokomerc' had provided jobs, schools, clinics and roads for an impoverished locality, and the thing to do was to press on with the good work, he said. Judged by prevailing political norms, he had a point. Although guilty of a criminal offence (his sentence of three years, incidentally, was not only light, but suspended), Abdić was only doing what others did, looking after his own patch and presenting the bill to the federation when the party ended.

Janko Smole, a former federal finance minister and Governor of the Yugoslav National Bank, made the same point liberally coated with irony, observing that there was little sense in complaining about 'Agrokomerc' when the Federal Assembly, only a month earlier, had done exactly the same thing by writing off the debts of two republics and one autonomous province (Macedonia, Montenegro and Kosovo). He described the situation as 'all-out civil war by financial means', without any way of controlling the money supply. Yugoslavia's internal debt, though at least as serious a threat to stability as foreign borrowing, was simply unknown, because nobody wanted to construct a mechanism for monitoring it. The system stood Marx on his head – politics determined the character of the economy. Politico-managerial coteries (Abdić was himself a member of the Bosnian Central Committee) eager for their own local economic miracle had little difficulty in persuading the banks to invest without too many questions being asked – in the case of 'Agrokomerc' the reputable Ljubljana Bank was involved. Communist functionaries were in effect printing money, and hyperinflation was taking hold. Smole, a Slovene, did not speak with the direct authority of the leaders of Slovenia, but he said what they were thinking, as Kučan made plain in his more guarded comments.

The fall of 'Agrokomerc' exposed the honeycomb of cronyism and nepotism which was all that was now left of the Party. A Bosnian Muslim, Hamdija Pozderac, who was in line to become chair of the Yugoslav state Presidency when the news broke, was forced to resign because of his brother's arrest for complicity in covering up the fraud. Abdić remained a hero to his followers, who blamed the Serbs for the collapse of the prosperity which 'Agrokomerc' had brought to the region. The Serbs were glad of the opportunity to reassert their muscle, and Serbs everywhere found a willing leader in Milošević, who was beginning to find in nationalism a source of legitimacy and political dynamism to replace the worn slogans of official marxism. A defining moment came in April 1987. Sent by Stambolić, who was nervous about the encounter, to meet the Kosovo party leadership, Milošević watched as thousands of Serbs besieged the building, beaten back by the (mainly ethnic Albanian) civilian police. Apparently on impulse, Milošević stepped forward to tell the demonstrators, 'Nobody should dare beat you, no one has the right to beat *you*', and then spent hours listening to their grievances. From this time on, he exploited the cause of martyred Serbdom to consolidate his power.

At the Eighth Plenum of the League of Communists of Serbia, held on 23–24 September 1987, Milošević became effectively sole ruler of the republic by ousting the 'liberal' Belgrade Communist faction, with the sympathetic silence of the military. The charge against his opponents was that they were soft on Kosovo, and so had betrayed Serbian interests. Milošević destroyed the career of his old friend and political mentor Stambolić, whose end came in a peculiarly nasty televised confrontation, reflecting the tightening grip of the Milošević camp on the mass media. On 11 January 1988, the Serbian assembly moved a motion calling for revision of the republic's constitution, and in May Azem Vllasi, the ethnic Albanian Communist leader elected in 1986, an ardent admirer of Tito, was demoted in the hierarchy in favour of Kaqusha Jashari. But if Milošević hoped to find a more compliant Albanian in Jashari, he was mistaken. She repeatedly complained about the aggressive tactics of Kosovo Serbs, including Communists, who were only interested in the 'reunification' of Serbia by abolishing the autonomous status of Kosovo.

Milošević, the quintessential Party bureaucrat, now proclaimed himself the leader of 'anti-bureaucratic revolution', and so granted licence to an ugly tide of anti-Muslim sentiment. Psychological pseudo-science was invoked to prove that the anal-retentive personalities of Muslims disposed them to treachery and stealth. Orthodox churchmen called for a crusade against the dark forces of Mohammedanism in language and imagery that nineteenth-century Serbs would have understood at once. The spirit of the legend of the 'Kosovo Maiden' was summoned up, an image of purity to set against the prurient theme of the defilement of Serbian women.[20] Even by the archaic standards of

Serbian nationalist discourse, it was a bit late in the day to rail against 'the Turk', but Kosovo's Muslim Albanians supplied the demonized other required to nourish nationalist hatred, conveniently linked to the hallowed legends of Serb suffering and heroism during the rule of the Islamic conquerors.

Kosovo was the barometer by which the Slovenian leadership gauged the coming of storms. The Thirteenth Congress of the Party had barely raised the problems of governing the province, leaving that nettle to be grasped by the Central Committee, which did not in fact meet for the purpose until June 1987, a whole year later. The meeting was besieged by thousands of Serb demonstrators demanding the 'unity' of Serbia, and was wound up a day early as a consequence of the disturbances outside the building. The representatives of the Yugoslav People's Army on the Central Committee in any case insisted that Kosovo was a 'defence problem', so there was not much left to discuss.[21] The leaderships of Slovenia and Croatia were confirmed in their disinclination to tangle with the Serbs by what amounted to a warning not to go poking their noses into security matters, but the increasingly high profile of the military in Party decisions produced a decisive reaction within Slovenia itself.

As in Serbia, the Slovenian party re-grouped around the national intelligentsia. The attack by Slovene intellectuals took off in 1987, in the pages of *Nova Revija*. Beginning with the February issue of the journal, a stream of articles appeared (many authored by people who were to become politically prominent after independence) which examined Slovenia's past and present position within Yugoslavia. The economy, the constitutional role of the military, the residual bolshevism of Party rule, were among the subjects discussed, and the conclusion was that the current organization of the Yugoslav federation was holding back Slovenia's development. Issue 57 of *Nova Revija* argued openly that Slovenia would be better off outside Yugoslavia. Slovenia's leaders tried prudently to distance themselves from these ideas, but without disavowing them, and they found support for their stand against Belgrade in strong currents of single-issue political activism within Slovenia, which combined with a popular youth culture to form a generic 'Alternative' movement.[22] A political storm struck early in 1988 when the Slovene Peace and Ecology movement used the pages of *Mladina* to attack Admiral Mamula as a 'merchant of death' for selling arms to famine-stricken Ethiopia, and accused him of gross personal corruption.

When the Slovenian courts failed to take action against *Mladina*, the Military Council (the political arm of the Yugoslav People's Army), meeting in Belgrade on 25 March 1988, ordered the Commander of the Ljubljana military district to sound out the Slovenian leaders about their attitude to possible intervention to suppress 'counter-revolutionary' activity in the republic – specifically, if they would be able to contain any demonstrations that might follow the arrests of Slovene dissident intellectuals. Even Dolanc condemned the move as unconstitutional, and by a combination of legal argument and filibustering Kučan just succeeded in preventing a secret session of the Party Presidium (29 March) from instigating a process of 'differentiation' (the new euphemism for a purge) in Slovenia.[23] Frustrated, military intelligence (KOS) brought charges under military law against four individuals at the end of May. One of them, a serving NCO, was accused of betraying state secrets to the other three, all of them *Mladina* journalists. The effect on public opinion in Slovenia was electrifying. A Committee for the Protection of Human Rights was formed, which organized a mass protest demonstration, and the general sense of outrage swelled to bursting when the court stupidly insisted on conducting the trial in Serbo-Croatian, the language of military command.

The imprisonment of the 'Ljubljana Four' turned out to be the beginning of an escalating confrontation between Slovenia and the federal authorities. In May, Mamula was replaced as Defence Minister by General Kadijević, a man known as a hard-line dogmatist, and in June Šuvar became chairman of the Party Presidium. Sensing that the tide was running with him in federal circles, Milošević on 11 June made public the draft of a new Serbian constitution which would abolish the federal status of the Vojvodina and Kosovo. His first target, as it turned out, was not Kosovo but the Vojvodina. The Serbs there formed a majority of the population, but only just (56 per cent), and anyway the province had a long tradition of autonomy. There was no issue of policy at stake – the Vojvodina daily *Dnevnik* dutifully sided with the army against the Slovenes. It was simply that the dominant core group of Serbs within the Vojvodina leadership had no stomach for signing away their autonomy, and therefore they had to go. Isolated and without allies elsewhere within the federation, they were subjected to screeching charges of betraying the Party by the Serbian mass media, and intimidated by demonstrations of Serbs bussed in from Kosovo, who paraded in front of the public buildings in Novi Sad.

The meeting of the Presidium called to discuss the situation in the Vojvodina has a strong claim to stand as the point of no return for the Party's federal leadership. The Presidium not only failed to censure Milošević, even indirectly, but actually endorsed the principle of reform of the Serbian constitution, and criticized the Vojvodina party leaders for not negotiating with the demonstrators.[24] A pattern was set, with Milošević pulling the strings of the Presidium by means of populist violence. On 5 October, the Vojvodina leadership resigned after mass demonstrations by 100 000 agitators, and two days later the leaders of Montenegro were facing angry crowds in Titograd demanding a stronger line on Kosovo.

At a Central Committee Plenum held on 17–20 October, Šuvar belatedly rebuked Milošević for his activities, and found some support, but it was all bluster. Having delegated to Milošević the dirty work of restoring centralism, the federal Party leaders had to accept his rules. A process of 'differentiation' was set in motion in Kosovo, but the anticipated pushover was checked when, on 17 November, the miners of Trepča emerged from their pits to set off on a 30-mile march to Priština in defence of Azem Vllasi and Kaqusha Jashari. They were joined the next day by factory workers and students, and even Radio/TV Belgrade, run by Milošević's sidekick Dušan Mitević, numbered the marchers at 100 000. Stung by this defiance, Milošević summoned a 'meeting of all meetings', calling on a million Serbs to gather in Belgrade. About a third of that number were present on November 19 to hear him tell them that 'Every nation has a love that eternally warms its heart. For Serbia, it is Kosovo.'[25]

Actually, the northern Serbs never showed much affection for the place. The historic religious sites in Kosovo were considered worthy destinations for gymnasium students on school trips, but most people preferred the attractions of the Adriatic or foreign travel. Soggy sentiment does not explain how an educated, secularized population of city-dwellers became mired in a campaign of racial hatred directed against ethnic Albanians. Only a small part of the answer lies in individual prejudice, fed by distorted history and folk-myths, against the 'Shiptars'.[26] To this must be added the fear and desperation of a population utterly demoralized by the onset of hyperinflation. In early 1988, annual inflation stood at 160 per cent; in December 1989 the monthly inflation rate was 64.3 per cent, annualized at 2500 per cent.[27] Milošević added a third ingredient to the brew: the means of mass mobilization and ideological control. His 'meetings' and 'happenings of the people' were anything but spontaneous. He used the existing ruling bureaucracy, with its increasingly heavy police presence, to lay on transport, pluck employees from factories and supply them with placards to wave. The Serbian media applauded his every move, and poisoned the wells of public information with nationalist propaganda.

They denounced the party leadership in Titograd (Podgorica), which in early January 1989 resigned in the face of more mass protests, to make way for Momir Bulatović, Milošević's choice to bind Montenegro to Serbia. The Trepča miners proved far harder to intimidate. Following the unanimous adoption in Belgrade of the amendments to the Serbian constitution which extinguished Kosovo's autonomy (22 February), 1500 miners stayed underground, some of them on hunger strike, demanding no change and a reversal of the purges in the provincial party organization. On 27 February, a thousand people gathered in Ljubljana's Cultural Centre (Dom Kulture) to express solidarity with the miners. Both Kučan and Jože Smole, head of the Socialist Alliance in Slovenia, spoke in their support, and Mitević, the Belgrade media boss, took care to relay the televised proceedings of the rally on Serbian television. In response to the damning criticisms they heard of themselves and their leaders, hundreds of thousands of Serbs massed outside the Federal Assembly in Belgrade, where, that same evening, the state Presidency declared a state of emergency in Kosovo. Army units in Priština took up positions on the streets, and federal security forces moved into the province in strength.

The meeting of the Party Presidium the next day was effectively run by Milošević. The mood among the republican leaders swung against him, with Kučan leading the way in condemning Milošević's blackmailing tactics, and the Presidium censured 'street politics' as a mode of conducting Party business. But more significant was the silence of the army, and Milošević got most of what he wanted. The Presidium again endorsed the principle of constitutional revision, and during the same evening Milošević appeared before the crowd to tell them that the 'anti-Yugoslav' malefactors in Kosovo would be named and punished. On 23 March, the end came. Surrounded by armoured personnel carriers, the Kosovo assembly passed the constitutional amendments that surrendered the province's autonomy, confirmed on 28 March by the Serbian assembly, in a rare holiday mood. In the subsequent riots, 22 ethnic Albanians and two policemen were killed, and the Kosovar victims may have numbered a hundred by the end of April. Arrests and trials of Albanians ran into thousands.[28]

On the 600th anniversary of Kosovo Field, 28 June, Milošević addressed a million chanting and cheering Serbs at Gazimestan.[29] He spoke of their 'final return' to the sacred places of Serbdom, but warned that in the future 'armed struggles' could not be ruled out. Milošević well understood that the crushing of Kosovo's independent federal status was only one battle in a campaign for a unitary state, and his message was clearly received in Slovenia and Croatia, where the Party's monopoly of power was dissolving. An opposition coalition, the Slovenian Democratic Alliance ('Demos') had been in unofficial existence since January 1989, and in February Franjo Tudjman's Croatian Democratic Union made its first public appearance in Zagreb. On 27 September, the Slovenian assembly passed 54 amendments to the republican constitution, including the unilateral right of secession (if Serbia could rewrite the laws of the federation without consulting the other members, why not Slovenia?), and in November legalized opposition parties.

The Fourteenth (Extraordinary) Party Congress (20–22 January 1990) was summoned by Milošević, who intended to bring the Slovenes to heel. For months past, Slovenia had displaced Kosovo as the prime target of hostile Serbian propaganda, to the point where the Slovenian leaders made secret contingency plans for an exit from the capital when they had to visit it on federal business. Staged in Belgrade, the Congress was from the first minutes a procedural shouting-match in which it became clear that the Slovenes would not be allowed to put forward their plans for reform of the federation, and they left within hours. What Milošević had not reckoned with was that the Croats would go too. Now headed by Ivica Račan, the Croatian leaders were thoroughly disenchanted by the behaviour of their federal representatives (Šuvar's mandate to the state Presidency was withdrawn in August), and they had no wish to remain in a League of Communists without Slovenia. With both Slovenes and Croats absent, the delegates of Bosnia-Hercegovina and Macedonia declined to take any further part in the business of Congress, until the problem was resolved. Nonplussed, the chairman of the proceedings called for a brief recess, from which the Party failed to return.

9
Back to Kumanovo*

World war destroyed the first Yugoslavia. The second Yugoslavia expired more slowly, with the waning of the last great European empire, the USSR. As the Gorbachev years ran their course, western governments no longer needed to cultivate a special relationship with Belgrade. Yugoslavia was demoted in NATO's security priorities to its pre-1949 status in April 1989, and the destruction of the Berlin Wall in November brought competition for western attention from the post-Communist states of Central Europe. The traditional conception of Yugoslavia as straddling the fault line between east and west reasserted itself: Poland, Hungary and Czechoslovakia were all considered more suitable candidates for inclusion in a new European order than a troubled Balkan state. The 'velvet revolutions' in Eastern Europe paved the way to a relatively smooth incorporation of the Catholic periphery of the Soviet empire within the ambit of the European Community and NATO, adding a new sense of urgency to the efforts of Croatia and Slovenia to 'disassociate' themselves from the Yugoslav federation.

Following the aborted Fourteenth Congress, Slovenia and Croatia announced that they would hold multi-party elections for both parliament and the office of President of the republic in April 1990. These elections gave the victory to the Demos coalition in Slovenia (headed by the Christian Democrats), and returned Kučan as President with 59 per cent of the vote. In Croatia, a rather surprised Tudjman found himself in control of both chambers of the Sabor, his Croatian Democratic Union having gained two-thirds of all seats after a second round of voting. As soon as the results of these elections became known, the Army began disarming the Territorial Defence forces of both republics, without the authority or even knowledge of the Commander-in-Chief, the chair of the state Presidency, who was, inconveniently, a Slovene. The Slovenian leaders quickly brought the army's operations to a halt, and in Croatia 50 000 police reservists were called up to reverse the Serb–Croat ethnic imbalance. Both republics also began buying arms illegally, shipped in mainly through Hungary. A military dimension had now been added to the conflicts within the federation.

Milošević was the key ally of the Army in resisting democratization. Serbia held the chair of the state Presidency after 15 May, in the person of Borisav Jović, and also retained (against all constitutional logic and fairness) the votes of Kosovo and the Vojvodina. When the voice of Montenegro was added, Serbia could not be outvoted on the eight-strong federal Presidency. Milošević appeared to bend to the winds of change: the League of Communists of Serbia was renamed the Socialist Party of Serbia in July, a gesture in the direction of the 'reform' communism sweeping through Eastern Europe. His real purpose, however, was to establish an unassailable power-base among the Serbs, since the chances of restoring a unitary federation were receding fast. Unable to ignore the sprouting of fractious opposition parties within Serbia, Milošević called a referendum on changes to the republic's constitution (1–2 July), which he contrived to represent as a popular vote on the future of Kosovo. A massive 97 per cent of voters approved the changes, ratified on 28 September, which conferred great powers on the president of Serbia, including the role of 'commander' of the armed forces, at the expense of parliamentary institutions.

The corollary was the building-up of the armed forces over which Milošević had direct control, that is to say, paramilitaries. In October, he authorized the formation of the Serbian Volunteer Guard, commanded by Željko Ražnjatović, better known as 'Arkan' – murderer, political assassin, bankrobber, poseur and psychopath. Šešelj also re-established the Serbian Chetnik Movement in June, and was briefly imprisoned in October for fomenting rebellion among the Serbs in Croatia. The seeming contradiction is easily explained. Milošević had not yet given up on the Army as an instrument of policy, and he made great play with the Partizan myth to butter up the High Command. At the same time, he connived at barely concealed assistance to Serb para-military formations in Croatia. In the elections, the Croatian Serbs gave solid support to the reform communists led by Ivica Račan, and in order to outflank him Tudjman edged closer to the ultra-nationalist wing of the Croatian Democratic Union, driving the Serbs into the arms of the Serbian Democratic Party (SDP). Founded in February 1990, the SDP also established itself in Bosnia in June, and the two leaders, Milan Babić in Croatia, Radovan Karadžić in Bosnia, emerged as crucial allies for Milošević in his strategy of building up armed support among the prečani Serbs.

Memories of Ustasha genocide flared up among the Croatian Serbs, which cannot be explained away simply as hysteria manufactured and manipulated by their leaders. Anyone over the age of 55 had terrible stories to tell of the Ustasha massacres and the death camps; that generation, including many thousands of orphans, bore the collective scars of persecution. Tudjman's new Croatia deprived Serbs of their status as a constituent nation of the republic, leaving them without minority rights, and his well known view that the Independent State of Croatia was a legitimate expression of Croatian state-right, despite its crimes, was chilling.[1] Rebellion broke out in early May, in Knin, in the Krajina, when Serbs led by Milan Martić protested against the reintroduction of the centuries-old red-and-white 'chessboard' insignia of Croatia, which had been used by Pavelić. This was the origin of the self-styled Serb Army of the Krajina, which received substantial material and moral support from General Ratko Mladić, the local YPA commander.

The career of Ante Marković provides a glimpse of the 'other' Yugoslavia, which might under different circumstances have made a peaceful transition from monopolistic Party rule. In March 1989, Marković succeeded Mikulić as head of the Federal Executive Council and proceeded to bring the Yugoslav National Bank under control. Marković secured the jettisoning of the Law on Associated Labour, and introduced a series of market reforms that brought an inflow of hard currency during the first months of 1990, and a reduction of the inflation rate to zero by April. He also tried to build up an all-Yugoslav political coalition by announcing the formation of the Alliance of Reform Forces of Yugoslavia, a liberal, pro-market party not associated with a narrow nationalist programme, and openly expressed the view that the country would be better governed by a multi-party system.

The Belgrade press spoke piteously of a 'stab in the back for democracy', and called on Marković to remember that he owed his position to the Party. Despite soothing words and a general expression of support for free markets, Tujdman made it clear that Marković would get no help from him if that meant the strengthening of federal institutions at the expense of Croatia. In the remaining elections, which took place in November and December, the Alliance of Reform Forces was beaten out of the ring. In Bosnia-Hercegovina, Alija Izetbegović's Party of Democratic Action won 86 of the 240 seats (38 per cent of the vote);

the Croatian Democratic Union, 44 seats (15 per cent); and the Serbian Democratic Party, led by Radovan Karadžić, 72 seats (27 per cent). Izetbegović became President, although he was in fact bested in the polling for that office by Fikret Abdić, who stood aside. In Montenegro, Momir Bulatović's League of Communists did not even bother to change its name, but still won two-thirds of the 125 seats, and he was elected President by a similar margin. Only in Macedonia did the Marković candidates put up a moderate showing – they got 19 seats in a six-way split that left the Internal Macedonian Revolutionary Movement the strongest single party in government with 37 seats out of 120, headed as President by the reform communist Kiro Gligorov.

Serbia was the last to go to the polls, on 9 December. Milošević scored a personal triumph, being elected as President with two-thirds of the vote – the Marković candidate got just 8 per cent, half that of second-placed Drašković. In the polling for the new unicameral Assembly, the Socialist Party of Serbia took 194 (78 per cent) of the 250 seats, but won only 44 per cent of the vote. Through his control of the media and the old party bureaucracy Milošević had established a firm grip on the system, but opposition was far from immobilized. Many Serbs (16 per cent) voted for the Serbian Renewal Movement (SRM), which took 19 seats (and second place) in the elections. Founded by Vuk Drašković and Vojislav Šešelj in March 1990, the SRM initiated a rush to occupy the extreme nationalist wing in Serbian politics, which Šešelj won hands down when he parted company with Drašković to found the Serbian Radical Party in February 1991. Among the youngest doctoral candidates in the history of Yugoslav higher education, Šešelj was an intellectual thug who invoked 'good old Hegel' to justify Serbian aggression and notoriously described the Kosovar Albanians as 'tourists'.

Meanwhile, the Marković reforms were inflicting great hardship throughout Yugoslavia, and in fact it was the advanced republics which first asked for new emissions of money to soften the blows. Eclipsed electorally, Marković now saw his economic recovery programme scuppered. The Serbs had for months been complaining that Serbia had been plundered to create the economic basis of the Yugoslav federation, when the war ended. The entire 11 August 1989 issue of the weekly *Intervju* (the cover page read 'The Sinking of Serbia') was devoted to showing that most of Serbia's industry had been transported, plant and people alike, Stalin-style, to other republics. An impressive witness to this supposed laying waste of Serbian economic and social life was Svetozar Vukmanović-Tempo, one of Tito's few surviving comrades-in-arms: Tito's reputation in Serbia was by this time quite destroyed. With elections safely over, Serbia raided the Yugoslav National Bank, making off with half the drawing rights of the federation in order to buy foreign currency and pay wages, without consulting the other republics. Slovenia and Croatia immediately informed the state Presidency that they would not recognize any federal financial obligations incurred after the date of the unauthorized Serbian 'loan'. Slovenia also upped the stakes by organising a referendum (23 December) in which nine out of ten voters, in an 85 per cent turnout, said 'yes' to an independent Slovenia.

It was effectively the end of Ante Marković, and of the state Presidency, which followed the Party into oblivion. The Presidency now lacked all power except the formal authority to order the Yugoslav People's Army (YPA) into action. The YPA was by this time in a difficult situation, committed to maintaining the integrity of Yugoslavia in obedience to the 1974 Constitution, but without a civil power to work alongside. In an attempt to regain a toehold in politics, the military top brass formed the League of Communists–Movement for Yugoslavia (LC–MY), in November 1990. The LC–MY harked back to the monolithic Party of Ranković, and its chief ideologue was Mirjana Marković, Milošević's wife, a dogmatic and inflexible marxist sociologist at Belgrade University. General Kadijević, successor to Admiral Mamula as Minister of Defence in 1988, and his Chief of Staff, General Adžić, headed a group of officers who assumed the role of defenders of socialism shamefully cast aside by Gorbachev – they pinned great hopes on his fall. For them the Partizan myth expressed a legitimating truth that could not be abandoned without destroying military morale. They refused to believe that Yugoslavia would go the way of the other communist states in Europe, because the Yugoslav peoples had made their own revolution, and out of that revolution the People's Army was born.

There is some evidence that the High Command contemplated the possibility of an army coup, but Kadijević in the end gambled on the restoration of hard-line authority in the USSR as the source of salvation.[2] The smuggling of arms into Slovenia and Croatia was quite another matter. The threat of armed rebellion clearly fell within the proper authority of military counter-intelligence (KOS), which was alerted to the activities of the energetic Martin Špegelj, a former YPA Commander of the Fifth Military District, now Tudjman's defence adviser, who was secretly organising Croat nationalist officers into an alternative command structure. Summoned to account for Špegelj's activities at a meeting of the state Presidency on 9 January 1991, the Croatian representative, Stipe Mesić, was saved by a constitutional deadlock. The delegates of Bosnia-Hercegovina and Macedonia refused to vote for the immediate disarmament of the Croatian forces at the hands of the YPA, leaving the voting tied at four to four. The dispute turned on the precise meaning of 'illegal' paramilitaries. Špegelj was guilty of a high crime (he went into hiding), but the illegally imported arms were not in illegal hands. The Territorial Defence forces were entirely constitutional formations, and the army could have no authority to disarm them without the consent of a majority of the republics.

A further meeting of the Presidency on 25 January failed to end the deadlock, and Kadijević refused to act against Slovenia and Croatia without the necessary orders. By the middle of March, Milošević's mind had therefore turned decisively to the creation of a Great Serbia. At the end of February, armed units of the self-styled 'Serb Autonomous Region of Krajina' occupied the Plitvice National Park in Croatia, and Croatian special forces moved in to dislodge them. The even-handed behaviour of the army in the confrontation drew praise from the Croat side. Twenty-nine Serb rebels were arrested, driving the remainder into public defiance, and Martić rallied his followers by telling them that Milošević had promised to send weapons, a public acknowledgement of Belgrade's direct involvement. In July it was revealed that arms were also being supplied to the Bosnian Serbs, who by now had set up three 'Serb Autonomous Regions' within the republic.

Events on 9 March diverted attention to Serbia itself, where the opposition parties, led by Vuk Drašković, brought 40 000 protestors out on to the streets of the capital, demanding freedom for the state-controlled media, and an end to what they derided as pseudo-democracy. Brutal retaliation by riot police inflamed the situation, and tanks were ordered in, but the army was uncomfortable about the propriety of the telephone-vote of the state Presidency that Jović claimed had authorized its intervention, and withdrew the next day. For ten days Belgrade's city centre was occupied by crowds, led by students, which at times numbered 500 000, and the disturbances spread to other cities in Serbia. On 15 March, Milošević ordered Jović to resign from the state Presidency because it could no longer function. And defunct it certainly was. Four of the six republican presidents were absent from the meeting between Tudjman and Milošević, held at Karadjordjevo on 25 March, held ostensibly to discuss the constitutional crisis, but really concerned to agree the carving-up of Yugoslavia into successor states.

Extremists on both sides began to dictate the course of events, since it was obvious that the division of territory between Croatia and Serbia would not be achieved by negotiation. An attempt by Croatian police to disarm the Serb enclave of Borovo Selo, and the Serb response to it

(1–2 May), ended with 12 Croats dead and 22 wounded, just one major incident in a pattern of mounting threat and mistrust fuelled by both sides. On 3 May, Tudjman spoke on the radio of warfare against the 'new Croatia', and the Croats followed the example of the Slovenes by voting nine to one for independence in a referendum, on 19 May. In reply, the Krajina Serbs voted to join Serbia and established a Serb National Council to represent their interests in an assembly. The Yugoslav People's Army was caught in the middle. The army's 'Yugoslav' scruples were now an annoyance to Milošević: he only wanted a federal army in order to fight Serbia's battles with some semblance of legitimacy.

The countdown began to 26 June, the date set by Slovenia and Croatia to declare their sovereignty. The Slovenian leaders were well aware that the Army was preparing to act, and they pre-empted the situation by declaring independence a day earlier, on 25 June, when the federal border posts were taken over by Slovenian guards, and the Slovenian flag hung out over them. Kučan persuaded General Kolšek, Commander of the Fifth Military District in Zagreb, that the army should not move immediately, for fear of enraging the people during their celebrations. On the night of 25–26 June, Kolšek set in motion a limited operation, involving about 2000 troops, to reinstate federal authority at the Slovenian borders. Meeting with resistance, the High Command decided on 27 June to mount a much larger operation, intending to deploy crack units to do the job which a simple 'police action' had failed to achieve. It was a fiasco. The Slovenes decided to defend their territory. Their first move, simple but effective, was to cut off the electricity, water and telephones servicing the YPA bases in Slovenia, and on the afternoon of 27 June Slovene defence forces shot down a helicopter carrying bread to the garrisons. The army itself was under siege.

The crushing blow that Kadijević and Adžić had been threatening for weeks never came, and it is a commentary on the surreal confusion of Slovenia's ten-day war that the Slovenian leaders were in constant contact with the army commanders, with both sides discussing each other's moves, as though it were some kind of gigantic board-game.[3] The army faced a number of problems. The dispersal of troops among various garrison towns meant that units in Slovenia and Croatia had to fight their way out of their barracks against a hostile civilian population, and the reliability of the conscript other ranks was questionable. In 1990, the Fifth Army District was made up of 20 per cent Croats, 8 per cent Slovenes, 10 per cent Muslims and 15–20 per cent Serbs and Montenegrins; ironically, the largest single contingent, 30 per cent, was composed of ethnic Albanians.[4] There was also a continuing constitutional dilemma. Orders could not be issued by the Commander-in-Chief, because there was none. Stipe Mesić should have become chair of the state Presidency on 15 May, but was blocked by Jovic, using the technicality that the President should be 'elected', not just installed as a matter of routine. The order to move against Slovenia, though duly published in the *Official Gazette*, was signed by Ante Marković, head of the Federal Executive Council.

Marković's position was temporarily strengthened by the intervention of the western powers, who were at last taking a close interest in Yugoslavia. Overwhelmed by the completeness of their victory in the Cold War – the Gulf conflict and German reunification were just two of the more urgent problems occupying their attention at the time – western governments were also overweening in their conviction that the Yugoslav crisis could be resolved by 'banging heads together' (the phrase was actually used many times), and telling the Yugoslavs to sort things out by negotiation. They spoke almost exclusively to Marković, encouraging his misplaced optimism that a short, sharp military shock and a dose of the market could pull the federation together. But although the military achieved most of their objectives in Slovenia, the cease-fire brokered by the European Community (through OSCE) on 2 July did no more than secure a three-month moratorium on independence for Slovenia and Croatia, and hapless army conscripts had taken all but a handful of the casualties of the war, losing 45 dead and 123 wounded. It was a defeat, however you looked at it.

The cease-fire suited everyone. On 30 June, Milošević withdrew his support for intervention in Slovenia – he wanted the army out in good shape to fight in Croatia, and the High Command wanted to extricate itself from an unwinnable war against a hostile population. Western governments, at first committed to keeping the Yugoslav federation together, were unwilling to support the use of force to do it, so that the moratorium was meaningless. Slovenia was now free to rejoin the Habsburg Europe from which it parted in 1918. Croatia had to fight much longer and harder for its independence, and this time the European Community had no success in peacemaking, despite repeated cease-fire agreements – 14 of them in all. The Serbs in Bosnia-Hercegovina and Croatia were now in open revolt and the YPA abandoned its role of policeman in the conflict. The Partizan red star emblem disappeared from the YPA insignia on 16 October, and army units fought alongside Šešelj's Chetniks for control of Slavonia. The army became a Serbian army, and was eventually submerged in a Serbian paramilitary state.[5]

Eastern and western Slavonia, where there were concentrations of Serb population, were not the only YPA targets. The army also laid siege to Dubrovnik (out of sheer spite, artillery units amused themselves by lobbing shells into the ancient city), and blockaded the major ports in Croatia, part of a general plan to withdraw Army garrisons and their weaponry intact, under cover of cease-fires. However, despite its immense firepower, the YPA was brought to a standstill in Slavonia, and it was not until 17 November that the charred ruins of Vukovar fell, after 86 days of brutal fighting and atrocities. In the meantime (8 October), Slovenia and Croatia declared their independence, and the war became internationalized. A European Community peace conference convened on 3 September at The Hague, chaired by Lord Carrington, was now tasked with studying the Yugoslav situation in all its complexity, in order to bring forward proposals for ending the war in Croatia and settling the question of the successor states. The weapons embargo imposed by the EC in July was repeated in the Security Council's Resolution 713 on 25 September, and UN Secretary-General Perez de Cuellar was asked to mediate in the conflict.

Unfortunately, it was at least two years too late to hope for a measured response from the warring Yugoslav republics to the crisis, and in any case the Hague Conference started from the premise that Serbia was the aggressor – this was the position taken by the EC foreign ministers on 27 August. The effect was to encourage the Serbs to keep on fighting, since they had nothing to gain by negotiation. By early December, the Conference's proposal to create a confederal Yugoslavia had still failed to overcome the objections of Serbia, despite Carrington's efforts to secure the autonomous status of ethnic minorities, a provision intended to soothe the fears of the Serbs in Croatia. While the Conference talked, the process of fragmentation accelerated. The Macedonians, in a referendum boycotted by the Albanian minority, opted for independence; the Kosovar Albanians voted in their own unofficial referendum to leave Yugoslavia (30 September); and in Sarajevo the republican assembly proclaimed the sovereignty of Bosnia-Hercegovina (15 October), after the Serb deputies had walked out in protest.

The west (for by now the United States was being drawn into the mêlée) assumed the role of fairy godmother, bestowing sovereignty upon deserving applicants. The EC heads of government, meeting at Maastricht on 10 December, agreed to the principle of recognizing the Yugoslav successor states, subject to a satisfactory report from a Commission, headed by the French jurist Robert Badinter, concerning the merits of each case. The Badinter Report rested on two principles, legally dubious and politically myopic. By inventing the concept of a state 'in the process of dissolution', previously unknown to international law, Badinter justified dismantling the borders of a sovereign state (Yugoslavia), while proclaiming the borders of the successor states (the republics) inviolable.[6] The combined effect was to deny the legal existence of Yugoslavia, so cutting the ground from under the feet of the Serbs, and to make lines on maps the object of diplomacy. The Titoist constitutions made peoples, not territorial entities, the bearers of sovereignty in Yugoslavia. By conflating the right of peoples to self-determination (the subject of huge controversy in international law) with the right of republics to secede unilaterally, Badinter created a formula for assisting the break-up of the federation.

To be sure, Badinter drew distinctions – recognition was conditional on western approval – but the results made little juristic or political sense. Slovenia was confirmed as an independent state. Kosovo, although now probably 90 per cent Albanian and suffering great repression, was ruled out on the grounds that it was not an existing Yugoslav republic, precisely the argument the Serbs used for wielding the whip. Bosnia-Hercegovina was put on hold, pending a referendum in which all three ethnic communities voted in significant numbers to secede, an event so unlikely that it could be discounted for all practical purposes. Macedonia was rejected for extraneous reasons – Greece objected to the formation of a state of that title, using disputed state symbols. Croatia was told that recognition would be granted once certain assurances had been given about respect for democracy and ethnic minorities. In fact, however, Croatia did not have to wait. Without lingering for the Badinter Commission to publish its report, Germany unilaterally recognised Slovenia and Croatia, on 23 December. Fearing what was coming, the self-styled Serb Republic of the Krajina pre-empted Bonn by four days, declaring its independence under Milan Babić on 19 December; the Serbs of Slavonia and Srem voted to join it on 24 December; and on 9 January 1992, the Bosnian Serbs rejected the authority of the Sarajevo government, completing the sequence of revolt.

The European Community, keen to appear united and decisive during the transition to full European Union, hastened to tidy up where it could. Macedonia brought independence a step closer by amending its constitution on 6 January, to meet the criteria for recognition, although (following Badinter logic) no attention whatever was paid to the self-organized referendum (11–12 January) in which the Albanian minority voted to secede. On 15 January, the EC recognized Croatia and Slovenia as independent states. The Yugoslav People's Army withdrew from

Macedonia during February and March without any fighting, to concentrate its forces on the growing conflict in Bosnia, where a referendum, boycotted by the Serbs, returned an overwhelming vote in favour of independence, which was endorsed by the assembly in Sarajevo on 3 March. On 6 April the EC and the United States recognized Bosnia-Hercegovina as a sovereign state, and also recognized Croatia and Slovenia. Faced by this united front, the Federal Assembly in Belgrade (27 April) approved a constitution for a new Federal (but no longer Socialist) Republic of Yugoslavia. The second Yugoslavia, Tito's Yugoslavia, had ceased to exist.

To Bosnia's Muslims, independence brought terrible suffering. The first blow was delivered by the EC, meeting in Lisbon on 18 March, in the form of proposals to divide Bosnia and Hercegovina into ten ethnic cantons. The basic principle of the plan was emphatically rejected by Izetbegović's Party of Democratic Action, bitterly disappointed by the decision of western governments to support the parcellization of the republic, because it sent entirely the wrong signals to Tudjman and Milošević, encouraging them to think in terms of partition, not a political settlement. The fears of all those who hoped for a peaceful, multi-ethnic Bosnian state (they included Serbs and Croats, as well as Muslims) were completely justified. On 27 March the Bosnian Serbs proclaimed a Serb Republic (Republika Srpska), with its isolated mountain capital at Pale, 20 kilometres south-east of Sarajevo, and Serbian paramilitary units moved into the republic, among them Arkan's 'Tigers' and Šešelj's Chetniks, to begin the process of ethnic cleansing.

The war in Bosnia now began in earnest, and until the end of 1994 the Bosnian Serb forces had it mostly their own way. They controlled 70 per cent of the territory of the republic, thanks to their overwhelming superiority in numbers and heavy weapons. On 19 May 1992, the Yugoslav People's Army was renamed the Army of Yugoslavia, and made a show of pulling out, but left behind some 50 000–80 000 troops of purportedly Bosnian Serb origin, together with their armoury, to form the Army of Republika Srpska, commanded by General Ratko Mladić. The Sarajevo government was attacked from two sides. The Croat inhabitants of five communes in western Hercegovina, led by Mate Boban, proclaimed the mini-state of Herceg-Bosna on 5 July, despite an agreement between Tudjman and Izetbegović to cooperate against the Serbs – there were Croats as well as Serbs who choked on the very idea of sharing a state with Muslims, and Tudjman could not be trusted to keep them in check. The Croatian Defence Council, the military force of Herceg-Bosna, controlled 20 per cent of Bosnia-Hercegovina, but did nothing to help the Bosnian Army, except where its operations happened to hold the Serbs at bay.

The United Nations recognized Bosnia-Hercegovina as an independent state on 22 May 1992, and imposed sanctions on the Federal Republic of Yugoslavia, but it could do no more on the ground than extend to Bosnia the mandate of UNPROFOR, the UN Protection Force which had just begun its operations in Croatia. In contrast to their reaction over Slovenia and Croatia the previous year, western governments pretended not to notice that the Serb offensive in Bosnia was in effect an invasion planned in Belgrade, for which there was ample precedent to justify armed international intervention. Instead, the West sent humanitarian aid, and kept up the arms embargo of 1991, so that the 50 000-strong Army of the Republic of Bosnia-Hercegovina (the Bosnian Army for short) was poorly equipped, and government territory was reduced to the Sarajevo–Tuzla–Travnik triangle in central Bosnia. By November, 1.5 million people, a third of the population, were refugees, and the western media were reporting on detention camps, some of them killing centres; the butchering of helpless civilians; mass rape, torture, maiming; the systematic elimination of the Muslim intelligentsia, and the wholesale destruction of Islamic cultural artefacts, from mosques to books.

The number of victims by the end of 1994 was 200 000 casualties and missing, and there were more than 500 000 displaced persons.[7] War crimes were committed on a scale unknown in Europe since 1945, violations of human rights were a daily occurrence. Most atrocities were the calling card of the Serb forces as they rampaged through Bosnia-Hercegovina, even though the lapse into barbarism inevitably spread, and all the combatants committed war crimes. Slowly, very slowly, the West was driven to respond. The economic blockade of Yugoslavia was tightened. The European Union leaned heavily on Greece, a major sanctions-buster because of its opposition to a Macedonian state, and Macedonia was finally recognized at the United Nations in April 1993, under the title of the Former Yugoslav Republic of Macedonia (FYROM), though the Greeks remained suspicious of the new entity on their frontier. NATO also gave its cautious backing to the limited use of air power to aid UN efforts, but still the dominant thrust of western policy was the use of coercive diplomacy to end the war.

A new permanent Geneva conference on Yugoslavia, chaired jointly by Lord Owen (for the European Union) and Cyrus Vance (for the UN), presented plans for the cantonization of Bosnia-Hercegovina, on 2 January 1993. The Bosnian government was in no position to reject the Vance–Owen Peace Plan, and the Croats got from it pretty well all they wanted. Milošević was the key player, because he could, it was thought by Owen in particular, persuade the Bosnian Serbs to accept the plan. Milošević was willing to cooperate, given certain guarantees: Serb control of the Posavina corridor, consensus agreement (that is to say, an effective veto) on those few matters left within the purview of Bosnian 'federal' institutions, and UN control of territory ceded by the Serbs. In Athens, on 2 May, Radovan Karadžić was pressured into signing an agreement incorporating these conditions, but he stipulated that the assembly in Pale must ratify it. Stirred up by their intransigent leaders, Biljana Plavšić and Momčilo Krajišnik the most prominent among them, the Bosnian Serbs rejected the Vance–Owen Plan by a majority of five to one.

Owen blamed the United States for its lukewarm support of the plan, but it is hard to see how the irrational imaginings of the Serbs in Pale could have been made to yield to sense – General Mladić even threatened to take the war to western capitals. The failure to bring the Bosnian Serbs into line was a major blow for Milošević. Inflation in Yugoslavia was running at 286 billion per cent, and the rift over Vance–Owen between the Socialist Party of Serbia (SPS) and the Serbian Radical Party led by Šešelj destroyed the political equilibrium in Belgrade. The Serbs within Serbia lost their best chance of escaping from Yugoslavia's international isolation, and Šešelj's minority party in the Belgrade assembly began effectively to set the political agenda. Because Milošević no longer spoke for a pan-Serb community, he was now a leader who could not be relied on to deliver the goods in international negotiations, but unfortunately the lesson was never absorbed by the West.

The failure of Vance–Owen spelt more disaster for the Bosnian government. On 16 June, Milošević and Tudjman met to discuss the partition of Bosnia-Hercegovina, and Milošević was pushed by Šešelj into purging 43 generals of the Army of Yugoslavia, including the Chief of Staff, in order to secure his hold on power by pre-empting the high ground of nationalist fervour. Renewed offensives brought Mount Igman, overlooking Sarajevo, under Serb control (4 August), and on 24 August the Croatian Republic of Herceg-Bosna was proclaimed. On 27 September, Fikret Abdić (of 'Agrokomerc' fame) announced the formation of the Autonomous Province of Western Bosnia, his old stamping ground around Bihać, rejecting the authority of the Sarajevo government. Fighting erupted between Muslim and Croat forces for control of the Neretva valley, ending in the capture of Mostar by Croatian forces in November. Mostar, the capital of Hercegovina and religious centre of the Muslims for centuries, was divided into two ethnic ghettos separated by the gap-toothed remains of the legendary bridge, destroyed by Croatian fire, which had stood for 400 years and gave Mostar its name.

The reputation of the United Nations was in tatters, and there was talk of ending the UNPROFOR operation. Hostage-taking, the routine penetration by Serb warplanes of the no-fly zone over Bosnia, refusal to allow passage to humanitarian convoys, all demonstrated the simple truth, that the UN would continue to be brought into contempt as long as it was hobbled by the role of peacekeeper. The fall of Srebrenica to the Serbs in April roused the UN commander General Philippe Morillon to such a pitch of angry compassion for the Muslim population that Security Council Resolution 819 declared Srebrenica a 'safe area', followed by five others: Sarajevo, Goražde, Žepa, Tuzla and Bihać. But since the UN had no means to defend or supply them, they were anything but safe, and the shepherding of Muslims into these enclaves did the work of ethnic cleansing for the Serbs, putting them all tidily into a demilitarized limbo for later mopping-up. Bosniak forces used the 'safe areas' in eastern Bosnia (Srebrenica, Goražde and Žepa) to launch offensives, but they too were unable to defend them. That was left to the UN, which had only a fifth of the 35 000 troops promised for the task. UNPROFOR's Commander-in-Chief, General Jean Cot, criticized both the UN and NATO for passivity, and at the end of January 1994 another French general, François Briquemont, resigned as UN commander in Bosnia, saying the military's task there was impossible.

Sarajevo caught the imagination of western publics. Through the television lens they shared the experience of peace monitors, who literally 'observed' helplessly as the Serbs shelled the remaining beleaguered inhabitants of a once cosmopolitan city, united at the beginning of the war in multi-ethnic demonstrations of solidarity against nationalist hatred. After an explosion in a market killed 69 people and maimed 200 more as they went about their morning business on 5 February 1994, NATO acted to enforce an exclusion zone for heavy weapons around the city, and on 28 February shot down four Serbian fighters in the no-fly zone. Attitudes in the White House were hardening as the Clinton administration shook down after a year in office, and on 18 March, Tudjman and Izetbegović signed an agreement in Washington to form a Muslim–Croat Federation for the governance of those areas of Bosnia-Hercegovina which had a Muslim or Croat majority at the beginning of the war. On 26 April, a Contact Group was formed (the US, France, Britain, Russia and Germany) which superseded Vance–Owen, and on 6 July its plan for peace was accepted by the Bosnian assembly.

This plan awarded 51 per cent of Bosnia-Hercegovina to the Muslim–Croat Federation, leaving 49 per cent to the Serbs.

Milošević also accepted the plan, in return for limited relief from the sanctions which were crippling Yugoslavia. Again the Bosnian Serbs refused the deal, which would force them to give up a third of the territory they controlled, but their military advantage was weakening. The Bosnian Army had almost doubled its fighting strength as a result of the influx of refugees, and had two years' experience of fighting for Muslim survival. The western arms embargo was lifted only after the Dayton Agreements ended the war, despite the vote in the US Senate to end it, on 11 May 1994, but light weaponry became much easier to obtain, some of it reputedly supplied by Saudi Arabia and Turkey, some smuggled in through Croatia.[8] On 20 August, Fikret Abdić's fiefdom was overrun by the Bosnian Army, and fierce fighting broke out to control the 'safe area' of Bihać. Although Mladić's forces continued to cock a snook at the West, again taking UN hostages and bombarding Sarajevo, they could not retake Bihać.

The battles raged on for almost another year, and in the end it was the Croatian Army that tipped the scales. Having twisted Tudjman's arm to sign up to the Muslim–Croat Federation, the United States turned a blind eye to the expansion and arming of the Croatian armed forces: the Croatian Army numbered 65 000 by the time of Dayton, and could call on reservists, Home Defence Forces and paramilitary police – some 350 000 men in all.[9] Croatia became the proxy which allowed the West to circumvent the problems of military action by NATO forces, although its policy became noticeably more resolute after the Serbs took 370 UN personnel hostage as a reprisal for NATO airstrikes on their positions around Sarajevo, at the end of May. In the spring and summer of 1995, offensives by Bosnian and Croatian forces began rolling the Serbs back; they retaliated by taking Srebrenica and Žepa during the first two weeks of July, and in Srebrenica committed the worst single atrocity of the war. Bosnian Serb troops led by General Mladić brushed aside the tiny contingent of UN Dutch soldiers, taking 32 of them hostage, and then massacred 6000–7000 Muslim men. For this act Mladić was indicted at the International War Crimes Tribunal as a war criminal.[10]

The effect of the UNPROFOR mandate was to freeze the situation in Croatia, leaving the Serbs in possession of a third of Croatian territory, from which they were able to launch air support for their Bosnian Serb brothers. In March 1995, Tudjman ended the mandate, and a new agreement (22 July) between Izetbegović and Tudjman on military cooperation brought instant results. At the end of July Croatian forces took the key Bosnian towns of Grahovo and Glamoč, cutting off Knin, which fell on 5 August. The Serbs now maintained a foothold only in eastern Slavonia. The mortaring of Sarajevo's main market on 28 August (37 dead, 85 injured) finally produced a proportional response from NATO: two weeks of bombing inflicted major damage on the Serb forces besieging the city, compelling Mladić to withdraw his heavy weapons. By the end of September, Muslim–Croat forces controlled central and western Bosnia, and the major Serb stronghold of Banja Luka came under threat. On 12 October, a cease-fire came into force throughout Bosnia-Hercegovina, and the signing of the Dayton Agreements at Versailles (14 December 1995) at last allowed a sullen and exhausted peace to settle on the republic.

Now it was the turn of Kosovo to come under the hammer. The signal for revolt was given by the Kosovars in the proclamation of a Republic of Kosovo, on 2 July 1990. On 7 September, in the wake of a mass strike, the Albanian representatives of the dissolved provincial assembly proclaimed a new constitution for a 'shadow' state, meeting in Kačanik under conditions of utmost secrecy. Fired from their jobs in thousands and harassed by police reinforcements brought in from Serbia, the Kosovars created a surrogate public sphere in private space. In May 1992, using their homes as polling stations, they staged elections throughout Kosovo, which returned a 'government' headed by Ibrahim Rugova and his Democratic League of Kosovo.

The strategy of the Democratic League while the war in Bosnia raged was to mount a passive resistance that grew into the semblance of a parallel state and society. Silence and violence were all that was left of relations between Serbs and Albanians. Driven deep into a self-sufficient world, the Kosovars built up informal networks for teaching their children and delivering basic health care. The dense weave of traditional Albanian extended kinship ties was well suited to the purpose, and the barrier of language completed the apartheid, but the financial support essential to even such a rudimentary alternative society had to come from outside. It was supplied by the large Kosovar communities living abroad, estimated at around half a million people, who were asked to pay a 3 per cent levy on their incomes, channelled through the Democratic League.[11] The Kosovars paid a high price for their stand, with perhaps a quarter of a million of them dependent on charitable relief for their basic needs.[12]

Three-quarters (at least) of the population of Serbia were also plunged into destitution. An average monthly salary in November 1993 bought just four ballpoint pens, and a single German Mark exchanged for a billion dinars. In January 1994, inflation peaked at 313 billion per cent, and a new banknote with a face value of 500 billion dinars came into circulation.[13] Bled dry by the war, with trade reduced to 20 per cent of its pre-sanctions level and unemployment already in excess of 50 per cent by the middle of 1993,[14] Serbia had already absorbed 458 000 refugees. Hitherto proud to boast that the peasants would see the Serbian people through the war by growing more, the government drove basic foodstuffs out of the shops by imposing a ceiling on prices, and in desperation Milošević called in the veteran international banker Dragoslav Avramović to head the Yugoslav National Bank.

Like Ante Marković before him, Avramović applied the same fundamental principle of economic stabilization: he stopped printing money. He also proposed economic reforms that would allow Serbia to re-join the international trade regime, but (again like Marković) Avramović had no independent political base. He owed his position to Milošević, who was always at heart a state-ownership apparatchik, hostile to all forms of capitalist-style accounting, except as short-term relief in times of extreme crisis. Avramović's success in reducing inflation to single figures by April brought temporary relief from hyperinflation without a parallel in modern Europe (it dwarfed the Weimar experience), but no economic recovery. Milošević ruled a pauperized population, which somehow managed to survive by smuggling and barter, supplemented by soup kitchens and the support of social networks. What they craved was security, an end to the daily struggle for existence.

The Serbian polity was by now totally criminalized. The point is not that legitimate government was subverted, Mafia-style, by organized crime, but that state functionaries were themselves gangsters, living high on the hog off illegal monopolies, notably the control of supplies of petrol and cigarettes. Institutionalized corruption bred fraudulent investment and banking schemes, used to fund a nationwide network of favours and bribes that translated into votes, or rent-a-crowd demonstrations. The distinctions between politicians, paramilitaries, businessmen and the ordinary crooks ceased to have any meaning.[15] Arkan bought the Red Star Belgrade football club with the proceeds of looting and extortion, and he was an intimate of senior political figures. When occasion required, his services were used by Milošević, whose son Marko was a playboy with an expensive passion for motor racing, financed by drug deals. Arkan's wife Ceca was the self-styled queen of folk turbo-rock, who set the tone of popular culture in the cafés and hotels.

To break such a cycle requires a realistic alternative programme, and the main opposition parties provided none. As the successor to the

League of Communists, Milošević's SPS controlled not just the mass media but also the bureaucratic resources essential to continuity of rule. The former apparatchiks claimed authority in the name of the 'people' now, not the 'proletariat', but it was simply one form of authoritarian collectivism substituted for the other. The Serbian constitution of 1991 not only conferred great powers on the President at the expense of the assembly; it was also unelaborated by substantive laws guaranteeing free political association – political parties, for example, had to be registered by the government. Underpinning this mock pluralization was a police force estimated at 80 000, and the paramilitaries who now roamed unchecked.[16] But the mechanics of coercion only partly explain how Milošević retained his grip on power. Another key factor was the character of the three main opposition parties, which helped to sustain the nationalist frenzy on which Milošević fed.

Šešelj's Serbian Radical Party supported the government whenever the politics of chauvinist extremism beckoned, and attacked Milošević only for being too soft. The effect was to make Milošević look reasonable in the west, desperate for an end to the war in Bosnia and willing to blink the fact that he started it in the first place. Milošević crushed Šešelj's attempt to mobilize opposition on the streets of Belgrade, and the authorities jailed him for 30 days in September 1994, followed by another two months the following June, for offences against public order. The sense of relief in western capitals was compounded by the fact that his Serbian Radical Party hosted several visits by Vladimir Zhirinovsky, who promised a renewed Russian-backed Slav alliance against them. Following its electoral failure in 1991, the Democratic Party became anxious about its nationalist credentials, and was the first to reject the Vance plan for Bosnia in January 1992. Even so, the party split when Vojislav Koštunica broke away to form the Democratic Party of Serbia, in July 1992, to campaign for the interests of the Serbs within Serbia more effectively. Both parties maintained cordial links with Pale, so that Milošević's pressure on the Republika Srpska to sign up to Dayton heightened the illusion of a man determined to bring nationalism to heel in the interests of peace.

Only Drašković welcomed the efforts of the Contact Group to end the war in Bosnia, and for a time he received considerable attention from western leaders. In the end, however, the fate of the Serbian Renewal Movement illustrated the contradictions by which the any opposition was beset while the war lasted. Drašković tried to move in two opposite directions at once, and sank into impotence. Committed to a state for all the Serbs, his support for Dayton led to massive defections from his party. A nationalist opposed to the continuation of the war, his call for inter-ethnic tolerance and civil liberties came oddly from the author of *The Knife*, who promoted the cult of Draža Mihailović and preached a romanticized, 'pure' peasant nationalism that became his trademark. No wonder nobody knew what to make of him. His willingness to do deals with Milošević in return for a share of power also provoked the hostility of the other opposition leaders, whose relations were in any case bedevilled by strong personal animosities.[17]

Milošević's acceptance of Dayton seriously weakened his position. Refugees continued to pour into Serbia, including most of a single wave of 150 000–200 000 Serbs fleeing the Krajina in the summer of 1995, proof of his betrayal in the eyes of many supporters. Economic hardship was also taking its toll. During April and May 1996, the SPS stronghold of Niš was shaken by mass demonstrations by workers, which spread to other towns throughout Serbia. The opposition took new heart. The Democratic Party, led since 1994 by Zoran Djindić, agreed to link with Drašković's Serbian Renewal Movement, and later with the reluctant Democratic Party of Serbia, in the formation of Zajedno ('Together'), to contest the Serbian parliamentary and municipal elections of 3 November 1996.

The coalition was dealt a severe blow on 7 October by the withdrawal of Avramović from the Zajedno campaign, ostensibly on health grounds. Although a Milošević appointee, Avramović's insistence on the need for economic reform led him to run for the Serbian premiership, and he enjoyed cult status among workers for his war against inflation. His departure was a setback for the Democratic Party, which was now trying to regain its traditional role as a modernizing party by putting questions of social and economic reform higher on the political agenda. Serious differences with the Serbian Renewal Movement remained, but Drašković's call for democracy as the essential foundation of a strong, internationally respected Serbia combined an appeal to progressive nationalism with an attack on the corrupt, authoritarian regime. Drašković was a veteran leader of mass demonstrations, politically vacillating, but a commanding and charismatic figure who had been beaten up, imprisoned, and the victim of at least one government murder attempt. His role was to spearhead a popular revolt against Milošević.

Zajedno fared badly in the federal parliamentary elections, winning only 22 seats, compared with the 64 seats gained by the 'left coalition' headed by the Socialist Party of Serbia, while the Serbian Radical Party took 16 seats, exploiting the post-Dayton nationalist backlash. However, Zajedno was more successful than any other party in tapping the votes of the major cities. In the municipal voting, Šešelj was elected Mayor of Zemun (just over the water from Belgrade), but Djindić won Belgrade City itself, and Zajedno candidates claimed victory in a dozen more towns. Milošević promptly refused to accept the results of the municipal elections on the ground of 'irregularities' (his term), triggering a wave of demonstrations.

What decided the outcome of the dispute was that the opposition won the battle for the streets in the capital city. A crowd of 200 000 turned out on 27 November in mass protest, and on 24 December 300 000 Zajedno supporters outnumbered a government sponsored rally, which ended with shootings by SPS supporters. On 27 December, the West stepped in. An OSCE mission, invited as observers by Milošević on the mistaken assumption that he could control the situation, declared Zajedno candidates the winners in 13 towns (including the major prizes of Niš and Kragujevac), as well as in Belgrade City and in eight of the Belgrade electoral districts. On Christmas Eve, 6 January 1997, half a million Zajedno supporters defied the bitter winter weather in mass protest, and they were led peacefully by the Patriarch to a celebration in St Sava's Cathedral.[18] Milošević tried to tough it out, but this time the opposition was organized for the long haul. Mass confrontations with the riot police gave way to multiple convergent 'walks' and 'happenings' with a carnival atmosphere, avoiding violence, which the authorities found far more difficult to deal with. Their manpower resources were stretched to the limit day after day, and the only excuse they could find for intervening was that the walks were obstructing the traffic.

Once the aura of impregnability sustained by force and electoral cheating began to evaporate, cracks appeared everywhere. The welcome (if belated) moral backing for democratic reforms by the Orthodox hierarchy was echoed by Serbian national-liberals, among them Dobrica Ćosić, along with other members of both the Serbian Academy of Sciences and Arts, and the Serbian Writers' Club. Students were prominent among the demonstrators, and it was to their leaders that the army Chief-of Staff, General Perišić, gave an assurance that the military would remain faithful to the constitution, effectively rebuffing Milošević, who wanted a positive statement of support for the government. In mid-February he was forced to concede all but two of the municipalities claimed by the opposition. Mass desertions from the Socialist Party of Serbia followed, including many big names now willing to expose the corruption of government. In April, the Minister for Police, 'Big Guy' Radovan Stojičić, was murdered in a restaurant. Though certainly not the first political killing, it was significant as marking the beginning of gang warfare for control of the state, rather than just a falling out among thieves.

Milošević was easily able to secure his own election as President of the Federal Republic of Yugoslavia (FRY) on 15 July 1997 by the captive votes of the Federal Assembly. This was a crucial first hurdle in maintaining his grip on power, because he had already served the maximum two terms as president of Serbia, but his position remained precarious. What saved him was the fragmentation of the opposition. Zajedno might well have expected to make a major impact on the Serbian elections scheduled for 21 September, but in fact the issue was never put to the test. In late May, Koštunica's Democratic Party of Serbia, and the small Civic Alliance of Serbia led by Vesna Pešić decided to boycott the contests on the grounds that electoral conditions were unfair (so what was new?). The Democratic Party followed suit later, and in the end only the Serbian Renewal Movement went on the campaign trail. The Zajedno coalition was dead in the water.

Even so, Milošević's plan to swap desks with Zoran Lilić, the outgoing FRY President, ran into trouble. In the elections, Lilić polled only 36 per cent of the votes for president of Serbia, Šešelj 29 per cent, and Drašković 22 per cent. Milošević's attempts to regain his influence within the Republika Srpska began to push him once more towards the hothouse nationalism of the Serbian Radical Party. The drift also reinforced divisions in Montenegro. The intensification of repression and censorship within Serbia, and talk of constitutional changes that would give Serbia the whip hand over the far smaller republic, produced a victory in the Montenegrin presidential elections for Milorad Djukanović, in October 1997. Still only 35, but already an astute and experienced politician, Djukanović defeated Bulatović, a sign that autonomist forces in Podgorica were waxing stronger with the fading of Milošević's fortunes.

After second and third rounds of the Serbian presidential elections, a new Milošević candidate, Milan Milutinović, managed to poll the required absolute majority (58.6 per cent) needed to secure victory, on 21 December, although only 50.9 per cent of voters turned out. Šešelj was runner-up, with 38 per cent. Drašković was ousted in the second round, gaining only 15 percent of the vote. Contradictory to the end, he tried to do deals with Milošević that would give the Serbian Renewal Movement, the main opposition party, substantial ministerial representation, but it was his final fling. Ostracized by his erstwhile Zajedno allies, Drašković had nothing to offer Milošević except a further dilution of his power over a Serbian assembly already split three ways. The rising star was Šešelj. His wild, chauvinist bombast offered a lifeline linking Milošević once again to the Serbs of Kosovo, whose loyalty was ebbing fast. On 24 March 1998, the Serbian Radical Party accepted the offer of 15 government posts, including the appointments of Šešelj and Tomislav Nikolić as Deputy Prime Ministers.

By this time, the Kosovo Liberation Army (KLA) was carrying out significant armed attacks against Serbian forces, with a degree of military organization and political vision that marked a new phase in the Kosovars' struggle against Serbian repression. They were disillusioned by Rugova's policy of passive resistance, especially when it became clear that Dayton had done nothing to improve their chances of autonomy within Yugoslavia, let alone eventual independence. The collapse of all government in Albania in the spring of 1997 removed any hope of diplomatic or military aid from Tirana. The west spoke strong words about not repeating the tragedy of Bosnia in Kosovo, but the same old problems of securing agreement and formulating a plan for NATO intervention supervened, complicated by the insistence of Russia that any international action must be approved both by the Security Council and Belgrade. Encouraged, the Radical-Socialist government sent the Army and security forces into Kosovo to eradicate the KLA, killing 700 people and creating a quarter of a million homeless by mid-September 1998.

Appalling stories of ethnic cleansing repeated themselves. This time, western statesmen could not afford to ignore the affront to western public opinion. By the night of 11–12 October Richard Holbrooke, the US special envoy to Yugoslavia, was closeted with Milošević in what were officially described as 'very heated' discussions. Milošević prevaricated and continued to pour reinforcements into Kosovo – despite promises to Holbrooke to reduce the Serbian forces to 12 500, they more than doubled that number by March 1999. On 6 February, therefore, the Contact Group invited representatives of the Yugoslav government and the Kosovars to Rambouillet, to discuss plans for peace in Kosovo. The Contact Group wanted 'extensive autonomy' for Kosovo short of outright independence, free movement for all international persons under the auspices of the UNHCR, the suspension of federal authority in matters injurious or discriminatory to the Kosovars, and the stationing of NATO troops in the province. It was, in effect, a demand for a free hand for the Implementation Mission, and Belgrade rejected the proposals as an intolerable assault on the sovereignty of the state. The Kosovars signed on 23 February, provoking a new offensive by the Serbian security forces, and so in the early hours of 24 March, NATO launched the first airstrikes against targets in Kosovo, and later in Serbia.

During 78 days of continuous bombardment involving about 13 000 sorties, NATO knocked out perhaps a third of Yugoslavia's military capability, but also extended the campaign to 'militarily significant' targets. Under cover of the attacks, Milošević escalated the policy of ethnic cleansing, and on 27 May he was indicted at The Hague as a war criminal, together with the army Chief of Staff, the Minister for Internal Affairs and two others. Some 5000 Kosovars lost their lives, and more than 800 000 of them became refugees, mainly in Albania and Macedonia. Ordinary Serbs were made to pay a heavy price. Serbia was deprived of electricity and water, and communications were severely disrupted. Casualties ran into many hundreds, most of them civilians. Normal life came to a dead stop. On 10 June 1999, in a tented NATO encampment near Kumanovo, the Yugoslav Army commanders signed a document authorized by Belgrade, which set in motion the immediate withdrawal of their forces from Kosovo.

The following night, a contingent of Russian soldiers from the UNPROFOR forces in Bosnia occupied Priština airport, the command centre of Serbian military operations, but the incident was soon discounted as a 'misunderstanding' in Moscow, where an embattled Boris Yeltsin was in no position to come to the aid of Milošević. Completely isolated diplomatically, Serbia resumed its descent into violent anarchy and renewed hyperinflation. Another attempt on the life of Drašković in October (a staged traffic accident) was followed on 15 January 2000 by the murder of Arkan, as he arrived late on Saturday afternoon at Belgrade's biggest hotel. This killing initiated a pattern of one-a-month shootings: by the end of May, the Defence Minister, another political gangster in the Arkan mould ('Lanky' Lainović), the head of Yugoslav Airlines and the prime minister of the Vojvodina had been gunned down. To date, none of the twenty-odd similar murders have been solved.

Milošević did his best to cast suspicion on Otpor ('Resistance'), a movement claiming 20 000 activists, mainly among students, which took on the leading role in demonstrations after the Zajedno coalition ceased to function. Milošević proposed new 'anti-terrorist' legislation to deal with the situation, but dropped it in the face of opposition from his deputy Šešelj, who probably saw himself as a target of repression, and from the leadership of Montenegro. Milošević was now forced onto another tack. In July he tried to change the way the President of the Federal Republic of Yugoslavia was elected, bypassing the Assembly in favour of a direct vote. Although his current mandate still had over a year to run, Milošević wanted to re-insure his position. The effect was to galvanize 18 opposition parties into forming the Democratic Opposition of Serbia, and a wave of popular protest, including the working-class supporters who had been the mainstay of his vote, cornered Milošević into calling elections for 24 September. He lost, but refused to concede, and was only ejected from power by huge crowd gathered from all over Serbia, which stormed the Federal Assembly building on 5 October 2000.

In April 2001, Milošević was arrested on multiple charges of abuse of power. The fact that he is currently in prison awaiting trial suggests that the essential task of bring the security forces under control is progressing, and the Yugoslav Army appears to accept the new order. However, the indictments relate mostly to financial gangsterism, and the government is resisting calls to extradite Milošević to the International War Crimes Tribunal for the Former Yugoslavia at The Hague. What critics see as the obstruction of international justice is the clue to much else. President Koštunica took office on the back of a popular rising. His political strength is that he is a heartfelt Serbian nationalist, with a wide popular appeal to the voters. The Federal Republic of Yugoslavia was a pariah state for a decade. Koštunica represents the desire of Serbs for a restoration of national pride, and resistance to western demands for collective punishment and disgrace. A solution to the Balkan crisis must include a stable, democratic Yugoslavia, and achieving that will depend on the outcome of a series of thorny and interrelated problems.

The politicians in Belgrade and Podgorica have little power to shape events, and the position of Serbia will be weakened still further if Montenegro leaves the rump federation. In the Montenegrin elections held on 22 April 2001, Djukanović's ruling coalition won by a margin of 42:40 per cent. Djukanović is committed to holding a referendum on independence, though he has expressed an intention to proceed cautiously, not least because western governments now urge that Yugoslavia should be kept intact for fear of further destabilization in the Balkans. Already NATO seems ready to allow Yugoslavia a greater military role in maintaining the security of the buffer zone with Kosovo, following armed clashes in the Preševo valley. Security considerations may therefore prompt the West to try and keep Montenegro and Serbia together through a combination of economic aid and determined diplomacy.

Even if this does happen, formidable difficulties remain. It does not now seem even remotely possible that the Kosovars will accept forever their present formal constitutional status as an integral part of Serbia. The province is barely kept in a state of relative passivity by NATO forces, with the UN trying (very unsuccessfully) to create the infrastructure necessary to civilian government. But eventually the troops will have to leave, and either a future Yugoslav government will have to persuade its people to relinquish Kosovo or fighting will break out again. Montenegrins as well as Serbs will look askance at an independent Kosovo, and they are likely to find a strong ally in Macedonia, because the question of a Great Albania is back on the international agenda.

The uncontrollable consequence of the West's humanitarian intervention in Kosovo was to send hundreds of thousands of refugees flying into western Macedonia, where the large indigenous ethnic Albanian population has now been stirred into demands for autonomy within the weak and beleaguered state. Continuous fighting is presently going on (May 2000), notably in the Bitola region, and around Macedonia's second city of Tetovo, where the intervention of the Macedonian Army was needed to dislodge rebels from the surrounding high ground. While the Kosovo Liberation Army remains officially committed to a negotiated solution to the demands of their Macedonian kinsfolk, there can be no doubt that some fractions within the Kosovo leadership have been fomenting armed rebellion over the border. Elementary geo-political facts underpin the logic of an enlarged Albanian entity, and moves towards to create one will certainly elicit a response in the form a Slav coalition to prevent it.

Finally, but by no means least, the settlement in Bosnia-Hercegovina is coming apart at the seams, as most people always thought it would. The Dayton Agreements were a defeat for Milošević, but he salvaged something from the wreckage, in the form of a weak state in Bosnia-Hercegovina. Dayton created a federal Croat–Muslim entity in one half of the Republic, with the Republika Srpska making up the other half. Defence and taxation, the backbone of state authority, are not in the hands of the Sarajevo government. In essence, the Bosniaks are under the continual threat of the partition of the state, the catastrophe that has haunted them since 1918.[19] The Special Agreement on Parallel Relations concluded between Belgrade and Pale in February 1997 was illegal (Krajišnik signed it without the authorization of the federal government), and it showed that the Republika Srpska cherishes ambitions of a de facto independent alliance with Yugoslavia, under cover of international agreements. In recent days, threats by the Croat officers within the Bosnian military to 'secede' in favour of an autonomous Herceg-Bosna demonstrates that not all the threats come from the Serbs. Ironically, Dayton has done least for the Bosnian Muslims, the people it was supposed to protect.

Stop Press: 28 July 2001. Today, St Vitus' Day, the anniversary of Kosovo Field, the government of Serbia extradited Slobodan Milošević to The Hague to stand trial on a range of charges, including crimes against humanity. There he joins Momčilo Krajišnik and Biljana Plavšić, while Radovan Karadžić and General Ratko Mladić, of the 'most wanted' category, remain at large. Milošević refuses to acknowledge the authority of the International War Crimes Tribunal for the Former Yugoslavia.

Western opinion is delighted by the extradition of Milošević, and British press estimates put the reward for his head at £900 million of immediate aid for Serbia. However, the domestic politics of the Federal Republic of Yugoslavia may be entering another phase of turmoil. The surprise operation to spirit Milošević away to The Hague was master-minded by Zoran Djindjić, the Prime Minister of Serbia, who invoked emergency powers to overrule a decision of the federal Constitutional Court the previous day, which opposed the extradition. The FRY President, Vojislav Koštunica, claims he was not informed of the Serbian government's intentions, and has spoken of 'lawlessness' in the conduct of the affair. Koštunica's Democratic Party of Serbia is set to leave the ruling coalition, and the split has extended to Montenegro, where the narrow victory of President Djukanović in the 22 April elections has left the republic without an administration. His pro-independence coalition has become hostage to the minority Liberal Party, which wants a swift and radical break with Serbia, causing the US Congress to withhold promised aid of US$89 million.

In Macedonia, Bosnia and Kosovo the Balkan crisis continues.

Notes

1 Prologue: the road to Kumanovo

1. The term 'South Slav' ('Jugo-' = 'south' in Serbo-Croatian) is in its origins a philological term coined in the late nineteenth century, and included the Bulgars, in addition to the Serbs, Croats and Slovenes. Since then, the expression has become fixed in its modern political meaning, to include only the three founding peoples of the first Yugoslavia.
2. Mallat, *La Serbie Contemporaine*, vol. II, p. 130. See, for a modern study, R.F. Byrnes (ed.), *Communal Families in the Balkans: the Zadruga* (Notre Dame, IN, 1976).
3. The sequence of Serbia's begins with Miloš Obrenović (1817–39), who abdicated under pressure from the unruly clans. He was succeeded by his brother Mihajlo, aged 16, deposed in 1842 by a coup which brought Aleksandar Karadjordjević (the son of Black George) to power, from 1842 to 1859. Deposed in turn by the Skupština, Aleksandar made way for the return of Miloš Obrenović, then aged 79, who died the following year. Mihajlo Obrenović now succeeded his brother for the second time, ruling from 1860–8, when he was assassinated. The Skupština elected his cousin Milan Obrenović (aged 14) as Prince, and in 1882 he became the first King of an independent Serbia. Milan abdicated in 1889 in favour of his son Aleksandar Obrenović, who was murdered by army plotters in 1903. Petar Karadjordjević, the son of Aleksandar Karadjordjević, was installed as King. In 1914, Petar handed over the powers of Regent to his son Aleksandar Karadjordjević, who presided over the founding of the first Yugoslavia in 1918, and succeeded to the throne in 1921.
4. Banac, *The National Question*, pp. 66–8.
5. Malcolm, *Kosovo*, chapter 8; cf. Vickers, *Between Serb and Albanian*, chapter 2, on the period of the 'Great Migration'. Paja Jovanović's painting *Migration of the Serbs* (1896) is one of the two supreme icons of Serbian nationalist romanticism – the other is *Kosovo Maiden*, by Uroš Predić (1920), which depicts a damsel cradling a fallen Serbian hero on the stricken field.
6. Raymond Pearson, *Ethnic Minorities*, p. 32, is the source of this saying. Ivo Goldstein, *Croatia*, chapter 6, provides a brisk introduction to the development of Croatia, 1790–1918. Elinor Murray Despalatovic, *Ljudevit Gaj*, is a useful introduction to the man and his milieu.
7. Glenny, *The Balkans*, pp. 97–106.
8. W.D. MacLellan, *Svetozar Marković and the Origins of Balkan Socialism* (Princeton, NJ, 1964), makes very interesting reading, not just for the 'life' but also the 'times' in which Marković was active. The idea of a communitarian peasant state gave rise to a distinctive, pre-modern conception of politics, which both Pašić and Radić never entirely shook off.
9. Glenny, *The Balkans*, pp. 154–60.

10. Malcolm, *Kosovo*, pp. 224ff.
11. Eric Hobsbawm, *Bandits* (Harmondsworth, 1972), discusses the 'Haiduks' of the Balkans in chapter 5. He characterizes them (p. 71) as 'robbers by trade, enemies of the Turks and popular avengers by social role, primitive movements of guerrilla resistance and liberation'. Driven by poverty and disaster to banditry, the hajduks became a powerful symbol of freedom to settled peasant populations living in conditions of servitude.
12. Lampe, *Yugoslavia*, p. 63.
13. Ibid., p. 75.
14. P.F. Sugar, *The Industrialization of Bosnia-Hercegovina, 1878–1918* (Seattle, WA, 1963), and R. Donia, *Islam under the Double Eagle, 1878–1914* (New York, 1981), are two important studies in this context. For a general survey of Bosnia in the nineteenth century, see Malcolm, *Bosnia*, chapters 10 and 11. The name 'Bosniak' (Bošnjak) is a means by which the Bosnian Muslims have from time to time tried to distinguish themselves from the Serbs and Croats in Bosnia. In 1994, the Sarajevo government adopted the term officially, and it has come into common usage during recent years.
15. Glenny, *The Balkans*, pp. 293–302.
16. Malcolm, *Kosovo*, pp. 252–8.

2 War and unification

1. Singleton, *Yugoslav Peoples*, pp. 290–1, gives some sources in English for the military aspects of the Great War.
2. Ostovic, *The Truth about Yugoslavia*, opens with a view of the process of unification and the work of the Yugoslav Committee. The text of the Corfu Declaration can be found here.
3. Lampe, *Yugoslavia*, pp. 106–7.
4. Lederer, *Yugoslavia at the Paris Peace Conference*, pp. 49–50.
5. See David MacKenzie, *The 'Black Hand' on Trial, Salonika, 1917* (Boulder, CO, 1995).
6. The Croats saw things completely differently. Ostovic, *The Truth about Yugoslavia*, p. 125, notes that taxes were three times higher in Croatia than in Serbia. See Lampe, 'Unifying the Yugoslav Economy: misery and early misunderstanding', in Dimitrijević (ed.), *Creation of Yugoslavia*, for a compressed, analytical account of the economic mess confronting the early post-unification governments.
7. These figures are given by Mustafa Imamović and Rusmir Mahmutcehajić, in *The Genocide Against the Bosnian Muslims* (Sarajevo, 1991), p. 13.
8. Malcolm, *Kosovo*, pp. 276–7.
9. Ibid., pp. 196–9.
10. Lampe, *Yugoslavia*, pp. 123–5. I can find no warrant for Lampe's claim that the Croat draft envisaged six *territorial* units. Čulinović, *Jugoslavija Izmedju Dva Rata*, vol. 1, p. 328, is the authority for the Croats' use of the term 'proper national state' in their draft. The 'semi-tribal' peoples are those not descended from a pleme ('tribe', 'branch', 'stem') of the original South Slav inhabitants, and clearly implies their subordination to the 'historic' peoples. It is not clear, anyway, how (say) a Macedonian could have voted to join Croatia or Slovenia, and the real object of the exercise must have been to partition Bosnia-Hercegovina.

3 The brief life of constitutional government

1. The observation is made by Čulinović, *Jugoslavija Izmedju Dva Rata*, vol. 1, pp. 356 7.
2. Ibid., p. 395.
3. One of the major gaps in the history of the first Yugoslavia is an appreciation of the role of the army in politics; nor is there a modern study of King Aleksandar. But see Glenny, *The Balkans*, pp. 428–30, for a cameo portrait.
4. The reference to the rarity of beds as a household item is the opening sentence of chapter 19 in the study by Rudolf Bićanić, *How the People Live*. Imprisoned as a young man for his association with the Croatian Peasant Party in the early 1930s, Bićanić emerged from his experience fired up with enthusiasm for understanding the life of the peasantry at first hand. He paints a stark contrast between the isolation and backwardness of the 'passive regions', and the life of the 'gentlemen' (gospoda) in the cities.
5. This way of looking at Radić and his party was first suggested to me by Nicos Mouzelis, in *Politics*. His comparative study of semi-peripheral states in the course of modernization includes a sketch of Bulgaria's peasant politics, and the parallels are striking. Mark Biondich's *Stjepan Radić* tells the story in detail. Latinka Perović considers the whole question of what she calls 'The Flight from Modernization' in the history of Yugoslavia, in Nebojša Popov (ed.), *Road to War*.
6. Smiljana Djurović, 'Industrializacija Srbije', in Latinka Perović et al. (eds), *Srbija*, p. 136.
7. The commercial dominance of Zagreb is all the more remarkable because, in 1910, Croatia's industrial base was hardly more developed than Serbia's. Less than 1 per cent of enterprises employed more than 20 workers and 68 per cent were family craft concerns. See Goldstein, *Croatia*, p. 106. The 'great leap forward' after 1918 goes some way towards explaining Serb perceptions of Croatia as the Trojan horse of their former enemies.
8. Lampe, *Yugoslavia*, p. 149.
9. Ibid., p. 138.
10. Allcock, *Explaining Yugoslavia*, pp. 111–12. Tomasevich, *Peasants*, p. 471, also stresses very forcibly the traditionalism of the Yugoslav peasantry, rooted in the economic and social conditions in which peasant communities lived and worked – holdings larger than 10 hectares were rare, and most were less than 5 hectares in extent.
11. Allcock, *Explaining Yugoslavia*, pp. 59ff.
12. Lampe, *Yugoslavia*, p. 130.

4 Encirclement and destruction of the first Yugoslavia

1. Hoptner's *Yugoslavia in Crisis* deals with the international situation from a Yugoslav perspective. Singleton, *Yugoslav Peoples*, chapter 8, is a good summary of Yugoslav international diplomacy during the 1930s. Keylor, *The Twentieth-Century World* (New York, 1992), chapters 2–4, is excellent on the European context.
2. Allcock, *Explaining Yugoslavia*, p. 57.

3. Olive Lodge, *Peasant Life*, gives a panoramic view of daily life in the southern, least-developed parts of the country, and her earlier technical ('Socio-biological') articles written for the journal *Population* in the 1930s are packed with vital statistics.
4. Lampe, *Yugoslavia*, p. 144.
5. Banac, *With Stalin*, pp. 67ff.
6. Rudolf Bićanić (ed.), *Ekonomska Podloga Hrvatskog Pitanja ('Economic Background of the Croat Question')*, published under the auspices of the Croatian Peasant Party in 1938.
7. Vladimir Maček, *In the Search for Freedom* (University Park, PA, 1957).
8. Milan Stojadinović, *La Yougoslavie entre les deux guerres: ni le pacte, ni la guerre* (Paris, 1979).
9. Harriet Pass Freidenreich, *The Jews of Yugoslavia*, is the source of the above sketch of the position of Yugoslav Jewry.
10. Tomasevich, *The Chetniks*, pp. 119–20.
11. Vickers, *Between Serb and Albanian*, pp. 117ff; Malcolm, *Kosovo*, pp. 283ff.
12. The text of the Memorandum is translated in Elsie (ed.), *Kosovo*, pp. 400–24.
13. The statistical argument can be found in Roux, *Les Albanais*, pp. 223–4; and cf. Malcolm, *Kosovo*, p. 286; Vickers, *Between Serb and Albanian*, p. 119.
14. Djilas, *Contested Country*, pp. 131–3.
15. Ibid., p. 93.
16. Pavlowitch, *Yugoslavia*, p. 107.

5 War, civil war and revolution

1. Vladimir Žerjavić, *Population Losses; Bogoljub Kočović, Žrtve*. Žerjavić's study is a sort of history in its own right, chronicling the bigoted refusal of some Serb historians to accept that the subject of war losses could be the subject of rational debate.
2. Djilas, *Contested Country*, pp. 146–7.
3. Tomasevich, *The Chetniks*, pp. 166–70.
4. Glenny, *The Balkans*, pp. 489–93; Browning, *Fateful Months*, pp. 41ff.
5. Tomasevich, *The Chetniks*, chapter 7; cf. Matteo Milazzo, *The Chetnik Movement*, pp. 11ff.
6. Žerjavić, *Population Losses*, table 36, p. 156.
7. Djilas, *Contested Country*, p. 210, note 35.
8. Ibid., chapter 4. Goldstein, *Croatia*, chapter 8, covers the war years in a way that places greater emphasis on the Croatian contribution to the Partizan movement.
9. Tomasevich, *The Chetniks*, p. 107; Lampe, *Yugoslavia*, p. 206.
10. Singleton, *Yugoslav Peoples*, pp. 178–81; Lampe, *Yugoslavia*, p. 208.
11. Malcolm, *Bosnia*, p. 179.
12. Ibid., p. 188. Malcolm neatly sums up the utter confusion of the guerrilla war, pointing out that the Muslim Volunteer Legion, 4000-strong in October 1942, 'fought more against the Partisans than against the Četniks, distrusted the Ustaša government (from which, however, it obtained its weapons), and tried to deal directly with the Germans'.

13. This is the burden of *The Rape of Serbia* by Michael Lees, who accuses Churchill of a purely 'whimsical' interest in the Balkans. See especially chapter 6.

14. These figures are taken from Lees (pp. 221ff.), who points out that even Party historians later conceded the figure of 60 000 Chetniks in Serbia.

15. Čavoški and Koštunica, *Party Pluralism or Monism*, tell the story of the tightening grip of the Party in detail.

16. Malcolm, *Bosnia*, p. 193.

17. Lampe, *Yugoslavia*, p. 223.

18. Banac, *With Stalin*, p. 20.

19. Lampe, *Yugoslavia*, p. 235.

20. Christopher Bennett, *Yugoslavia's Bloody Collapse* (London, 1995), p. 50.

21. Miron Rezun, *Europe*, p. 83. There is much anecdotal evidence that the coarseness and brutality of their Partizan liberators shocked the inhabitants of Belgrade. A friend (she was a gymnasium student at the time) told me that the commissars came into classes picking out young men to be sent to the Srem front, telling them to 'get out there and see what dying's like' (idite tamo, pa vidite kako se gine). There was also the question of property. The new Communist elite requisitioned buildings at will, and most substantial domestic dwellings were sub-divided forever, without compensation, to accommodate overbearing newcomers.

22. Malcolm, *Kosovo*, p. 312.

23. See Stefan Troebst, 'Yugoslav Macedonia 1943–1963', in Bokovoy et al. (eds), *State–Society Relations*.

24. Shoup, *Communism*, chapter 4, contains a lucid summary of the tangled issues surrounding the development of Macedonian national consciousness, in the context of war and the rivalries between the Bulgarian, Yugoslav and Greek Communists. Poulton, *Who are the Macedonians?*, chapter 7, reviews the controversies concerning the ethnogenesis of Macedonian identity. The contributions by Troebst and Drezov, in Pettifer (ed.), *New Macedonian Question*, delve more deeply.

25. Allcock, *Explaining Yugoslavia*, p. 126.

26. Banac, *With Stalin*, pp. 116ff., reviews the problems posed for the Party by the decision to collectivize. Melissa Bokovoy's *Peasants and Communists* is a recent work dealing with the peasantry in Croatia.

27. Djilas, *Conversations with Stalin* (Harmondsworth, 1962), p. 111.

6 The long march of revisionism

1. The term 'people's democracy' was introduced by Tito at the founding of the post-war Yugoslav state, and soon became the subject of ideological confrontation. Stalin approved it, because it helped conceal the activities of Communist parties seeking to consolidate their power. Tito resented the demand that he should in fact share power with bourgeois politicians, and the implication that such states were not yet 'properly' Communist. Among the revisionist-minded leaders of the satellite states, it thus became a coded way of justifying 'national' communism, and the right to depart from the Soviet model of socialist development. See Ghita Ionescu, *Break-Up*, pp. 24ff.

2. These figures are cited by Dušan Bilandžić, in *Historija SFRJ*, pp. 157–8. They tally pretty well with those given by Banac, *With Stalin*, p. 150.
3. Banac, *With Stalin*, pp. 138–9.
4. Djilas recalls the moment of revelation in *The Unperfect Society*. Johnson, *Transformation*, is the definitive study of the evolution of the theory of Yugoslav socialism.
5. The single word 'samoupravljanje' combines various shades and levels of meaning. Always translated as 'workers' self-management' (radničko samoupravljanje) when referring to decision-making by enterprise collectives, it can also mean 'self-government', or even 'self-determination', according to context.
6. Research in Slovenia in the 1960s showed that non-combatants who joined the Party after the war had the highest rates of inter-generational mobility, ahead of Party war veterans, then followed by non-Party veterans. See Stane Saksida, in *Gledišta* (11–12), 1971, p. 1545.
7. Djilas, *The New Class*, p. 101.
8. Bilandžić, *Historija SFRJ*, pp. 223–8.
9. The full text of the Programme is available in English as *Yugoslavia's Way*, translated by Stoyan Pribichevich (New York, 1958).
10. Malcolm, *Kosovo*, p. 321; developments in Croatia are summarized in the early pages of Ante Cuvalo, *Croatian National Movement*.
11. Shoup, *Communism*, chapter 6, is the best concise account of the battle for economic reform.
12. Ibid., p. 250; cf. Carter, *Democratic Reform*, pp. 12–13, who cites a rumour that the Serbs and Macedonians drew guns on each other.
13. Shoup, *Communism*, p. 259.
14. Marko Milivojević, 'The Role of the Yugoslav Intelligence and Security Community', in Allcock et al. (eds), *Yugoslavia in Transition*, passim.

7 Reform – and reaction

1. Stipe Šuvar, who was in a position to judge (he later held the highest offices in the Party, and became President of Yugoslavia), wrote in his 'Young Turk' phase that 'all important federal and republican functions in this country are discharged by about a hundred people at the most. All possible functions are earmarked for them'. *Naše Teme* (5), 1968, p. 759.
2. Branko Horvat recalls a local Party meeting where the subject of corruption came up. One participant wanted to know what all the fuss was about, remarking that everybody gave bribes to get things done. Horvat comments: 'What impressed me was not that a degenerate bureaucrat had lost all feeling for basic moral distinctions, but that of the fifty or so Communists present not one reacted to his statement, and that the man was later elected to the secretariat of the organization.' See *Ogled o Jugoslavenskom Društvu*, p. 242, available in English as *An Essay on Yugoslav Society*. An in-house study of Party members in the early 1960s, carried out by Miroslav Pečujlić, revealed that two-thirds of them had joined for 'career' rather than 'ideological' reasons; see his *Politička Sociologija* (Beograd, 1965), p. 107.

3. Quoted in Nikolić (ed.), *Savez Komunista*, p. 143. This collection of articles is a representative sample of currents of opinion within the Party elite at the time.

4. In a report to the LCY Central Committee, Ante Jurjević noted: 'While the majority of work organizations try by grinding effort to increase incomes by adjusting to economic reform, we find some where employees earn 10 000 dinars a month without any exertion. While a cleaner in a bank makes 1000 dinars, there are graduate teachers earning 700. This is becoming a political issue ... .' Cited in *Borba*, 11 January 1967.

5. Leslie Benson, 'Class, Party and the Market in Yugoslavia 1945–68'. unpublished PhD thesis, University of Kent at Canterbury, 1973, Section I, contains a detailed analysis of the radical changes in the structure of inequalities brought about by economic reform.

6. Leslie Benson, 'Market Socialism and Class Structure', in Frank Parkin (ed.), *The Social Analysis of Class Structure* (London, 1974), passim.

7. Bilandžić, *Historija SFRJ*, p. 411.

8. Carter, *Democratic Reform*, chapter 11, gives a penetrating analysis of press activity during the post-Ranković thaw. Gertrude Joch Robinson's *Tito's Maverick Media* contains much interesting material.

9. B. Jakšić, 'Jugoslovensko društvo izmedju revolucije i stabilizacije', *Praxis* (3–4), 1971, p. 423.

10. Ivo Baučić, *Effects of Emigration*, conveys some sense of the enormous scale and social impact of the exodus. By 1968, there were three permanent commissions in Belgrade (West Germany, France and Austria) concerned with channelling migrant labour to those countries.

11. Malcolm, *Kosovo*, p. 3, explains that Metohija was the name given by Serbs to the western region of Kosovo, which contains many of Serbia's most sacred religious sites, and derives from the Byzantine Greek word for a monastic estate. Hence the connotation, anathema to the Albanians, of Serbian Orthodox lordship dating back to medieval times.

12. On the sweeping changes in the composition of the Party after 1968, see Burg, *Conflict*, pp. 84–9. Carter, *Democratic Reform*, p. 262, table V, makes the point about the failure to oust Ranković supporters from the lower levels of the party-state apparatus.

13. Dušan Bilandžić, 'Problemi samoupravljanja danas', *Naše Teme* (5), 1968, p. 717.

14. Stipe Šuvar, *Samoupravljanje*, p. 102.

15. The detailed figures can be found in Bogdan Denitch, *Legitimation*, p. 114.

16. Marković and Kržavac, *Liberalizam od Djilasa do Danas*, vol. 2, p. 213. The title of their work (*Liberalism from Djilas to the Present Day*) is evidently intended to convey something quite at odds with the contents. Purporting to be a rehearsal of the Party line on the evils of anarcho-liberalism, it contains what are evidently verbatim reports from various closed forums, which has the effect of presenting the views of Party critics fully and fairly. This enormous work of reportage (analytically it is hopeless) appears to be a massive 'leak' by Party dissenters, disguised as an academic tribute to ideological orthodoxy. This interpretation is supported by the date of publication, when reformers were regrouping for the Eleventh Congress, after a very difficult period of censorship.

17. Carter, *Democratic Reform*, pp. 218ff.
18. Marković and Kržavac, *Liberalizam*, at various places.
19. Jure Petričević, *Jugoslavija*, p. 51.
20. Bilandžić, *Historija SFRJ*, pp. 443–4.
21. The term 'ninth partner' is used by James Gow in *Legitimacy and the Military*, his key study of the role of the Yugoslav People's Army in politics.
22. Complaint by a highly skilled worker, made at an open forum at which visiting functionaries answered questions, about his poor housing conditions (in Yugoslavia, work organizations were the main source of housing funds): 'I've got a wife and two children. I've been with the firm 32 years (together with my wife we've got 50 years' service). I've been on the housing list 11 years, but instead of a three-roomed apartment I've been allocated a single room. I complained to the municipal and republican Courts of Associated Labour and they brought in a verdict in my favour. Recently there was another allocation of apartments, but the decision of the two courts has not been implemented. Who's responsible for the fact that court decisions are ignored, and how long shall I have to wait?' There was no response. Reported in *Politika*, 22 August 1982, p. 9.
23. Zukin, *Beyond Marx and Tito*, chapters 4 and 5.
24. Edvard Kardelj, *Socialist Planning* (Beograd, 1982).
25. *NIN*, 13 June 1982, p. 25.
26. Berislav Šefer, *Socijalna Politika*, p. 71.
27. See Ljubo Sirc, *The Yugoslav Economy*, on the basic failures in agricultural policy (pp. 203ff.), and the idea of 'mass planning' (pp. 210ff.). On the 'Green Plan', see Allcock, *Explaining Yugoslavia*, pp. 137–9.
28. *NIN*, 6 June 1982, p. 17.
29. M. Schrenk et al., *Yugoslavia: Self-management, Socialism and the Challenge of Development* (Baltimore, MD, 1979).
30. *Politika*, 2 July 1978; *Borba*, 21 September 1978.

8 The end of Titoism

1. Lampe, *Yugoslavia*, p. 311.
2. Burg, *Conflict*, p. 343.
3. Lampe, *Yugoslavia*, p. 334.
4. *Intervju*, 28 August 1987, p. 8.
5. On the reverberations of this incident, see *NIN* 15 November 1981, pp. 8–9; 13 June 1982, pp. 8–10.
6. *NIN*, 21 March 1982, pp. 10–12; 23 May 1982, pp. 16–17.
7. Magaš, *Destruction*, p. 78.
8. Bilandžić, *Jugoslavija*, pp. 53ff.
9. Lampe, *Yugoslavia*, pp. 336–8.
10. I was there. Ranković's obituary notice in *Politika* was relegated to second place on a page which also reported, more prominently, the death of Miloš Minic, the organizer of the Seventh Congress. It was still too soon for a Serbian nationalist rehabilitation of Ranković in public.
11. See Muhamedin Kullashi, 'The Production of Hate in Kosova', in Duijzings (ed.), *Kosovo/Kosova*, p. 63, for a wry account of the 'numbers game'.

12. On appeal, all the sentences were reduced, because the court was forced to concede that none of the 'counter-revolutionary' acts of which they were accused had been the subject of any evidence. However, it upheld their 'convictions' for anti-state propaganda under another section of the criminal code, with which they had not in fact been charged. See Adil Zulfikarpasić, *Sarajevski Proces*, under the sub-section 'Presude' ('Judgements').
13. Meier, *Yugoslavia*, p. 67.
14. Bilandžić, *Jugoslavija*, pp. 200ff.
15. Vickers, *Between Serb and Albanian*, pp. 239–40.
16. On the new historiography of the 1980s, see Pavlowitch, *Improbable Survivor*, chapter 9.
17. Malcolm, *Kosovo*, p. 338.
18. Extracts from the Memorandum can be found in Grmek et al., *Le Nettoyage Ethnique*. The exact authorship is still a matter of some doubt.
19. Lydall, *Yugoslavia*, pp. 24ff.
20. A committee of Serb experts reported in 1990 that rape was less frequent in Kosovo than in Serbia proper, and in 71 per cent of cases the rapist and his victim were of the same nationality. See Malcolm, *Kosovo*, p. 339. Norman Cigar, in *Genocide in Bosnia*, traces out in chapter 3 what he calls the 'preparatory phase', the ideological softening up that preceded war and genocide.
21. Meier, *Yugoslavia*, p. 39.
22. Pavkovic, *Fragmentation*, p. 106.
23. Meier, *Yugoslavia*, pp. 62ff.
24. Ibid., pp. 74–5.
25. Silber and Little, *Death*, chapter 4, tell the story of Milošević's rise to power, and his manipulation of the Kosovo question. The book was first published in 1995, to accompany a TV series of the same name.
26. Šiptar is the derogatory, Serbianized version of the Albanians' own name for themselves.
27. US: Department of the Army, *Area Handbook*, 12 July 1993.
28. Meier, *Yugoslavia*, pp. 81ff.; Malcolm, *Kosovo*, pp. 343ff.
29. Silber and Little, *Death*, pp. 71–3.

9 Back to Kumanovo

* *Conflict in the Former Yugoslavia*, edited by John Allcock, Marko Milivojević and John Horton, is an excellent reference guide to the events dealt with in this chapter. I have also made use of a number of electronic sources, among which the Institute of War & Peace Reporting (info@iwpr.net) deserves special mention.

1. Svetozar Stojanović, *Fall*, pp. 91ff.
2. Silber and Little, *Death*, p. 126.
3. Ibid., pp. 154ff.
4. Meier, *Yugoslavia*, p. 179.
5. See Miloš Vasić, 'The Yugoslav Army and the Post-Yugoslav Armies', in Dyker and Vojvoda (eds), *Yugoslavia and After*, chapter 7.

6. Pavkovic, *Fragmentation*, pp. 149–50.
7. Burg and Shoup, *War in Bosnia-Herzegovina*, p. 171.
8. Allcock et al. (eds), *Conflict in the Former Yugoslavia*, 'Arms Transfers'.
9. Ibid., 'Croatian Army'.
10. Ibid., 'Srebrenica'.
11. Judah, *Kosovo*, chapter 3. Vickers, *Between Serb and Albanian*, chapters 13 and 14, covers the years leading up to catastrophe well, a useful foil to Judah, whose focus is closer to the ground. She gives the figure of 400 000 Kosovars abroad (pp. 239–40). A key source for the Kosovo conflict is OSCE Human Rights Report, *Kosovo/Kosova: As Seen, As Told*, at http://www.osce.org/kosovo/reports/hr/
12. Malcolm, *Kosovo*, p. 351.
13. Obradović, 'The Ruling Party', in Popov (ed.), *Road to War*, pp. 446–7.
14. Thomas, *Serbia*, chapter 17.
15. Ibid., chapter 16, where Thomas reviews the collapse of the Yugoslav economy in 1993, but notes (p. 171) that 'a significant proportion of foreign trade had survived despite the fact it was theoretically illegal. The criminalisation of foreign trade, however, meant that the handling and transportation of vital resources were placed in the hands of sanctions-busting "businessmen", war profiteers and gangsters with intimate links to government. The sanctions regime in Serbia cemented the triangular inter-linked relationship between political power, business and criminality.'
16. Ibid., chapter 9.
17. I am much indebted here to Dubravka Stojanović for her chapter on 'The Traumatic Circle of the Serbian Opposition', in Popov (ed.), *Road to War*.
18. Thomas, *Serbia*, p. 306.
19. Allcock et al. (eds), *Conflict in the Former Yugoslavia*, 'Dayton Agreements'.

Bibliography

What follows is a selection of key works used in the writing of this book, and does not pretend to be a source bibliography for any of the periods or themes covered. Articles and chapters in books have been excluded; they are given a full reference in the Notes.

General surveys from early modern to recent times

For the reader wishing to set the history of the South Slavs in its regional context, B. Jelavich, *History of the Balkans* (Cambridge, 1983), is a classic two-volume study, covering the eighteenth century onwards. M. Glenny, *The Balkans: Nationalism, War and the Great Powers, 1804–1999* (London, 2000), is very interesting and readable. J.R. Lampe, *Yugoslavia as History: Twice There was a country* (Cambridge, 1996), is a landmark, particularly strong on the economic history of what he calls the 'imperial borderlands' which made up Yugoslavia. J.B. Allcock's *Explaining Yugoslavia* (London, 2000), is a major contribution to historical sociology that ranges across a fascinating diversity of themes. F. Singleton, *A Short History of the Yugoslav Peoples*, (Cambridge, 1985), is accessible, and wears its learning lightly. The Admiralty handbook *Jugoslavia, Volume II*, published by the Naval Intelligence Division (1944), contains much information of historical value and useful maps. Parts of the handbook are incorporated in S. Clissold (ed.), *A Short History of Yugoslavia: From Early Times to 1966* (Cambridge, 1966), but the later sections dealing with events after 1941 are best skipped, being now outdated. Despite its title, I. Goldstein's *Croatia: A History* (London, 1999), functions quite well as a general introduction to the history of Yugoslavia, and contains chapters on the eighteenth and nineteenth centuries.

A number of works dealing with particular areas of the South Slav lands are of comparable chronological sweep. H. Poulton, *Who are the Macedonians?* (London, 1995), addresses his own question in a historical survey of the development of Macedonian national consciousness. Two authoritative studies by N. Malcolm, *Bosnia: A Short History*, (London, 1994), and *Kosovo: A Short History* (London, 1998), devote about half their length to the period after 1804. M. Vickers, *Between Serb and Albanian: A History of Kosovo* (London, 1998), is an uneven work, combining interesting narrative with some questionable judgements. A major recent addition to the history of the Slav Muslims is M. Imamović, *Historija Bošnjaka* (Sarajevo, 1998).

The South Slavs 1804–c. 1921

The huge theoretical literature on nationalism and the transition to modernity lie outside the scope of this bibliography, but mention may be made of the collection edited by G. Balakrishnan, *Mapping the Nation* (London, 1966), which contains important essays relevant to this book by Hroch, Gellner, Breuilly, Smith and

Hobsbawm. D. Djordjević, *Revolutions Nationales des Peuples Balkaniques 1804–1914* (Beograd, 1965), sets the Serbian national movements in comparative context. M.B. Petrovich, *The History of Modern Serbia 1804–1918* (New York, 1976), is an outstanding work, and G. Stokes, *Politics as Development: The Emergence of Political Parties in Nineteenth-century Serbia* (Durham/London, 1990), is in the same mould. J. Mallat, *La Serbie Contemporaine* (Paris, 1902) offers a compendium of interesting facts. I. Mužić, *Hrvatska Politika i Jugoslavenska Ideja* (Split, 1969), tells the story of Serb–Croat relations in the struggle for Bosnia-Hercegovina. There is no political biography of Pašić in English, and Pašić wrote little about himself, but the bald facts of his career are told by M. Vuković-Birčanin, in *Nikola Pašic, 1845–1926* (Munich, 1978). Radić is very well served in English by M. Biondich, *Stjepan Radić, the Croat Peasant Party, and the Politics of Mass Mobilization, 1904–1928* (Toronto/London, 2000). C. Rogel, *The Slovenes and Yugoslavism, 1890–1914* (Boulder, CO, 1977), examines the Slovenes' political response to their more powerful South Slav neighbours. I. Banac, *The National Question in Yugoslavia: Origins, History, Politics* (Ithaca, NY/London, 1984), pulls the various threads together in an analysis of nationalism during the critical period 1878–1921. The standard work on the events surrounding to the foundation of the first Yugoslavia is I.J. Lederer, *Yugoslavia at the Paris Peace Conference: A Study in Frontier-making* (New Haven, CT/London, 1963). D. Djordjević (ed.), *The Creation of Yugoslavia 1914–21* (Santa Barbara, CA/Oxford, 1980), contains a number of essays worth reading.

Yugoslavia c. 1918–c.1980

The best bird's-eye survey is by S.K. Pavlowitch, *The Improbable Survivor: Yugoslavia and its Problems, 1918–1988* (London, 1988), which is thematic in its treatment; see also his earlier *Yugoslavia* (London, 1971). The three-volume study by B. Petranović, *Istorija Jugoslavije 1918–1988* (Beograd, 1988), is massive but lacks analytical edge and a decent index. A view from a Slovene historian is J. Pirjevec, *Jugoslavija 1918–1992: Nastanek, razvoj ter razpad Karadjordjevičeve in Titove Jugoslavije* (Ljubljana, 1995).

The economic and social development of Yugoslavia is comprehensively covered by Lampe and Allcock, but F. Singleton and B. Carter, *The Economy of Yugoslavia* (New York/London, 1982), is a useful additional monograph. D.H. Aldcroft and S. Morewood, *Economic Change in Eastern Europe since 1918* (Aldershot, 1995), sketch the regional context in accessible form.

There is no comprehensive history of the Communist Party of Yugoslavia in English, and nothing worth mentioning in Serbo-Croatian. I. Avakumović, *History of the Communist Party of Yugoslavia*, volume 1 (Aberdeen, 1964), takes the story up to 1941, but there were no successor volumes. S.K. Pavlowitch, *Tito, Yugoslavia's Great Dictator: A Reassessment* (London, 1992) is a fine critical study of Tito's life. M. Djilas, *Tito: The Story from Inside* (London, 1981), offers an interesting personal account.

P. Shoup, *Communism and the Yugoslav National Question* (New York, 1968), is still a key work on the Party and the nationalities' question. Macedonia is examined by S.E. Palmer and R.R. King, *Yugoslav Communism and the Macedonian Question* (Hamden, 1971). E. Kofos, *Nationalism and Communism in Macedonia*

(New York, 1993), is an extended version of a book originally published in Thessaloniki in 1964. The question of the development of national identity among the Slav Muslims is covered by A. Purivatra, *Nacionalni i Politički Razvitak Muslimana* (Sarajevo, 1969), and A. Purivatra, M. Imamović and R. Mahmutcehajić, *Muslimani i Bošnjaštvo* (Sarajevo, 1991). M. Roux, *Les Albanais en Yougoslavie* (Paris, 1992), looks at the ethnic Albanians in Yugoslavia with the eye of a social scientist, adding a valuable extra dimension to the narrative histories by Malcolm and Vickers. Two good general works on nationalism are P.F. Sugar and I.J. Lederer (eds), *Nationalism in Eastern Europe* (Seattle, 1969), and P. Lendvai, *Eagles in Cobwebs: Nationalism and Communism in the Balkans* (London, 1970).

Yugoslavia 1921–41

J.A. Irvine, *The Croat Question: Partisan Politics in the Formation of the Yugoslav Socialist State* (Boulder, Co, 1993), and A. Djilas, *The Contested Country: Yugoslav Unity and Communist Revolution 1919–1953* (Cambridge, MA/London, 1991), span the lives of the first and the second Yugoslavia from different but overlapping standpoints, and neither should be missed. A.N. Dragnich, *The First Yugoslavia: Search for a Viable Political System* (Stanford, CA, 1983), and P.D. Ostovic, *The Truth about Yugoslavia* (New York, 1952), are readable general surveys. F. Čulinović, *Jugoslavija Izmedju Dva Rata*, 2 vols (Zagreb, 1961), is a mine of information, often quoting elusive primary sources. B. Gligorijević, *Demokratska Stranka i Politički Odnosi u Kraljevini SHS* (Beograd, 1970), and A. Purivatra, *Jugoslavenska Muslimanska Organizacija u Političkom Životu Kraljevine SHS* (Sarajevo, 1974), are useful studies of two of the main political parties. The general picture of parties and elections during the Vidovdan years appears in B. Gligorijević, *Parlament i Političke Stranke u Jugoslaviji, 1919–1929* (Beograd, 1979).

J. Tomasevich, *Peasants, Politics, and Economic Change in Yugoslavia* (Stanford, CA, 1955), addresses the life of the most important class of the population. O. Lodge, *Peasant Life in Yugoslavia* (London, 1942), is highly recommended for its vivid picture of daily peasant existence, and so is the somewhat later study by J. Halpern, *A Serbian Village* (New York, 1958).

J.B. Hoptner, *Yugoslavia in Crisis* (New York, 1962), records the years leading towards war. Yugoslavia's defeat by the Axis is analysed by F. Čulinović, *Slom Stare Jugoslavije* (Zagreb, 1958), and the 1941 coup is recalled by D.N. Ristić, *Yugoslavia's Revolution of 1941* (University Park, PA/London, 1966).

War and revolution, 1941–8

V. Žerjavić, *Population Losses in Yugoslavia 1941–45* (Zagreb, 1997), and B. Kočović, *Žrtve Drugog Svetskog Rata u Jugoslaviji* (London, 1985), have undisputed pride of place as scientific studies of war losses. J. Tomasevich, *War and Revolution in Yugoslavia, 1941–1945: The Chetniks* (Stanford, CA, 1975), remains unsurpassed as a scholarly account. M. Milazzo, *The Chetnik Movement and the Yugoslav Resistance* (Baltimore, MD/London, 1975), may also be consulted. The Partizan war is hopelessly under-researched, and has to be pieced together from other books, such as Malcolm's two studies on Bosnia and Kosovo. I. Banac, *With Stalin against Tito: Cominformist Splits in Yugoslav communism* (Ithaca, NY/London, 1988), gives a lucid analysis of the post-war crisis provoked by the split with Moscow. M. Djilas, *Conversations with Stalin* (Harmondsworth, 1962), tells some of the story from the inside. S. Clissold, *Yugoslavia and the Soviet Union, 1939–1973; a Documentary Survey* (London, 1975), is an excellent 'bridging' reference work, dealing with the Party's most important foreign patron during the years of struggle and consolidation of Yugoslav national communism. A.R. Johnson, *The Transformation of Communist Ideology: the Yugoslav Case* (Cambridge MA/London, 1972), analyses the ideological war against Stalin in an absorbing portrait of the Party elite. K. Čavoški and V. Koštunica, *Party Pluralism or Monism* (London, 1985), trace out the extinction of multi-party politics by 1950. M. Djilas, *The New Class* (London, 1957), is a celebrated analysis of how the Yugoslav revolution was diverted in its course.

Tito's Yugoslavia, 1948–80

G. Ionescu, *The Break-Up of the Soviet Empire in Eastern Europe* (Harmondsworth, 1965), and R.V. Burks, *The Dynamics of Communism in Eastern Europe* (Princeton, NJ, 1961), set Yugoslav national communism in context. A.Z. Rubinstein, *Yugoslavia and the Non-aligned World* (Princeton, NJ, 1970), deals with a central prop of Tito's foreign policy. The Party's relations with the Orthodox and Catholic churches are examined by S. Alexander, *Church and State in Yugoslavia since 1945* (Cambridge, 1979).

G.W. Hoffman and F.W. Neal, *Yugoslavia and the New Communism* (New York, 1962), and M.G. Zaninovich, *The Development of Socialist Yugoslavia* (Baltimore, MD, 1968), are valuable studies of what Lampe has called 'Yugoslavia Ascending'. W.S. Vucinich, *Contemporary Yugoslavia: Twenty Years of Socialist Experiment* (Berkeley, CA, 1969), is an interesting collection of essays, a kind of mid-term report. D. Rusinow, *The Yugoslav Experiment 1948–74* (London, 1977), was written after the tide of reformism had turned, and is the standard history of the period. D. Wilson, *Tito's Yugoslavia* (Cambridge, 1979), covers the same ground in a very readable account. D. Bilandžić, *Historija Socijalističke Federativne Republike Jugoslavije: Glavni procesi* (Zagreb, 1979, 2nd edn), has to be 'decoded' for its political judgements, but is authoritative on the economy, and studded with suggestive asides (listed as *Historija SFRJ* in Notes).

The complex institutional structure conventionally subsumed under the terms 'self-management' and 'market socialism' is set out by B. McFarlane, *Yugoslavia: Politics, Economics and Society* (London/New York, 1988). Two studies by B. Horvat, *An Essay on Yugoslav Society* (New York, 1970), and *The Yugoslav Economic System* (New York, 1976), give the views of sympathetic but highly critical scholar who remained a convinced 'Yugoslav' to the end. L. Sirc, *The Yugoslav Economy Under Self-Management* (London, 1979), is damning.

S. Zukin, *Beyond Marx and Tito* (Cambridge, 1975), testifies to the sclerosis of 'direct democracy' at the grass-roots. The problems of reforming the apparatus of the party-state are the subject of two important studies by S.L. Burg, *Conflict and Cohesion in Socialist Yugoslavia: Political Decision-making since 1966* (Princeton, NJ, 1982), and A. Carter, *Democratic Reform in Yugoslavia* (London, 1982). To these should be added P. Ramet, *Nationalism and Federalism in Yugoslavia 1963–1983*, (Bloomington, IN, 1984). D. Marković and S. Kržavac, *Liberalizam od*

Djilasa do Danas, 2 vols (Beograd, 1978) is a major source on Party in-fighting, but is sprawling and unscholarly. M.K. Bokovoy, J.A. Irvine and C.S. Lilly, *State–Society Relations in Yugoslavia 1945–1992* (London, 1997), contains a number of useful essays.

Yugoslavia and after, 1980–2001

D.A. Dyker and I. Vejvoda (eds), *Yugoslavia and After* (London/New York, 1996), is excellent as a survey of key themes. N. Beloff, *Tito's Flawed Legacy* (London, 1985), reviews the Tito years in a controversial study. H. Lydall, *Yugoslav Socialism: Theory and Practice* (Oxford, 1984), and *Yugoslavia in Crisis* (Oxford, 1989), are analyses of the weaknesses of 'self-governing socialism'. J. Gow, *Legitimacy and the Military: The Yugoslav crisis* (London, 1992), shows why the Yugoslav People's Army played the role it did in the events leading to collapse. D. Bilandžić, *Jugoslavija poslije Tita 1980–1985* (Zagreb, 1986), examines the fateful transition to overt nationalism. B. Magaš, *The Destruction of Yugoslavia: Tracking the Break-up 1980–92* (London, 1993), and M. Glenny, *The Fall of Yugoslavia: The Third Balkan War* (Harmondsworth, 1996), are both of interest. A. Pavkovic, *The Fragmentation of Yugoslavia* (London, 1997) is a first-class analytical introduction. A. Danchev and T. Halverson (eds), *International Perspectives on the Yugoslav Conflict* (London, 1996), is concise and helpful. J.B. Allcock, M. Milivojević and J.J. Horton (eds), *Conflict in the Former Yugoslavia: An Encyclopedia* (Denver, CO/Santa Barbara, CA/Oxford, 1998), is a tour de force. S.L. Woodward, *Balkan Tragedy: Chaos and Dissolution after the Cold War* (Washington, DC, 1995) places the events of Yugoslavia in their context.

N. Popov (ed.), *The Road to War in Serbia: Trauma and Catharsis*, (Budapest, 1999), and R. Thomas, *Serbia under Milošević: Politics in the 1990s* (London, 1999), are two important scholarly sources in a somewhat neglected field.

Other works consulted

Allcock, J.B., Horton, J.J. and Milivojević, M. (eds) *Yugoslavia in Transition* (New York/Oxford, 1992).

Bićanić, R., *How the People Live: Life in the Passive Regions* (Department of Anthropology, University of Massachusetts at Amherst [1934] 1981).

Bogosavljević, S. (ed.) *Bosna i Hercegovina Izmedju Rata i Mira* (Sarajevo, 1992).

Bokovoy, M.K., *Peasants and Communists: Politics and Ideology in the Yugoslav Countryside 1941–1953* (Pittsburgh, PA, 1998).

Bougarel, X., *Bosnie: Anatomie d'un conflit* (Paris, 1996).

Browning, C.R., *Fateful Months: Essays on the Emergence of the Final Solution* (New York/London, 1991).

Brubaker, R., *Nationalism Reframed: Nationhood and Nationalism in the New Europe* (Cambridge, 1996).

Burg, S.L. and Shoup, P., *The War in Bosnia-Herzegovina: Ethnic Conflict and International Intervention* (Armonk, NY/London, 1999).

Ćerić, S., *Muslimani srpskohrvatskog jezika* (Sarajevo, 1969).

Cigar, N., *Genocide in Bosnia: the policy of 'ethnic cleansing'* (College Station, TX, 1995).

Cuvalo, A., *The Croatian National Movement 1966–72* (New York, 1990).
Denitch B., *The Legitimation of a Revolution* (New Haven, CT/London, 1976).
Donia, R., *Islam under the Double Eagle, 1878–1914* (New York, 1981).
Dragnich, A.N., *Serbia, Nikola Pašic, and Yugoslavia* (Rutgers NJ, 1974).
Duijzings, G. (ed.), *Kosovo/Kosova* (Nijmegen, 1996).
Elsie, R. (ed.), *Kosovo: In the Heart of the Powder Keg* (New York, 1997).
Freidenreich, H.P., *The Jews of Yugoslavia* (Philadelphia, 1979).
Grafenauer, N., *The Case of Slovenia* (Ljubljana, 1991).
Grmek, M., Gjidara, M. and Šimac, N. (eds), *Le Nettoyage Ethnique* (Paris, 1993).
   Published simultaneously in Zagreb as *Etničko Čišćenje*.
Jelavich, C., *South Slav Nationalisms: Textbooks and Yugoslav Union before 1914*
   (Columbus, OH, 1990).
Jelic-Butić, F., *Hrvatska Seljačka Stranka* (Zagreb, 1983).
Judah, T., *Kosovo: War and Revenge* (New Haven, CT/London, 2000).
Lees, M., *The Rape of Serbia* (San Diego, CA/New York/London, 1990).
Leković, M., *Martovski Pregovori* (Beograd 1983).
Mouzelis, N., *Politics in the Semi-Periphery: Early Parliamentarism and Late
   Industrialisation* (Basingstoke, 1986).
Nikolić, M. (ed.), *Savez Komunista Jugoslavije u Uslovima Samoupravljanja* (Beograd,
   1967).
Petričević, J., *Jugoslavija na optužbeničkoj klupi* (Brugg, 1978).
Pettifer, J. (ed.), *The New Macedonian Question* (Basingstoke, 1990).
Puljiz, V. (ed.), *The Yugoslav Village* (Zagreb, 1972).
Ramet, S.P., *Balkan Babel: The Disintegration of Yugoslavia from the Death of Tito to
   the War for Kosovo* (Boulder, Co, 1993, 3rd edn).
Rezun, M., *Europe and War in the Balkans: Toward a New Yugoslav Identity*
   (Westport, CT/London, 1995).
Robinson, G.R., *Tito's Maverick Media: The politics of Mass Communication in
   Yugoslavia* (Chicago, IL/London, 1977).
Rothschild, J., *Return to Diversity: A Political History of East Central Europe since
   World War II* (New York/Oxford, 1993).
Silber, L. and Little, A., *The Death of Yugoslavia* (Harmondsworth, 1995).
Stojanović, S., *The Fall of Yugoslavia* (Amherst, NY, 1997).
Šuvar, S., *Samoupravljanje i Alternative* (Zagreb, 1978).
Trouton, R., *Peasant Renaissance in Yugoslavia 1900–1950* (London, 1952).
Woodward, S.L. *Socialist Unemployment: The Political Economy of Yugoslavia
   1945–1990* (London, 1993).

Index